WEAR GIFFORD

A HISTORY OF EDUCATION

by
Peter Coad

Mrs Thirza Mancy
Headmistress
1912 – 1939

WEAR GIFFORD

A HISTORY OF EDUCATION

by
Peter Coad

First published in 1998 by
EDWARD GASKELL Publishers
6 Grenville Street
Bideford • Devon
EX39 2EA

ISBN 1 -898546 - 22 - 3

© Peter Coad

**Wear Gifford
A History of Education**

All rights reserved. No part of this publication may be reproduced, stored in a retrieval system, or transmitted in any form by any means, electronic, mechanical, photocopying, recording or otherwise, without the prior written permission of the publishers.

Typeset, printed & bound by
The Lazarus Press
Unit 7 Caddsdown Business Park
Bideford Devon EX39 2DX

DEDICATION

This book is dedicated to my dear wife, Prue, in grateful thanks for all her support and encouragement in the writing of it.

CONTENTS

SECTION ONE   Page

    General History of Education   1
    Part of the Original Will of John Lovering   2
    Education at Wear Gifford   3
    Lovering Scholarships   7
    Head Teachers, 1860 - 1944   8
    The Location of the Early Schools   9
    The New School, 1860   12
    Structural Changes, circa 1900   23
    Bibliography, References, Acknowledgements   24

SECTION TWO

    School Photographs, 1895 - 1940

SECTION THREE

    School Index, 1905 - 1945
    School Admission Register, 1905 - 1945
    School Log Book, 1900 - 1945

SECTION FOUR

    Miscellaneous Documents

FOREWORD

I was born in the village of Wear Gifford sixty-seven years ago where I was Baptised and Confirmed in the Church of the Holy Trinity. In my early years I attended the Methodist Chapel, only yards from where I lived. From 1939 to 1945 my family lived in School House making the church the nearest place of worship; my brother Allen and I attended regularly and sang in the choir.

I first enrolled in the local school January 1934 at the age of four years; for the following five years my education alternated between Wear Gifford and Plymouth. From 1939 my education continued at Wear Gifford until September 1940 when the award of a Bridge Scholarship took me to Bideford Grammar School.

I remember well my infant teacher at Wear Gifford, Miss Banbrook, who taught me the rudiments of reading, writing and arithmetic; she was very kind and patient. The memory of my introduction to a chalk and slateboard is vivid. The move to Mrs Mancy's senior class provided me with the necessary foundation for a scholarship. My debt to these two teachers is incalculable.

Peter Coad

April 1997

A GENERAL HISTORY OF EDUCATION

Until the end of the nineteenth century, education was available only to those who could afford it. Monasteries and other ecclesiastical establishments provided education for the privileged few in the early years; many such institutions provided residential tutors for the children of the aristocracy and the wealthy.

During the 12th and 13th centuries, the Universities of Oxford and Cambridge were established, soon followed by many residential public schools such as Winchester College (1382), Eton College (1440), Rugby School (1567), and Harrow School (1571), to name but a few. They were exclusively for those rich enough to pay the fees. The same period witnessed the establishment of many hundreds of grammar schools. By 1600 there were already ten such schools in the County of Devon: Bideford Grammar School (16th century), Colyton Grammar School (1546), Queen Elizabeth's Grammar School, Credition (1547), Exeter School (1332), Okehampton Grammar School (1591), The King's School, Ottery St Mary (1337), and Tavistock Grammar School (1509). Although most were fee paying schools for the sons of prosperous merchants, farmers et al, many provided scholarships for the education of talented children from the poorer classes. From the seventeenth century, increasing numbers of wealthy benefactors began providing for the education of some poor children. One such philanthropist was John Lovering of Wear Gifford who, in his Will of 1671, provided for the education of sixteen children of the poor in the parish.

PART OF THE ORIGINAL WILL OF JOHN LOVERING

In The name of God Amen — John Lovering

The Eighteenth day of March in the yeare of our Lord One Thousand Six Hundred Seaventy one, in the Twenty fourth yeare of the Reigne of our Soveraigne Lord Charles the Second by the grace of God King of England Scottland ffrance and Ireland Defender of the ffaith &c I John Lovering the elder of Greate Cliffton in the County of Devon Merchant being now in perfect memory and in Competent health (Prayse be given to my God and Gratious God) And calling to mind the frailty and uncertainty of mans life and the certainty of death hopeing that the disposeing of these my Temporall Blessings which God of his love and goodness hath bestowed on mee in this transitory life will fitt thee my preparation for my dissolution and for Eternall life, I doe therefore make this, my last will and Testament in manner and forme following First I Commit my Soule unto God my heavenly ffather and Creator who gave it, me Stedfastly beleiveing through the merritts of Christ my deare Lord and Saviour to have a full and ffree pardon of all my sinnes and to Enjoy him for ever in his Kingdome of Glory And my body to the Earth from whence it first came. Item I give devise and bequeath All that Messuage Tenement and Courtelage att Hard bart within the Burrough of Clifton Dartmouth Hardness whereof I stand seized as of ffee And my will and meaning is To have the said Tenements and Messuage Converted into severall Tenements or Dwellings for the use and benefitt of poore superannuated Seamen and Seamens widdowes And for the Rectifying thereof And for trussing up all manner Rent to discharge the yearly Reparacons thereof, And the overplus (is any such be) To be equally devided and distributed to such poore persons as shalbe placed and dwell there As by an Instrument or Indenture that shalbe drawne upp.

To which end and purpose more att large appeareth, I say I give ffive hundred pounds of which I appoint Three hundred pounds or thereabout for the enlargeing of the said Messuage And the overplus my will and meaning is to be forthwith laid out in Land for to raise annuall Rent for to discharge Reparacons and upholding of the foresaid dwellings but the remainder of said Rent to be equally distributed by the Trustees mentioned in the afforesaid Instrument of Item, I give and bequeath One hundred pound to such poore of said Towne of Clifton Dartmouth Hardness as are not in the poores booke of said Towne and to such as Constable and are esteemed to make knowne their Povertie (to witt) To ffive and Twenty widdowes that are Laborious in spinning knitting sewing or I say fforty shillings to each of such for a Stock to employ themselves with And to but one of such in a ffamily or house And the other ffifty pounds to such as are aged weake and impotent that for convenient necessities and wants not exceeding Twenty shillings to each And my will and meaning is that cheifly those that are pious and not those that are sober shall have the benefitt of this guift intreating my loveing ffriends Mr Acton Bayer Mr John Whiteway Mr John Whiterow Mr Jerome Stone and Mr Edward Elliott or any three of them for to distribute this guift of one hundred pounds aforesaid To be paid by my Executor within nyne months after my decease.

EDUCATION AT WEAR GIFFORD

The recorded beginnings of a school at Wear Gifford derives from the charity established by John Lovering, Merchant, who lived in the parish, presumably at Wear Hall. There is documentary evidence linking John Lovering with Lord Fortescue, owner of Wear Hall, concerning matters of a charitable nature.

John Lovering died in 1671; in his Will he left money for the education of sixteen children of the poor at Wear Gifford. An extract from the Will said, *I bequeath one hundred pounds for a schoole to be placed either in Wear Gifford, Hunshoe* (Huntshaw) *Alscott* (Alverdiscott) *or Great Torington there where it shallbe thought most convenient by my executor and overseers or any two of them for to teach poore peoples children for to Read such as are not able to pay their childrens schooling themselves. And my will and meaning is that this one hundred pounds shalbe laid out in land to raise a yearly rent for ever for to pay the person for his or her paines that shall teach such children and the person that shall teach them is to be nominated and appointed by my executor and overseers or by any two of them or by any other whom they shall appoint. And it is my desire that this land may be purchased with all convenient speed after my decease and the said one hundred pounds to be paid by my executor att the sealing of the writings which are to be drawn by the learned in the Law and setled according to law for a Schoole for ever. And my will and meaning is that the poore children of Wear Jifford shall principally have the benefit of this schooling and if there be not poore children enough for to make up the number of sixteene boyes and girles or twenty for soe many he or she are to teach that undertake this employment then to take out of the next parishes soe many as will make up that number and if they of Weare Jifford will not or shall neglect to send their children to this Schoole then to take them off other adjacent parishes that will have their children taught and this rent soe raised as aforesaid to be collected and paid quarterly by them whom my executor and overseers or any two of them shall nominate and appoint hoping they wilbe carefull to choose such a person as may take paines with the children to teach them well. And when they can read well and can well read over the Bible then to receive others in their Roomes successively.*

The Deed to provide the annual capital for the bequest was drawn up on the 12th March 1694 by his son and sole executor, John Lovering, Merchant, residing in Chittlehampton in the County of Devon. (It is not known why it took 23 years to arrange.)

Historical documents relating to the Lovering Educational Foundation have been difficult to find. The Devon County Charity Commissioners held an enquiry into matters concerning the Parish of Huntshaw on the 8th March 1907. For that enquiry, they referred to a previous Charity Commissioners Report dated 1824. It contains detailed information concerning the 'Lovering Gift'. The following is a complete transcription of that report.

Lovering's Gift

John Lovering, by his will, bearing date 18th March 1671, gave £100 for a school, to be placed in Wear Gifford, Huntshaw, Alverdiscott or Great Torrington, when it should be thought most convenient by his executors, to teach the children of such poor people to read as were not able to pay for their schooling; the said £100 to be laid out in land, to raise a yearly rent, for ever, to be paid to the person who should take such children, such person to be appointed by his executors or overseers, or any other whom they should appoint; and he directed, that the poor children of Wear Gifford should principally have the benefit of the school; and if there should not be poor children enough to make up the number of 16 boys and girls, or 20, there should be taken out of the next parishes so many as would make up that number; and if those of Wear Gifford should neglect to send their children to the school, then the children should be taken out of the adjacent parishes,

He also gave to the poor of Wear Gifford, £50; to the poor of Great Torrington, £40; and to the poor of Huntshaw, £10; to be distributed by the person whom his executors should appoint, to such poor as were not in the books of the collectors of the poor in any of the said parishes; and he directed, that the said £100 should be given in the three sums beforementioned, to the parishes of Wear Gifford, Great Torrington and Huntshaw, to employed in land with the aforesaid £100 given for schooling poor children, because it might be easier to meet with a parcel of land for £200 than for £100 the yearly rent and profits of such land to be paid, half for schooling poor children as aforesaid, and the other half to be divided to the poor of the said three parishes, in proportion to the sums given as aforesaid; and he appointed John Lovering, his son, sole executor.

In 1680, Owen Feltham, esq. and three others, in consideration of £287 conveyed to the said John Lovering, the son, and his heirs, three closes of land, containing, by estimation, 11 acres, in the parish of Barnstaple, called Pilland, or the higher part of a tenement formerly called Great Pilland, then in the tenure of Richard Salisbury.

By indenture, bearing date 12th January 1683, between the said John Lovering, the son, of the first part; Richard Crossing, and six others, overseers of the said will, of the second part; and Arthur Fortescue, esq. and six others, of the third part; reciting the said will; and that the said John Lovering, the son, in pursuance of the intent of the said will, but not having an opportunity of a purchase exactly suitable to the said £200 had employed the sum of £287 according to his best discretion, in the purchase of the feesimple of the above-mentioned land, containing 11A 1R 13P. The said John Lovering, with the consent of the said parties of the second part, enfeoffed to the said parties of the third part, and their heirs, 8A & 11P parcel of the above-mentioned land, upon trust, that one moiety of the yearly rents and profits of the said 8A & 11P should be paid by the said feoffees, according to the directions of the said will, for the use of a schoolmaster or schoolmistress to be nominated as the said will had appointed, for the teaching of 16 poor children at the least; and that the other moiety of the said yearly rents and profits of the said 8A & 11P should be paid for ever, according to the directions of the said will, for the uses of the said poor people of Wear Gifford, Great Torrington and Huntshaw, as in the said will was directed, with power of appointing new trustees, when the survivors of those then appointed should be reduced to four. And it was thereby declared, that the said 8A & 11P were proportionate in value to the said sum of £200 given by the said will.

The last trust deed bears date the 2d May 1806, by which this land was conveyed to seven persons, all of whom are now living.

The trust property consists of a field in the parish of Barnstaple, called Salisbury's Meadow, containing about eight acres, now in the occupation of John Wilkinson, under a lease for 14 years, commencing at Lady-day 1814, at the yearly rent of £50 the feoffees repairing the fences. An auction was held previous to the granting of this lease. The field had been previously let for £21. The present tenant, after having paid £25 for the rent of one half year, applied for a reduction, and the feoffees thinking the rent much too high, agreed to reduce it to £40 per annum. At Michaelmas 1816, the feoffees agreed to deduct £5 more from the rent of the preceding year. From Michaelmas 1816 to Michaelmas 1822, the rent has been £30 per annum; but the feoffees were obliged to distrain for the sum due at the last-mentioned period, in consequence of which a charge of 10s was incurred to a solicitor, but no part of the rent was lost. The rent of £30 is said to be the fair annual value of the land, In 1818 the field was exonerated from the land tax. Henry Stoneman, esq. one of the trustees, receives the rents; and after deducting such small sums as may have been required for the repairs of the fences, divides the residue as follows:-

One moiety is paid to a schoolmaster of Wear Gifford, appointed by the trustees for teaching about 16 poor children of that parish to read. In the case of there not being a sufficient number of children of Wear Gifford, the parishes of Great Torrington and Huntshaw, are entitled to have children taught in the school; this right, however, has not been exercised for many years.

One fourth part is paid to one of the trustees residing in Wear Gifford, and distributed by them, about Christmas, amongst the poor of that parish.

Of the remaining fourth part of the rents, four-fifths are distributed by one or more of the trustees residing in the parish of Great Torrington, about Christmas, amongst the poor of that parish; and one-fifth is transmitted to a feoffee residing in the parish of Huntshaw, who makes a similar distribution amongst the poor thereof. The benefits of the charity in each of the parishes are confined to such poor persons as do not receive constant relief.

The other early references to the existence of a school in Wear Gifford was in 1821 in the 'Replies to Queries for the Bishop's Visitation' an endowed school is mentioned and is referred to again in the '1833 Abstract of Educational Returns' as a Daily Endowed School at which children, other than charity children, were taught for a fee.

The Elementary Education Act 1870 (The Forster Act) provided for the setting of elected School Boards to serve one or more parishes to provide facilities for education where this was lacking or deficient, at public expense. Thus Board Schools were established. Wear Gifford already had a purpose built school for over a decade. By the passing of the Education Act 1902 (The Balfour Act) the 'dual' system by which the two different types of schools were recognised and provided for under the 1870 Act, became all the more firmly entrenched. The School Boards created under the old Act disappeared, the County and Borough Councils became local education authorities responsible for elementary education. In Devon, apart from the Devon County Council, the LEA's were Exeter, Plymouth, Barnstaple, Tiverton and Torquay.

All schools had a body of managers, the constitution of which depended on the type of school whether a Council School (formerly a Board School) or a Voluntary School (Church of England, Methodist or Roman Catholic). While the Local Authorities bore the cost of maintaining Council Schools, the expense of maintaining the fabric of the voluntary schools was divided between the Managers and Local Authority, roughly on a landlord and tenant basis.

The Education Acts of 1870 and 1902 virtually made the Lovering Education Bequest superfluous. However, from 1912 the School Log Book records pupils awarded Lovering Scholarships, boys to Bideford Grammar School and girls to Edgehill College. Even after the Education Authority in 1921 had introduced their own scheme providing scholarships and free places to grammar and secondary schools (as the term was then used), this scheme was supplemented as far as Wear Gifford children were concerned, by Lovering Scholarships which continued to be awarded up to at least 1940. By 1944 the numbers on the roll, apart from evacuees, had dropped to 15, and in 1945 when the evacuees had departed, the school was closed and the remaining pupils transferred to Torrington.

Extant records of the Lovering's Charity only go back to 1903; the current trustees felt unable to clarify my list of scholars who had been awarded a Lovering's Scholarship since 1903 on the grounds of confidentiality. Thus, if I have omitted the names of any of those awarded a scholarship, please accept my apologies. My list was mainly extracted from the School Log Book and some from memory.

The current objectives of the Lovering Educational Foundation, last amended 1992, are as follows:-

The granting to boys and girls resident in the beneficial area who, in the opinion of the Trustees, are in need of financial assistance: (i) exhibitions tenable for any form of advancement of education; (ii) financial assistance, outfits, clothing, tools, instruments or books to enable beneficiaries on leaving school to prepare for, or assist their entry into, a trade, profession or calling. (Area of benefit:- the Parish of Wear Gifford, the Borough of Great Torrington, the Parishes of Huntshaw and Alverdiscott).

LOVERING SCHOLARSHIPS

1911	Olive Moore	Edgehill College
1912	Reginald Wise	Bideford Grammar School
1914	Hilda Gomer	Edgehill College
1914	Gwendoline Wise	Edgehill College
1915	Marie Banbrook	Edgehill College
1916	Richard Moore	Bideford Grammar School
1919	Doris Beer	Edgehill College
1920	Jessie Jeffery	Edgehill College
1925	Eric James Beer	Bideford Grammar School
1926	Marjorie Moore	Edgehill College
1929	Joan Mancy (Lucy Mabel)	Edgehill College
1929	Wallace McKenzie	Bideford Grammar School
1935	Norman Mitchell	Bideford Grammar School
1935	Eric Busby	Bideford Grammar School
1937	Rebecca Mary Grigg	Edgehill College
1938	Desmond James Grigg	Bideford Grammar School
1940	Alan George Pidler	Bideford Grammar School

OTHER AWARDS

1924	Phoebe Mancy	Devon County Scholarship to Edgehill College
1926	Stella May Brownjohn	Devon County Scholarship to Edgehill College
1927	Ida Doreen Beer	Devon County Scholarship to Edgehill College
1940	Peter Coad	Bridge Scholarship to Bideford Grammar School
1942	Margaret June Gilder	Devon County Scholarship (at a Plymouth School)
1944	William Lancelot Grigg	Awarded a special place at Bideford Grammar School

WEAR GIFFORD CHURCH OF ENGLAND SCHOOL

Head Teachers from 1860 to 1944

W Dart	1860 – 1868
R Drewe	1868 – 1868
W E Turner	1868 – 1869
J Shapland	1869 – 1883
W Bowden	1883 – 1889
E Philips	1889 – 1891
David Rees	1891 – 1898
H M Etherington	1898 – 1898
W Ashton Jewell	1898 – 1901
J M Tucker	1901 – 1909
F L Wyatt, Mrs	1909 – 1910
E J Sobey, Mrs	1911 – 1912
T W Mancy, Mrs	1912 – 1939
P M Tuckett (Temp)	16. 4. 1939 – 26. 5. 1939
A C White (Temp)	5. 6. 1939 – 3. 8. 1939
A H Vorsden (Temp)	11. 9. 1939 – 25. 10. 1939
I D P Barl (Temp)	1.11. 1939 – 3. 11. 1939
A H Vorsden (Temp)	6.11. 1939 – 21. 12. 1939
Gertrude J Arnold, Miss (Temp)	8. 1. 1940 – 10. 5. 1940
E M Turner, Mrs	14. 5. 1940 – 16. 8. 1940
F Christopher	16. 8. 1940 – 5. 9. 1940
E M Turner, Mrs	9. 9. 1944 – 26. 10. 1944
K G Gerry	1. 11.1944 – 4. 12. 1944

THE LOCATION OF THE EARLY SCHOOLS

One of the remaining mysteries concerning the first Lovering School is its location. An examination of the records and legends clearly point to Wear Gifford. John Lovering lived in the village and it would be not surprising if he was biased in favour of it being sited in Wear Gifford. Indeed, his Will clearly states that 'the poor children of Wear Gifford shall principally have the benefit of this schooling . . .' He goes on to say that if there were insufficient numbers from Wear Gifford, the school could 'take them off other adjacent parishes that will have their children taught'. In 'The History of Great Torrington in the County of Devon' by J J Alexander and W R Hooper, (published 1948) it states unequivocally that the Lovering School was placed at Wear Gifford but recognised that Torrington children had a right to attend it, and had done so for more than a century. Quoting from the Charity Report of 1824, 'the right to do so had not been exercised for many years'. To support the notion that the School had been located at Wear Gifford, they cite as evidence that the road leading from Torrington to Wear Gifford was called in consequence 'School Lane'. Messrs Alexander and Hooper were wrong to use the naming of 'School Lane' as supporting evidence; land documents as early as 1614 refer to 'School Lane', many years before the establishment of a Lovering endowed school. Never-the-less, the evidence puts beyond all reasonable doubt that the Lovering School was located in Wear Gifford; but where?

In my research experience, legends dare not be ignored; they often turn out to be entirely true, partially true or indeed, without discoverable foundation or, at worse, entirely false. It is to legend I initially turn to identify the location of the school. I was born at a cottage called 'Bonifants', near the old Methodist Chapel. My grandfather, John Beer, was born in the village in 1880 and lived at 'Bonifants' from the time of his marriage, 1909. On a number of occasions he told me that 'Bonifants' was formerly 'old dame school', a title often used to describe village schools in the 17th/18th centuries. He could offer no supporting evidence but was emphatic that it was true. Until the idea of writing this book came to me, I had not given the matter much thought. What is beyond doubt is that this cob cottage was built well within the period of the first Lovering School. Thinking about it some years ago, I considered the possibility that 'Bonifants' was a corruption of the combination of the two French words, 'bons enfants' i.e. 'good children'. I was reasonably comfortable with that hypothesis until I discovered that a Margery Bonefants died in the village 1774 age 114. Thus she would have been born 1660 and would have been age 34 when the first Lovering School was established. It is possible that Margery Bonefants lived in the cottage now called 'Bonifants' and became known by that name simply because it was occupied by her. At the risk of seeming to be facetious, Margery Bonefants was well qualified in terms of age to be referred to as 'an old dame'. There is, however, rather more compelling evidence; 'Bonifants' was not built in the traditional proportions of the average village cottage. Over the years I have visited most cottages in the village; in only one respect is 'Bonifants' unique. Its living room is at least twice the average size, certainly big enough to house sixteen pupils. Its location is as close as it could be for pupils from the adjacent parishes of Torrington, Huntshaw and Alverdiscott to attend. I am firmly convinced that, with the combination of legend, factual and circumstantial evidence, 'Bonifants' was the first Lovering School.

From the 'Replied to Queries for the Bishop's Visitation' in 1821 we know that an endowed school existed in the village; it was again referred to in the 1833 'Abstract of Education Returns'. However, the Tithe Map of 1837 contains no reference to a school from which it could be assumed that schooling was being conducted in a schoolmaster's or schoolmistress's own house or cottage. From the 1841 Census, there was one schoolmaster and two schoolmistresses scattered around the parish. Some time before 1850 (from the Directory and supported by the 1851 Census) a William Bennet Caple, Schoolmaster, and his Schoolmistress wife with their two children, Augusta and Albert, lived at Wear Dock. The address encompassed a row of cottages starting at the Bideford end with Roadcliffe Cottage (now Birdshouse) to a pair of cottages, now converted into one and known as Little Hill Cottage. The Caples lived in the cottage nearest Torrington. It can be assumed that the Caples used their home as the school endowed by John Lovering. When the first purpose built school was opened 1860, a William and Elizabeth Dart were appointed as Schoolmaster and Schoolmistress to run it.

In his 'Historical Notes on Devon Schools' (published by the Devon County Council 1989) Robert Bovett suggests two other possible locations for early schools in Wear Gifford. One was Roadcliffe Cottage, Wear Dock, and the other was Corner House at the bottom of Park Hill. However, research reveals no supporting evidence.

Bonifants, Wear Giffard. c.1700

Little Hill Cottages, formerly Wear Dock. c.1840.

THE NEW SCHOOL
1860

The plans for the Church of England School and School House were drawn by the well-known local architect. Richard Davie Gould of Barnstaple and was completed in 1859. The following year, 1860, the Earl Fortescue and Hugh, Lord Fortescue, under the School Sites Acts, conveyed to the Minister, Churchwardens and Overseers, a site for a school for "labouring and poorer classes" to be in union with and conducted according to the principles of the National Society. The school was centrally placed at Wear Quay.

Wear Quay. 1800. TREVOR FROST.
THE ARROW POINTS TO THE SITE WHERE THE NEW SCHOOL WAS BUILT. 1860.

CONVEYANCE (DEED POLL) 1860

(NDRO.2617 add 3/4)

Rt Hon Hugh, Earl Fortescue and Hugh, Lord Fortescue (aka Viscount Ebrington) of Castle Hill (under authority of Acts 5 & 8 Vict for affording facilities for the conveyance and endowments of sites for schools) freely and without valuable consideration grant and convey unto the Minister, churchwardens and overseers of the parish of Weare Gifford all that piece of land containing about 40 perches in the village of Weare Gifford, bounded on the NW by land of the sd Earl Fortescue, on the N by glebeland, on the SE by land of Earl Fortescue and on the SW by a public road, distinguished by the tithe numbers 820, 821, 822, 824, 825 and parts of 761 and 775.

To hold to the use of the sd Minister, churchwardens and overseers and their successors for the purposes of the sd Acts, upon trust to permit the sd premises to be forever used as and for a school for the education of children and adults or children only of the labouring and other poorer classes in the sd parish and for no other purpose. And the school shall always be in union with and conducted according to the principles of the National Society for promoting the Education of the Poor in the Principles of the Established Church..

The school to be managed as follows:
The Principal Officiating Minister to have superintendence of religious and moral instruction of all the scholars. He may use or direct the premises to be used as a Sunday School. In all other respects, control to be exercised by a Committee consisting of the Minister, his licensed curate(s) and two other persons, of whom Earl Fortescue and the Hon Mark Rolle be the first appointed (each contributing at least 20s per annum). Such persons to be members of the Church of England and landholders within the parish. Vacancies to be filled by election of contributors. No person to be appointed as Master or Mistress or the school who is not a member of the Church of England. The Committee to elect a Secretary. Minister to be Chairman.
Date: 10 March 1860
Enrolled in High Court of Chancery, 5 April 1860)
(For copy of marginal plan see page 15)

COMMUTATION OF TITHES OF WEAR GIFFORD – 1837

The tithe numbers referred to in the above conveyance (Deed Poll) 1860 are identified in the 1837 Wear Gifford Tithe Map as follows:

Tithe Nos	820 House and garden
	821 House and garden
	822 House
	all occupied by John Loyd
Tithe Nos	824 House
	825 Garden
	occupied by Thomas Turner
Tithe No	761 Gribbey Hill
	arable land being part of Wear Barton occupied by James Ford
Tithe No	775 Waste land belonging to the Rt Hon Lord Fortescue

All the above property was owned by and rented from the Rt Hon Earl Fortescue

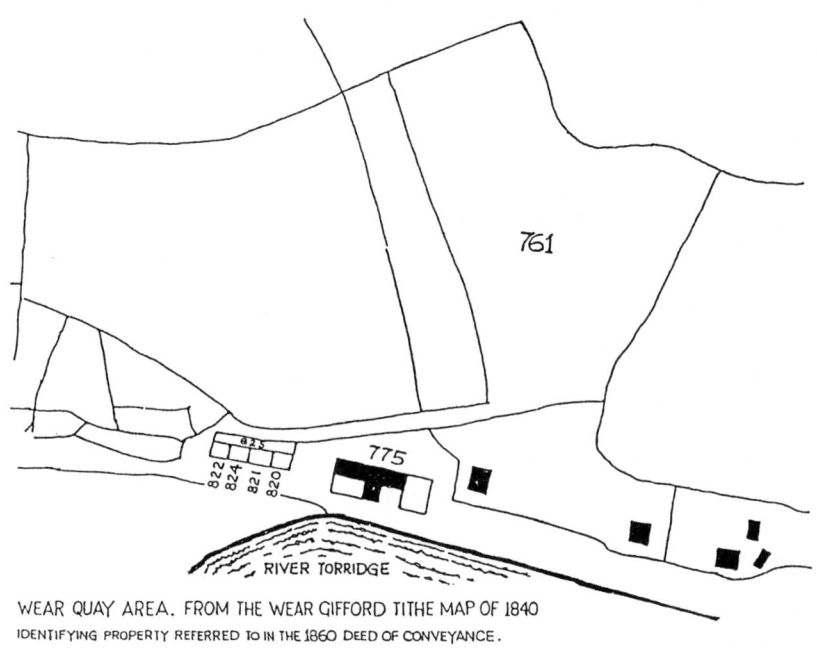

WEAR QUAY AREA. FROM THE WEAR GIFFORD TITHE MAP OF 1840
IDENTIFYING PROPERTY REFERRED TO IN THE 1860 DEED OF CONVEYANCE.

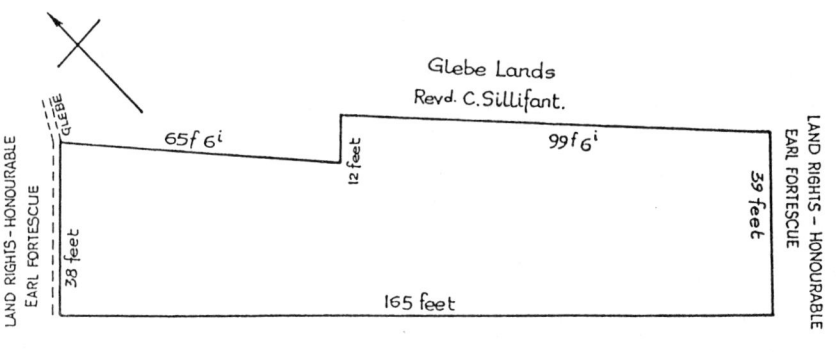

REDUCED COPY OF A PLAN REFERRED TO IN THE 1860 DEED OF CONVEYANCE.

PLANS OF WEAR GIFFORD CHURCH OF ENGLAND SCHOOL AND SCHOOL HOUSE

drawn by

TREVOR FROST
of Wear Gifford

from original plans by

RICHARD DAVIE GOULD

ARCHITECT – BARNSTAPLE

1859

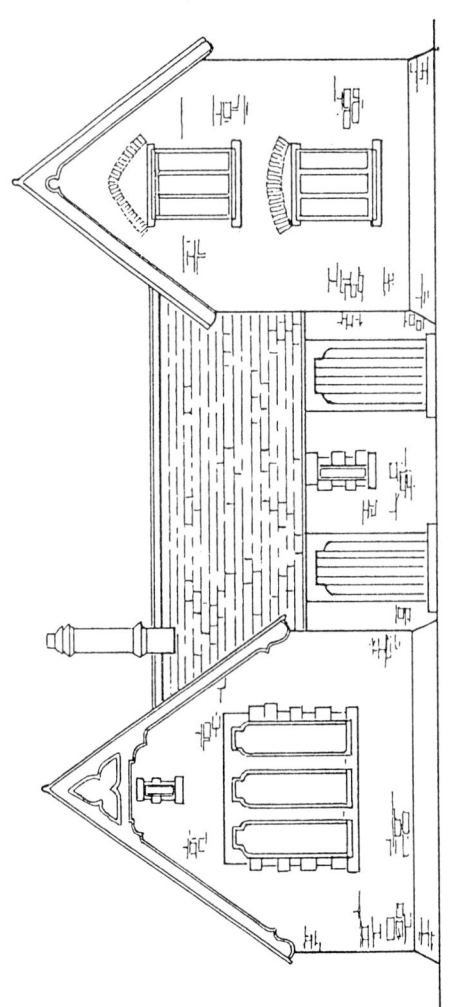

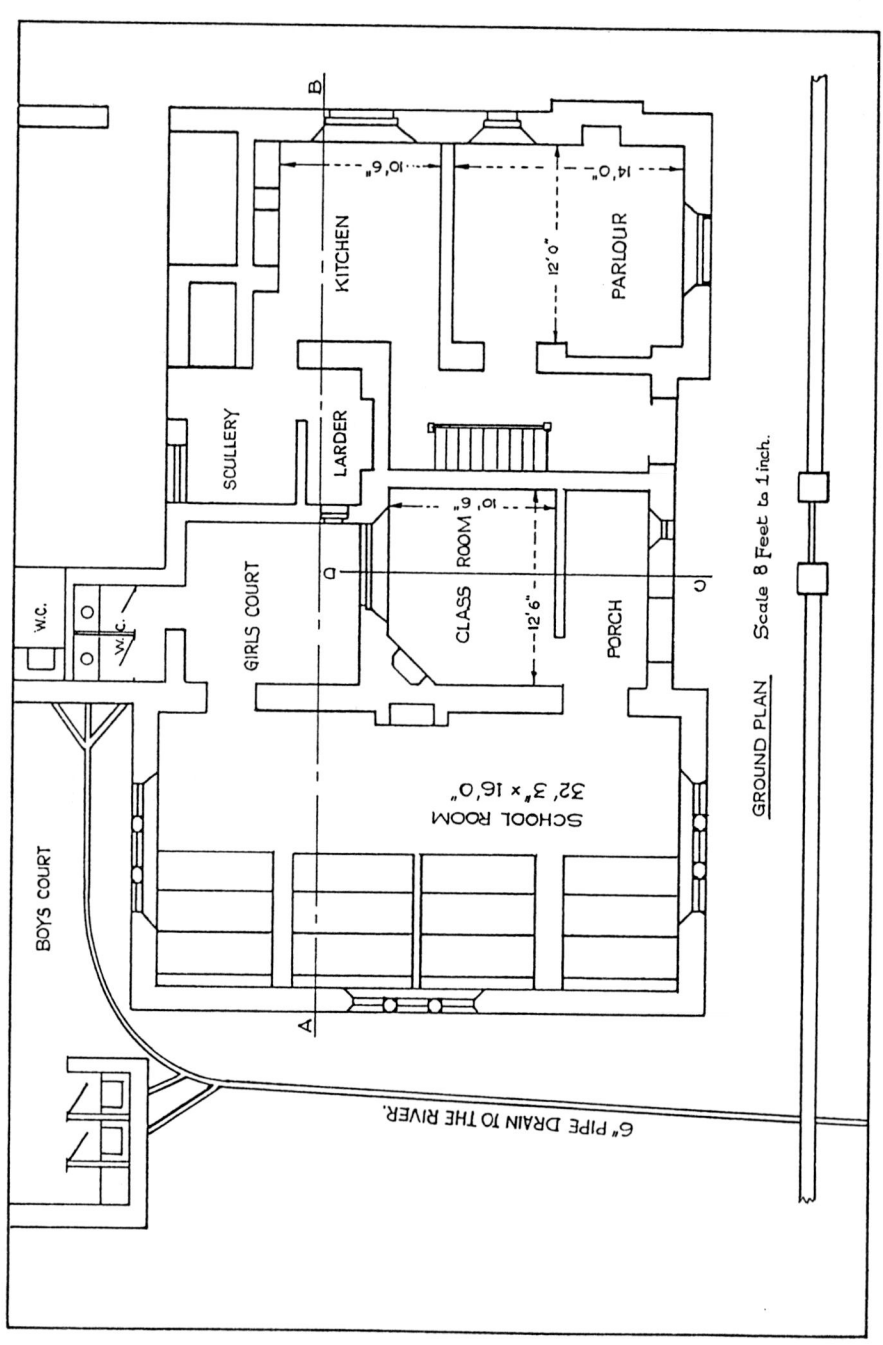

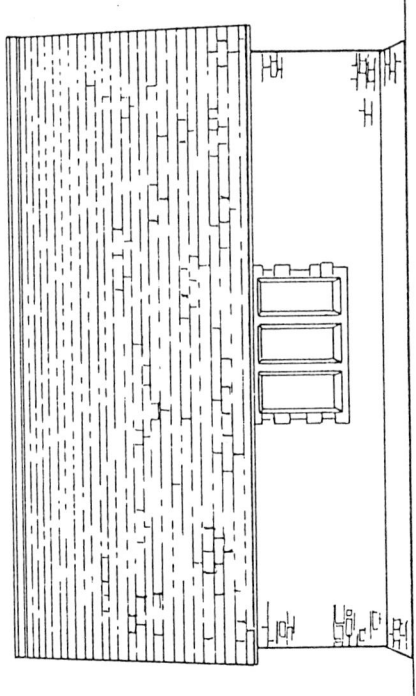

SIDE ELEVATION OF SCHOOL

Scale 8 feet to 1 inch.

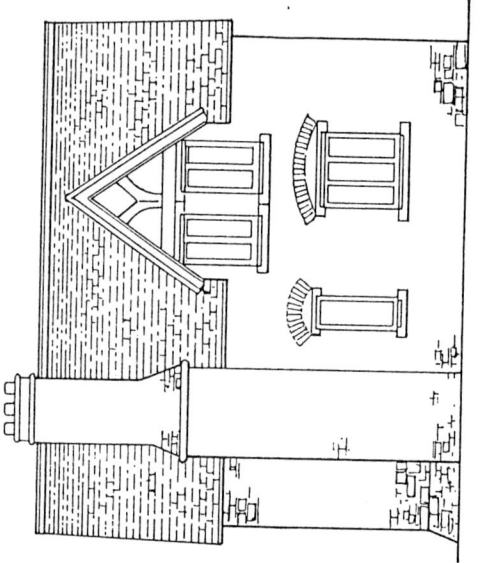

SIDE ELEVATION OF RESIDENCE.

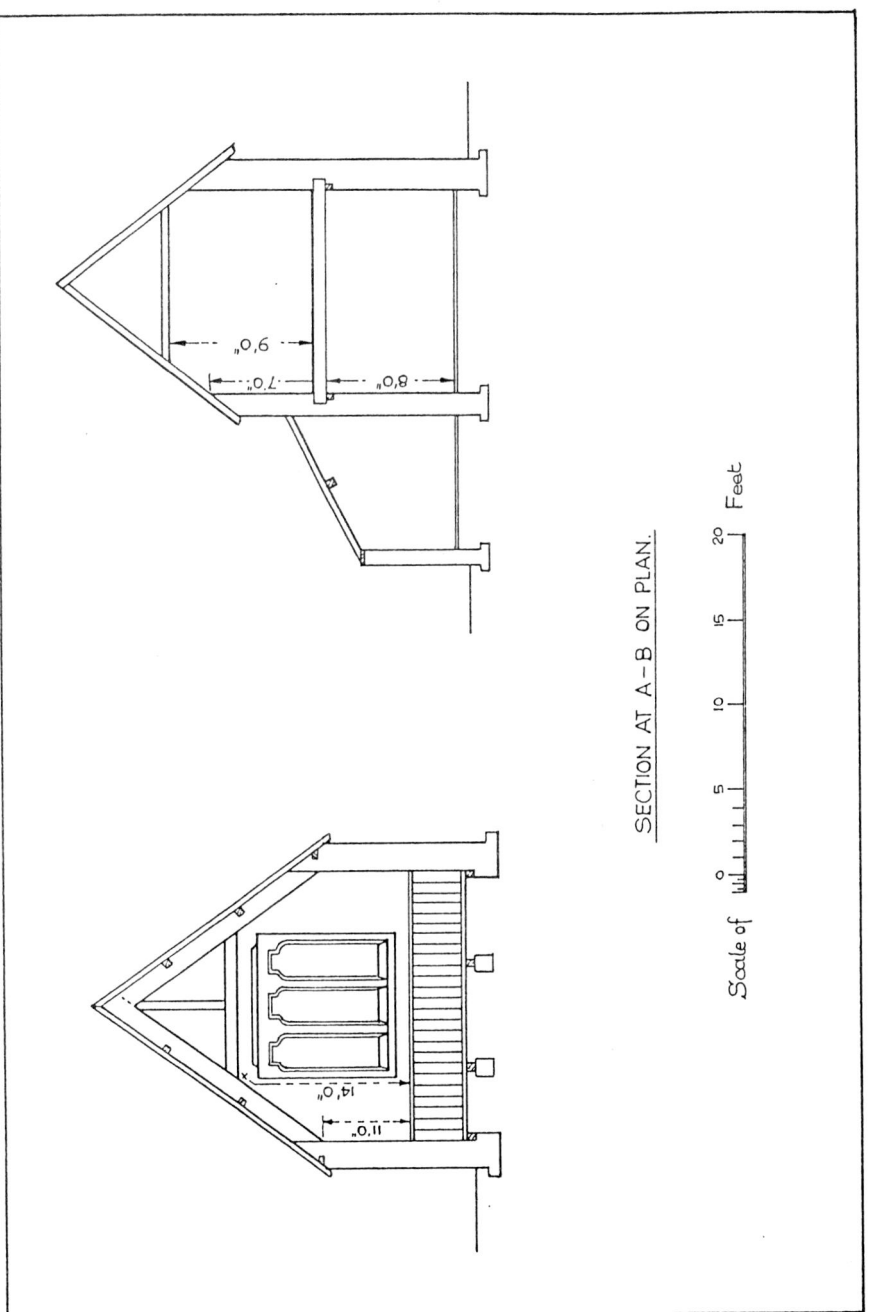

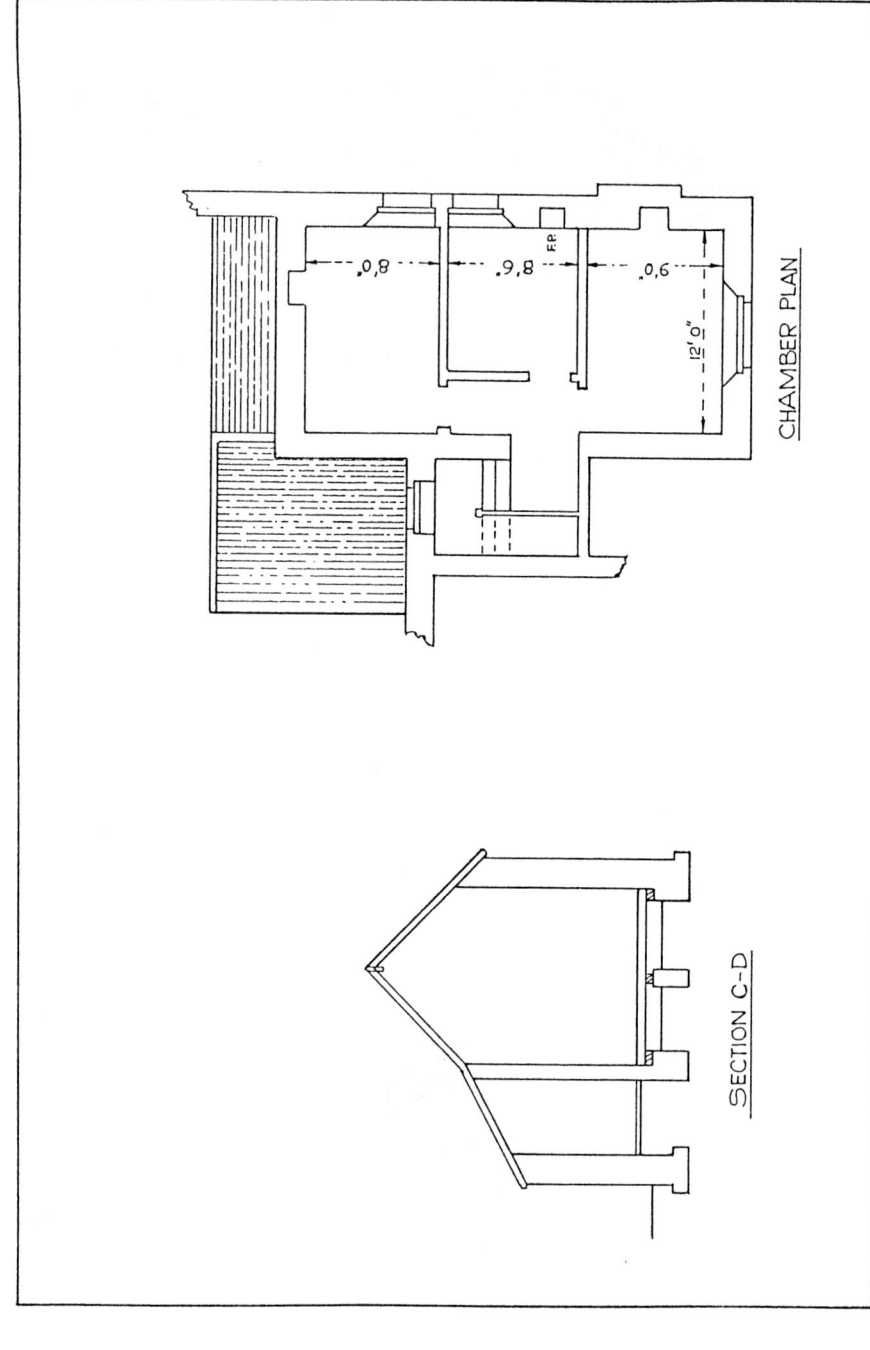

WEAR - GIFFORD ~ CHURCH SCHOOL ~ C1900.

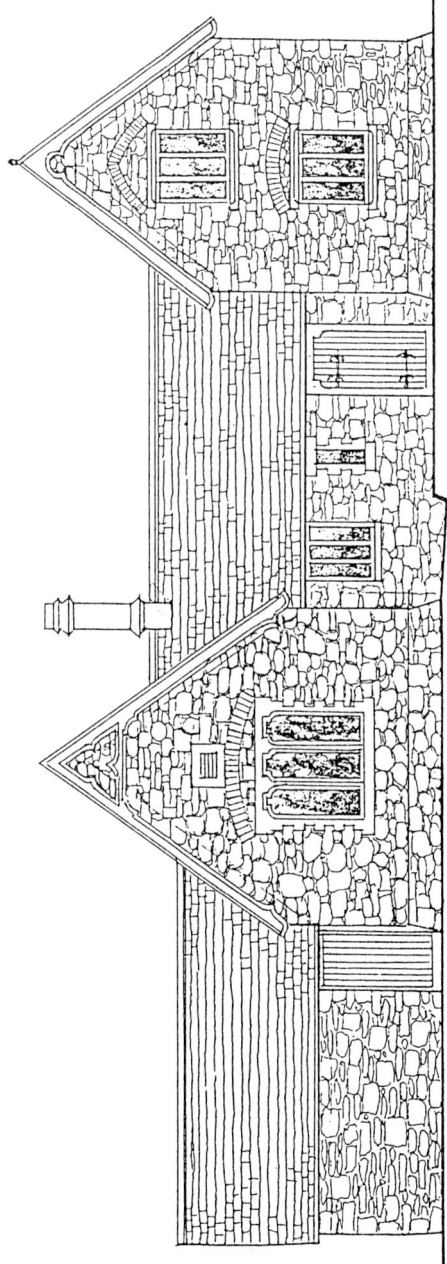

ELEVATION AGAINST ROAD

The drawing above illustrates the structural changes to the school circa 1900. Formerly the small wing on the right of the main school building provided the entrance leading immediately into the cloakroom. By transferring the entrance door to the new wing and replacing it with a window, the space was used to enlarge the infant classroom. The additional wing on the left functioned as the new cloakroom. The girls lavatories were made into a fuel shed and they took over the boys lavatories formerly located through and behind the new cloakroom. New lavatories for boys were built in the far corner of the playground.

BIBLIOGRAPHY

The Charity Commissioners Report concerning the 'Lovering Gift', published 1907.

The History of Great Torrington by J J Alexander and W R Hooper, published by Advance Studio, Sutton, Surrey, 1948.

Historical Notes on Devon Schools by Robert Bovett, published by Devon County Council, 1989.

REFERENCES

The Will of John Lovering, 1671, (Prob: 11/347) was obtained from the Public Record Office, Chancery Lane, London, WC2A 1L4.

The Wear Quay section of the Wear Gifford Tithe Map of 1840 was obtained from the North Devon Record Office, Barnstaple, Devon.

ACKNOWLEDGEMENTS

I acknowledge with thanks:

The kind permission given by the Devon County Council and Mrs Jean Bovett to quote freely from her late Husband's book, 'Historical Notes on Devon Schools'.

The Education Department of Devon County who kindly gave me permission to publish the Weare Gifford School Index, Admission Register, Log Book and miscellaneous documents. (N.D.R.O. 764C).

The kind permission given by the Reverend G J Hansford and the Parochial Church Council; of the Church of the Holy Trinity, Weare Gifford, to publish a copy of the school plans of 1859 and the Conveyance (Deed Poll) of 1860 with the marginal plan annexed. (N.D.R.O. 2617A 3/4).

The invaluable advice, information and photographs for this volume from: Miss Joan Mancy, Miss Phoebe Mancy, Mrs Violet Smart, Mr Howard Curtis, Mr David Rookes, Mrs Dulcie Nickels and Mrs Vera Griffin.

I also pay special tribute to Mr Trevor Frost whose artistic skills contributed significantly to this publication.

I am also grateful to Mr Tim Wormleighton, Senior Archivist at the North Devon Record Office, Barnstaple, and Mrs Margery M Rowe, formerly County Archivist, Devon Record Office, Exeter, who provided me with incomparable advice, assistance and encouragement.

Finally, without the dedication, hard work and long suffering of Mrs Rosemary Smith and Mrs Gill Leary who word-processed the book, it would not have been published.

PHOTOGRAPHIC SECTION

Wear Gifford School c. 1914

School Playground
Jubilee Day 1935   Dedication of the new Union Jack

1898

c. 1895 Girls
Front row: third from right, is Ellen Gomer, later Mrs Jack Beer At the back is Headmaster, David Rees

c. 1895 Boys

Second row from the front, third from the right, is George Gomer. On left is Headmaster, David Rees

c. 1904

1 Mr Tucker, Headmaster 2 ? 3 ? 4 Mary Parkhouse 5 Bert Clare 6 ?
7 Richard (Dick) Gomer 8 Minnie Start 9 ? 10 ? 11 ?
12 Florence Parkhouse (Mrs Prout) 13 Frank Braunton 14 ? 15 ? 16 ? 17 ? 18 ?
19 May Start 20 ? 21 Mabel Gomer 22 ? 23 Rose Start 24 ? 25 Percy Stapleton
26 ? 27 Hilda Gomer 28 ?

1912

1 ? 2 ? 3 Miss Ellis, Infant Teacher, 4 ? 5 Doris Beer, 6 ? 7 Dolly Hammett, 8 ? 9 Bruce Lake, 10 Gladys Start, 11 ? 12 ? 13 ? 14 Bill Chammings, 15 ? 16 Reggie Wise, 17 ? 18 ? 19 Lily Hammett, 20 Leslie Beer, 21 Jessie Jeffrey, 22 ?

c. 1923

Left to right

Back row: Eric Beer, Mrs Mancy, Reggie Beer, Frank Edworthy, Fred Cox, Jack Isaac, Leonard Beer.
Second row: Molly Cox, Dorothy Beer, Gladys Rooke, Ivy Edworthy, Phoebe Mancy, ?, Phyllis Beer, Florence Rooke.
Third row: Joan Moore, Joan Mancy, Ida Beer, Margery Beer, Vera Beer, Nita Beer.
Front row: Arthur Edworthy, Doris Moore, Marjorie Moore, Harold Edworthy.

c. 1924

Left to right

Back row: Miss Gertrude Banbrook, Alfie Tanton, Harold Edworthy, Freddie Beer, Willie Tyrell, Tommy Wooldridge, Eric Beer, Ernie Becklake.
Second row: Miss Bertha Parkhouse, Elsie Wise, Mollie Cox, ?, Lily Tyrell, Jessie Jeffrey, Doris Tanton, Winnie Henderson.
Third row: Ida Beer, Nita Beer, Elsie Beer, Barty Jelf, Margery Beer, Joan Moore.
Front row: Vera Beer, ?, ?.

1927

Left to right

Back row: Harold Edworthy, Frank Day, Frank Wilton, Alfie Tanton, Arthur Edworthy, William Moore, Wallace MacKenzie.

Second row: Margery Gilbert, Iris Day, Evelyn Beer, Phyllis Braunton, Hilda Dymond, Hilda Braunton, Vera Beer, Joan Mancy, Clara Becklake, Margery Beer.

Third row: Marjorie Squire, Winnie Lawrence, Gwen Braunton, Violet Curtis, Betty Busby, Dulcie Edworthy, Vera Braunton, Phyllis Squire.

Front row: Jack Braunton, Aubrey Braunton, George Gorvett, Sonny Braunton, Jimmy Martin, Ernie Becklake.

1928

Left to right

Back row: Billy Moore, Ernie Becklake, Jimmy Martin, Frank Wilton, Alfie Tanton, Arthur Edworthy, Wallace MacKenzie, Sonny Braunton, Harold Edworthy.

Middle row: Joan Moore, Joan Mancy, Phyllis Braunton, Elsie Beer, Margery Beer, Marjorie Gilbert, Hilda Braunton, Vera Beer, Evelyn Beer.

Front row: Jack Braunton, George Gorvett, Dulcie Edworthy, Clara Becklake, Violet Curtis, Gwen Braunton, Vera Braunton, Joyce Stevens, Aubrey Braunton.

1929

Left to right

Back row: Frank Day, Arthur Edworthy, Frank Wilton, Harold Edworthy, Jimmy Martin.

Second row: Eileen Grigg, Vera Braunton, Hilda Braunton, Iris Day, Phyllis Braunton, Vera Beer, Hilda Dymond, Evelyn Beer, Betty Busby, Margery Gilbert behind John Wooldridge, Jack Braunton, Gwen Braunton.

Third row: Clara Becklake, Winnie Lawrence, Dulcie Edworthy, George Gorvett, Sonny Braunton, Bill Dymond, Ernie Becklake, Joyce Stevens, Violet Curtis.

Front row: Kitty Braunton, Rosalie Beer, Mary Grigg, Marjorie Squire, Gwen Shute, Phyllis Squire, Harold Beer, Norman Mitchell.

1933

Left to right

Back row: Mrs Mancy and Miss Banbrook
Second row: Eric Busby, Ernie Becklake, Edith Gordon, Clara Becklake, Vera Braunton, Evelyn Stevens, Iris Day, Sonny Braunton, Aubrey Braunton.
Third row: Mary Prouse, Kitty Braunton, Winnie Lawrence, Phyllis Squire, Joyce Tanton, Eileen Grigg, Mary Grigg.
Fourth row: Olive Cole, Joan Braunton, Lily Stevens, Vera Beer, Evelyn Cole, Marjorie Squire.
Front row: Desmond Grigg, Dick Lawrence, Harold Beer, Billy Lawrence, Ernie Gorvett, Alec Parkhouse, Norman Mitchell.

1934

Left to right

Back row: Eric Busby, Evelyn Stevens, Gwen Braunton, Violet Curtis, Eileen Grigg, Vera Braunton, Norman Mitchell, Mrs Mancy.

Second row: Miss Banbrook, Clara Becklake, Ernie Gorvett in front of Clara Becklake, Rosalie Beer, Mary Grigg, Lily Stevens, Marjorie Squire, Joyce Tanton, Winnie Lawrence, Kitty Braunton, Olive Cole, Alec Parkhouse, Ivor Parkhouse.

Third row: Evelyn Cole, Edith Braunton, Mary Prouse, Jean Ortway, Jean Slee, Joan Braunton, Vera Beer.

Front row: Harold Beer, Derek Gibbons, Dick Lawrence, Bill Lawrence, Reggie Lawrence, Desmond Grigg, Ronnie Gorvett, Ernie Cole.

1935

Left to right

Back row: Lilian Stevens, Mary Grigg, Dorothy Netherway, Winnie Lawrence, Rosalie Beer.

Second row: Cecil Netherway, Harold Beer, Evelyn Cole, Mary Heddon, Olive Cole, Vera Beer, Joan Braunton, Desmond Grigg, Ernie Cole.

Third row: Betty Hunt, Gladys Lawrence, Queenie Cole, Edith Braunton, Betty Beer, Betty Grigg, Mary Prouse, Sheila Short, Kathleen Carter, Glenys Grigg.

Front row: Ernie Gorvett, Reggie Lawrence, Ronnie Gorvett, John Martin, Alan Pidler, Allan Coad, Albert Lawrence, Peter Coad, Howard Curtis, Bill Lawrence, Dick Lawrence.

1936

Left to Right

Back row: Mrs Mancy, Winnie Lawrence, Eileen Grigg, Violet Curtis, Vera Braunton, Joyce Heddon, Mary Grigg, Miss Banbrook.

Second row: Cecil Netherway, Harold Beer, Lavinia Plows, Rosalie Beer, Lilian Stevens, Kitty Braunton, Mary Heddon, Vera Beer, Joan Braunton, Olive Cole, Evelyn Cole, Kingsley Plows, Desmond Grigg.

Third row: Christopher Plows, Bill Lawrence, Derek Gibbons, Trevor Plows, Betty Grigg, Gwenneth Matthews, Edith Braunton, Merlin Matthews, Betty Beer, Ernie Gorvett, Ronnie Gorvett, Dick Lawrence, Ernie Cole.

Front row: Howard Curtis, Reggie Lawrence, Queenie Cole, Kathleen Carter, Gladys Lawrence, Mildred Matthews?, Sheila Short, Nancy Tucker, Iris Gibbons, Glenys Grigg, Margaret Tucker, Mary Prouse, Allan Coad, Peter Coad, John Martin.

1939

Left to right

Back row: Ernie Gorvett, Cecil Netherway, Kitty Braunton, Rosalie Beer, Lily Stevens, Mary Heddon, Vera Beer, Ena Trathen, Ernie Cole, Ronnie Gorvett.

Middle row: Mary Prouse, Betty Grigg, Queenie Cole, Betty Beer, Edith Braunton, Sheila Short.

Front row: George Prouse, Kathleen Carter, Phyllis Evans, Betty Hunt, Howard Curtis.

1940

1, 2 & 3 Mancy friends and relations, 4 John Martin, 5 Peter Coad, 6 Betty Grigg, 7 Mavis Allen, 8 Glenys Grigg, 9 Irene Ford, 10 Mary Tanton, 11 Kathleen Carter, 12 Billy Grigg, 13 Sheila Short, 14 Phyllis Evans, 15 Phyllis Tanton, 16 Betty Hunt, 17 Mary Martin, 18 Phyllis Prouse, 19 George Prouse.

WEAR GIFFORD RECTORY
Ascension Day Party
1924

1 Dorothy Beer   2 Lily Isaac   3 ?   4 ?   5 Frank Mancy   6 Willie Tyrell   7 ?
8 Dolly Hammett   9 Lily Hammett   10 Sydney Stevens   11 ?   12 Lily Tyrell
13 Walter Tucker   14 Phoebe Mancy   15 Nellie Henderson   16 Ida Beer   17 Jack Isaac
18 Elsie Wise   19 Doris Tanton   20 Phyllis Beer   21 Winnie Henderson   22 Alfie Tanton
23 ?   24 Joan Mancy   25 Vera Beer   26 Margery Beer   27 Eric Beer

WEAR GIFFORD RECTORY
Ascension Day Party

1 Winnie Henderson   2 Elsie Wise   3 Nellie Henderson   4 Sid Stevens   5 Jack Isaac
6 Lily Tyrell   7 Frank Mancy   8 ?   9 ? Gilbert   10 Eric Beer   11 Phyllis Beer
12 Millie Beer   13 Doris Tanton   14 Alfie Tanton   15 Joan Mancy   16 Margery Beer
17 Vera Beer   18 ?   19 Ida Beer

SCHOOL MANAGERS

Frederick James Beer
1871 - 1938

Thomas Wilton
1872 - 1964

Thomas Edward Wooldridge
1884 - 1976

Mrs Selina Armstrong
1855 - 1943

Landwaters (Floods) at Wear Gifford

SCHOOL SANITARY INSPECTORS

William Gomer 1858 - 1931
in the uniform of the 4th Devon Rifle Volunteers

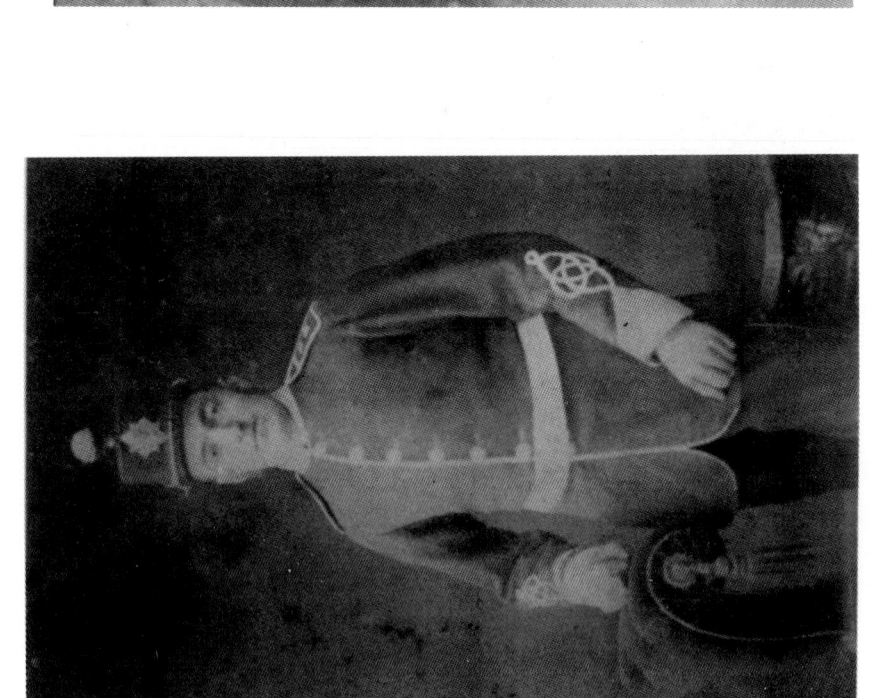

Richard Gomer 1863 - 1927
(brother of William Gomer)

The Reverend Richard Moyses Rector of Holy Trinity Church,
Wear Gifford 1921 - 1931
School Correspondent

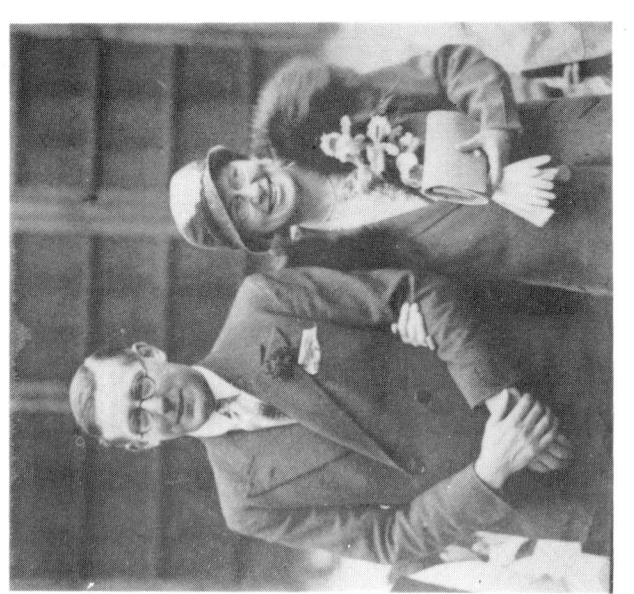

Mr & Mrs Lampard-Vachell of Wear Hall
who gave Christmas parties for all the schoolchildren

Torrington May Fair
1935

WEAR GIFFORD

CHURCH OF ENGLAND SCHOOL

INDEX TO ADMISSION REGISTER

1905 - 1945

WEARE GIFFARD CHURCH OF ENGLAND SCHOOL ADMISSION REGISTER, 1905-1945

INDEX

NAME IN FULL	ADMISSION NO	NAME IN FULL	ADMISSION NO	NAME IN FULL	ADMISSION NO
Allcock, Ellie	568	Babb, Winifred Mary	445	Beer, Rosalie May	732
Ackland, Frederick	647	Becklake, Edith Sarah	448	Beer, Harold Richard	735
Allin, Mavis Joyce	801	Brown, Dora	463	Braunton, Joan Madeline	736
Allin, Royston Owen	850	Braund, Winifred	479	Busby, Eric Donald	742
		Braund, Edwin	495	Braunton, Joan Madeline	736
		Beer, Nita	514	Ball, Bertie Douglas John	739
		Beer, Leslie	533	Ball, Leslie Cecil George	750
		Brownjohn, Stella May	542	Ball, Marjorie Mary	751
		Braunton, Phyllis May	543	Ball, Reginald Thomas	752
		Beer, Lilian Evelyn	545	Ball, Ethel May	753
		Braunton, John Thomas	546	Beer, Vera May (2)	756
		Braunton, Aubrey	547	Brodie, Kathleen	761
		Bailey, Joseph Edwin	548	Busby, Betty Nesta	706
		Bailey, Gwendoline Annie	558	Braunton, Beatrice Edith	765
		Bailey, Winifred Doris	570	Braunton, Beatrice Edith	765
		Bailey, Victor Douglas	514	Beer, Betty	768
		Bailey, Victor Douglas	479	Beer, Betty	768
		Becklake, Clara	543	Becklake, Mary	805
		Braunton, Vera Maud	542		
		Busby, Betty Nesta	598		
		Braunton, Gwendoline Mary	610		
		Banbrook, Gertrude Mary	619		
		Braunton, Gwendoline Mary	621		
Braddon, Elsie		Bailey, Winifred Doris	546		
Beer, Florence		Braunton, Alfred John	627		
Beer, Leonard Owen		Braunton, Hilda May	621		
Beer, Doris		Braunton, John Henry	635		
Banbrook, John		Braunton, Gwendoline Mary	636		
Beer, Nita		Braunton, Kathleen Joyce	637		
Beer, Leslie		Braunton, Kathleen Joyce	648		
Banbrook, Marie					
Banbrook, Edna					
Baker, Elsie					
Baker, Frances					
Baker, Alfred					
Baker, John					
Beer, Frederick Ernest					
Beer, Dorothy Mary					
Beer, Nita					
Beer, Doris					
Banbrook, Edna					
Banbrook, Marie					
Beer, Phyllis Mabel					
Beer, Reginald Albert					
Busby, Joyce					
Beer, Marjory Ellen					
Baker, Frances					
Banbrook, Gertrude					
Beer, Marjory Ellen					
Beer, Elsie Winifred					
Beer, Eric James					
Beer, Ida Doreen					
Beer, Vera May (1)					

INDEX

NAME IN FULL	ADMISSION NO	NAME IN FULL	ADMISSION NO	NAME IN FULL	ADMISSION NO
Clements, Horace	464	Davey, Thomas Wm	576	Edworthy, Ethel	450	Fisher, Walter	480
Chamings, Doris	477	Davey, Thomas Wm	576	Edworthy, Winifred	491	Furseman, William	567
Chamings, Wm Henry	531	Drowley, Albert John	614	Edworthy, Francis Wm	539	Fowler, Amy	590
Chamings, Alfred	538	Drowley, Wm George	615	Edworthy, Elizabeth Ivy	580	Fairhead, Grace	608
Cooke, Beatrice Mary	559	Davey, Thomas Wm	576	Edworthy, Winifred	491	Fairhead, Ralph Jeffery	623
Cooke, Frederick Wm Hanford	581	Drew, George	643	Edworthy, Mary	612	Fairhead, Ralph Jeffery	623
Chapman, Freda	604	Day, Frank	719	Edworthy, Mary	612	Ford, Irene May	822
Chamings, Emma	609	Day, Iris Jean	720	Edworthy, Arthur George	651		
Chapman, Evelyn	611	Dymond, William Douglas	723	Edworthy, Harold Henry	662		
Cox, Leslie	617	Dymond, Hilda Frances	724	Edworthy, Harold Henry	662		
Cox, Frederick	618	Day, Frank	719	Edworthy, Dulcie Violet Joy	710		
Chapman, Evelyn	611	Duncan, Margaret Mary	835	Evans, Phyllis Mary French	802		
Cox, Percy Wm	620			Evans, Vera	852		
Chamings, Emma	609			Egan, Gladys Mary	854		
Cox, Mary Ann	625						
Coniam, Percy Wm	646						
Coniam, Percy Wm	646						
Clarke, Albert	686						
Clarke, Dorothy	687						
Curtis, Violet	714						
Challice, Beryl	726						
Cole, Evelyn Florence	744						
Cole, Olive Gwendoline	745						
Cole, Ernest Francis	767						
Coad, Peter	769						
Cole, Queenie Doreen	772						
Curtis, Albert Howard Henry	780						
Coad, Peter	785						
Carter, Kathleen Ruby	792						
Coad, Allan James	794						
Clements, Desmond Reuben	797						
Coad, Allan James	794						
Coad, Peter	785						
Coad, Allan James	794						
Coad, Allan James	818						
Coad, Peter	819						

INDEX

NAME IN FULL	ADMISSION NO	NAME IN FULL	ADMISSION NO	NAME IN FULL	ADMISSION NO
Gomer, Hilda	441	Hammett, Dorothy ✗	500	Isaac, Lilian Ruby	549	Joliffe, Gladys	485
Gilbert, Florence	465	Huxtable, Charles	525	Isaac, John	556	Jeffery, Jessie	515
Gomer, Florence	575	Huxtable, Lily	526	Isaac, Brian Ernest John	825	Joliffe, Lily Matilda	572
Gerry, Elizabeth	577	Huxtable, Albert	527			Jewell, William	595
Gomer, Florence	575	Huxtable, Emily	529			Jewell, John	596
Gilbert, Roy	626	Hammett, Lilian ✗	532			Jeffery, Vera	607
Gilbert, Florence Susan	665	Huxtable, Annie	541			Jeffery, Vera	607
Gilbert, Mildred Adelaide	666	Heale, Walter	565			Jolliffe, Lily Matilda	572
Gilbert, Gladys Gertrude	667	Heale, Percy	564			Jelfs, Barry	634
Gilbert, Marjorie Frances	671	Heale, Beatrice	566			Jelfs, Barry	634
Gorvett, William George	716	Heale, Henry	571			Jelfs, Barry	634
Grigg, Eileen	729	Huxtable, Florence	574			Johnson, Alfred	681
Grigg, Mary	730	Henderson, Helen Lucy	644			Johnson, John	682
Gordon, Edith Mary	743	Henderson, Winifred	645			Jewell, Christine Winifred	804
Grigg, Desmond James	746	Hearn, Gladys May	696			Jeffery, Jean Pauline	816
Gorvett, Ernest	733	Husband, Marjory	738			Jeffery, Joel	817
Gorvett, Ronald Aubrey	760	Husband, Janie	739			Jenner, Peter	815
Grigg, Bettine Beryl	*773	Husband, Sheila	740				
Grigg, Glenys Linda	793	Husband, Walter	741				
Gibbons, Derek John	771	Hoblin, Peggy	757				
Gibbons, Iris Beryl	796	Hedden, Joyce Annie	783				
Gibbons, Derek John	771	Hedden, Mary Edith	784				
Grigg, William Lancelot	811	Hunt, Elizabeth Joan	799				
Goulding, Beryl	813	Huxtable, Marjorie	827				
Goulding, Joyce	814	Huxtable, Greta	828				
Gilder, Margaret June	823	Huxham, Donald A.	843				
Goulding, Diane	830	Huxham, Jean W.	844				
Griffin, Joan	833						
Grigg, Hilary	840						
Griffin, Robert John	851						

*This admission number has been duplicated; it also applies to Reginald George Lawrence.

INDEX

NAME IN FULL	ADMISSION NO	NAME IN FULL	ADMISSION NO	NAME IN FULL	ADMISSION NO
Lake, Bruce	524	Moore, Richard	453	Martin, Frederick Wm John	782	Nethercott, Vera	592
Langmead, George	560	Moore, George	540	Mathews, Mildred Esther	795	Nethercott, William	593
Langmead, Fred	561	Mancy, Frank Vernon	557	Martin, Betty Florence Mary	808	Netherway, Dorothy	777
Langmead, Frank	562	Martin, Frederick	501	Martin, Frederick Wm John	782	Netherway, Cecil	778
Langmead, Charles	563	Mancy, Phoebe	573	Martin, Betty Florence Mary	808	Netherway, Dorothy	777
Lake, Edith Mary	597	Moore, John Pickard	589				
Lewis, Bessie	602	Martin, Frederick	501				
Langmead, Charles	563	Martin, Flossie	603				
Lawrence, Winifred Amy	725	Moore, Doris Gertrude	624				
Lawrence, Richard John	732	Moore, Marjory Ellen	633				
Lawrence, Winifred Amy	725	Martin, Frederick	501				
Lawrence, William Henry	763	Mills, Marjory Phyllis	638				
Lawrence, Richard John	747	Manning, Cyril	656				
Lawrence, William Henry	763	Mancy, Lucy Joan Mabel	657				
Lawrence, Reginald George	*773	Moore, Joan Ann	660				
Lawrence, Gladys May	781	Martin, James W^m	664				
Long, Eric George	845	Mugford, Ivy	673				
London, James Anthony	847	Mugford, Amy	674				
Lee, Jeffrey	848	Mugford, George	675				
		Mugford, Barbara	678				
		Mugford, Amy	674				
		Manning, Ruth Lilian	684				
		Moore, William Heywood	691				
		Manning, Ruth Lilian	684				
		Martin, Ivor William	698				
		McKenzie, John Wallace	700				
		Manning, Myrtle	702				
		Manning, Cyril	656				
		Martin, Ivor W^m	698				
		May, Thomas Geoffrey	728				
		Mitchell, William Norman	734				
		Moyse, Eric	759				
		Matthews, Merlyn Saskadoc	774				
		Mathews, Gwendolyn Manadoc	775				

*This number has been duplicated; it also applies to Betune Beryl Grigg

INDEX

NAME IN FULL	ADMISSION NO	NAME IN FULL	ADMISSION NO	NAME IN FULL	ADMISSION NO
Orchard, Virginia	690	Parker, Maurice	737	Rew, Ernest	591	Squire, George	443
Oatway, Jean	*770	Parkhouse, Bertha	432	Rookes, Gladys Mary	594	Short, Thomas	454
Oatway, Jean	824	Pengilly, John	434	Rookes, Florence May	632	Squire, William	466
		Perryman, Daniel George	551	Redwood, Horace Ayre	803	Start, Gladys	483
		Perryman, Harry Roy	552			Smith, Rex	517
		Perryman, Richard	553			Stevens, Sidney	550
		Perryman, Minnie	554			Squires, Dorothy	569
		Pankhurst, Alfred	616			Squires, Violet	578
		Pearson, Kenneth Alfred	676			Stevens, Sidney	550
		Porter, Edward	709			Scott, Muriel Mary	600
		Parker, Maurice	737			Squire, Cora Mabel	606
		Parker, Maurice	737			Squire, Cora Mabel	606
		Parkhouse, Ivor Claude	754			Start, Gladys	483
		Parkhouse, Alec	756			Squire, Violet Annie	613
		Prouse, Ada Mary	762			Stevens, Rose	649
		Pidler, Alan George	779			Squire, Pamela	654
		Plows, Loveridge Jack	787			Squire, Muriel	655
		Plows, Kingsley Gordon	788			Squire, Charles Thomas	669
		Plows, Lavinia Christine	789			Squire, Frederick Arthur	670
		Plows, Trevor Newton	790			Squire, Charles Thomas	669
		Plows, Christopher John	791			Stevens, Kathleen Joyce	697
		Prouse, William George	800			Skinner, William Henry	699
		Poore, Raymond	807			Stevens, Evelyn Beatrice	705
		Poore, Raymond	807			Stevens, Kathleen Joyce	697
		Prouse, Phyllis Mabel	810			Squire, Phyllis Mary	715
		Prouse, Albert	839			Stevens, Evelyn Beatrice	705
		Pidler, June	849			Squire, Phyllis Mary	715
		Prouse, Sylvia Ann	853			Squire, Marjorie Ada	718
						Squire, Norman Trevor	722
						Shute, Gwendoline Mary Alice	727
						Stevens, Lilian	764
						Stevens, Evelyn Beatrice	705
						Slee, Jean	766
						Smith, Joan Audrey	776
						Short, Sheila Mary	786

*This admission number has been duplicated; it also applies to Margaret Rose Tucker

INDEX

NAME IN FULL	ADMISSION NO	NAME IN FULL	ADMISSION NO	NAME IN FULL	ADMISSION NO
Short, Sheila Mary	786	Tucker, Charles	459	Vinnicombe, Alfred James	772	Wise, Gwendoline	446
Short, Mary Frances	809	Tucker, William	484	Vanstone, Winifred	830	Wilton, Thomas	481
Short, Margaret	855	Tucker, Walter Henry	579	Vanstone, John	846	Wilton, William	537
Stroud, Moreen	841	Tithecott, Melbourne	588			Woolridge, Thomas	599
Stroud, Shirley	842	Tanton, Doris	605			Williams, Violet	601
		Tanton, William Alfred	628			Williams, Violet	601
		Tyrell, William John	630			Wise, Elsie May	622
		Tyrell, Lily Cory	631			Wheeler, Frances Maud	639
		Tithecott, Leslie	650			Wheeler, Reginald John	640
		Tithecott, Melbourne	588			Wheeler, Frank	641
		Tanton, Joyce	731			Wheeler, George	642
		Tanton, Joyce	731			Woolridge, Thomas	599
		Tucker, Margaret Rose	*770			Wilton, Frank Anthony	672
		Tucker, Nancy May	771			Williams, Reginald	683
		Trathen, Ena Nellie	806			Wilcox, William John	689
		Tanton, Phyllis Margaret	820			Wicks, Kenneth	701
		Tanton, Mary Christine	821			Williams, Gertrude	721
		Taylor, Shirley	826			Wooldridge, John Edward	733
		Tanton, Linda	834			Wicks, John	812
		Tucker, Ernest	838			Welbrock, Jean	829
						Worden, June	832
						Worden, Thomas Arthur	836
						Worden, Hazel Elizabeth	837

*This admission number has been duplicated; it also applies to Jean Oatway

WEAR GIFFORD

CHURCH OF ENGLAND SCHOOL

REGISTER

1905 - 1945

WEARE GIFFARD CHURCH OF ENGLAND SCHOOL ADMISSION REGISTER, 1905-1945 REGISTER

Admission No.	Date of Admission	Full Name of Child	Name of Parent or Guardian	Address	Date of Birth	Name of Last School	Date of Last Attendance at this School	Cause of Leaving and Remarks
432	3.4.1905	Parkhouse, Bertha	William	Ford View	31.3.1901	None	17.9.1915	Exempt by age. Employed as monitor.
434	5.6.1905	Pengilly, John	Douglas	The Hill, W.G.	8.11.1901	None	5.11.1915	Exempt by age. Employed at Annery House.
441	5.3.1906	Gorner, Hilda	Richard	The Post Office, W.G.	8.1.1903	None	6.8.1914	Gone to Edgehill College, Bideford. Won Lovering Scholarship.
443	7.3.1906	Squire, George	Thomas	Prospect Place, W.G.	8.7.1902	None	14.4.1916	Exempt by attendance. Employed by Mr T. Moore.
445	15.5.1906	Braddon, Elsie	William	Venton Cottage, W.G.	25.3.1901	None	24.3.1915	Exempt by age. Gone to service.
446	21.5.1906	Wise, Gwendoline	Frederick	Brookham, W.G.	10.1.1903	None	6.8.1914	Gone to Edgehill College, Bideford. Won Lovering Scholarship.
448	22.5.1906	Beer, Florence	Herbert	Weare Giffard	7.5.1902	None	4.5.1916	Exempt by age. Employed at home, gloving.
450	11.6.1906	Edworthy, Ethel	Charles	North Firs, W.G.	15.3.1902	None	30.3.1916	Exempt by age. Gone to service at Park Farm, Weare Giffard.
453	15.2.1907	Moore, Richard	William H.	Polkinghorne, W.G.	29.10.1903	None	27.9.1916	Gone to Bideford Grammar School. Won the Lovering Scholarship.
454	8.4.1907	Short, Thomas	William	Venton Farm, W.G.	20.1.1902	None	29.1.1915	Exempt by Labour Certificate. Working on father's farm.
459	3.6.1907	Tucker, Charles	George	Annery Kiln, W.G.	5.2.1903	None	14.4.1916	Exempt by attendance. Employed by Mr Nicholls.
463	22.10.1907	Beer, Leonard Owen	Herbert	Weare Giffard	16.11.1903	None	4.5.1917	Exempt by attendance. Employed by Mr T. Beer
464	13.1.1908	Clements, Horace	Frederick	The Hill, W.G.	11.2.1904	None	9.3.1917	Labour Certificate. Exempt by attendance. Employed by his father (market gardener).
465	10.3.1908	Gilbert, Florence	Arthur	Chope's Bridge, W.G.	26.9.1903	None	4.5.1917	Exempt by attendance. Employed at home.
466	26.3.1908	Squire, Miriam	Thomas	Prospect Place, W.G.	15.1.1905	None	17.1.1919	Exempt by age. Employed at home.
477	16.11.1908	Chamings, Doris	William	Little Weare, W.G.	12.12.1904	None	5.4.1917	Gone to Edgehill College.
479	16.3.1909	Beer, Doris	Herbert	Weare Giffard	10.1.1906	Huntshaw	13.5.1912	Removed to Huntshaw.
480	19.4.1909	Fisher, Walter	James	Addlehole, W.G.	8.1.1901	Huntshaw	12.2.1915	Exempt by attendance.Labour Certificate. Gone to farmwork, Mr Moore, Polkinghorne.
481	19.4.1909	Wilton, Thomas	Thomas	Cleave Farm, W.G.	11.4.1903	Huntshaw	13.10.1916	Exempt by attendance. Working on his father's farm.
483	19.4.1909	Start, Gladys	William	Chope's Bridge, W.G.	1.3.1905	Huntshaw	5.11.1917	Removed to Devonport (temporarily).
484	21.4.1909	Tucker, William	George	Annery Kiln, W.G.	7.12.1904	None	20.9.1918	Exempt by attendance.Labour Certificate.Employed as garden boy by the Rev. H.O.Cavalier.
485	27.4.1909	Joliffe, Gladys	Reuben	Park Farm, W.G.	11.4.1904	Huntshaw	5.4.1917	Gone to Bideford.
491	30.8.1909	Edworthy, Winifred	Charles	North Firs, W.G.	20.6.1904	Huntshaw	7.10.1915	Gone to West Worlington.
495	8.2.1910	Banbrook, John	Hedley	Marshbrook, W.G.	10.10.1900	Guildford	13.11.1914	Left. Over age. Working in factory.
500	23.5.1910	Hammett, Dorothy	Fanny	Ivy House, W.G.	18.10.1904	None	24.9.1918	Left. Exempt by age.
514	1.4.1911	Beer, Nita	Herbert	Weare Giffard	28.1.1908	None	26.7.1912	Left neighbourhood.

WEARE GIFFARD CHURCH OF ENGLAND SCHOOL ADMISSION REGISTER, 1905-1945 REGISTER

Admission No	Date of Admission	Full Name of Child	Name of Parent or Guardian	Address	Date of Birth	Name of Last School	Date of Last Attendance at this School	Cause of Leaving and Remarks
515	24.4.1911	Jeffery, Jessie	Charles	Cliffe Cottage, W.G.	4.1.1907	None	30.7.1920	Gone to Edgehill College, Bideford. Won the Lovering Scholarship.
517	26.6.1911	Smith, Rex	Edward	Annery Kiln, W.G.	11.6.1906	None	11.8.1916	Removed to Bideford.
524	11.3.1912	Lake, Bruce	Alfred	Huxwill, W.G.	7.3.1906	None	8.4.1919	Gone to Bideford Grammar School.
525	26.3.1912	Huxtable, Charles	Wm. Henry	Little Weare, W.G.	10.7.1906	Littleham	21.12.1915	Left the district. Gone to Bideford.
526	26.3.1912	Huxtable, Lily	Wm. Henry	Little Weare, W.G.	1.7.1907	Littleham	21.12.1915	Left the district. Gone to Bideford.
527	26.3.1912	Huxtable, Albert	Wm. Henry	Little Weare, W.G.	30.8.1902	Littleham	13.8.1915	Exempt by certificate. For period of the war.
529	1.4.1912	Huxtable, Emily	Wm. Henry	Little Weare, W.G.	14.1.1901	Littleham	13.1.1915	Exempt by age. Gone to service.
531	15.4.1912	Chamings, Wm. Henry	William	Little Weare, W.G.	26.8.1907	None	8.8.1918	Gone to Bideford Grammar School.
532	29.4.1912	Hammett, Lilian	Fanny	Ivy House, W.G.	13.10.1907	None	21.12.1921	Exempt by age and attendance.
533	3.6.1912	Beer, Leslie	John	Park Hill, W.G.	1.4.1909	None	6.11.1919	Illness. Medical adviser certifies unfit to attend school during this winter. Deceased. Died June 11th 1920 after acute rheumatism.
537	31.3.1913	Wilton, William	Thomas	Cleave Farm, W.G.	11.8.1907	None	29.7.1921	Exempt by age and attendance
538	9.6.1913	Chamings, Alfred	William	Little Weare, W.G.	15.6.1908	None	30.7.1920	Gone to Bideford Grammar School.
539	16.6.1913	Edworthy, Francis Wm.	Charles	North Firs, W.G.	20.6.1908	None	28.7.1922	Exempt by age and attendance. Gone to Westward Ho to work in kennels.
540	16.6.1913	Moore, George	William	Polkinghorne, W.G.	28.4.1908	None	30.7.1920	Gone to Bideford Grammar School.
541	30.6.1913	Huxtable, Annie	Wm. Henry	Little Weare, W.G.	27.3.1909	None	23.3.1914	Distance, delicate. Exempted from attendance by Committee (until 6 years of age)
542	1.7.1913	Banbrook, Marie	James	Hillside, W.G.	17.6.1904	Cheltenham	13.8.1915	Won Lovering Scholarship.
543	1.7.1913	Banbrook, Edna	James	Hillside, W.G.	30.11.1905	Cheltenham	9.12.1914	Left temporarily.
545	15.9.1913	Baker, Elsie	John	Rose Cottage, W.G.	5.1.1902	Barley Grove, Torrington	12.2.1915	Exempt by attendance. Labour Certificate. Gone to domestic service at Riversdale.
546	15.9.1913	Baker, Frances	John	Rose Cottage, W.G.	17.12.1904	Barley Grove, Torrington	24.4.1918	Illness (Doctor's Certificate) temporarily.
547	15.9.1913	Baker, Alfred	John	Rose Cottage, W.G.	4.3.1906	Barley Grove, Torrington	28.2.1919	Removed to Bideford.
548	15.9.1913	Baker, John	John	Rose Cottage, W.G.	16.6.1907	Barley Grove, Torrington	28.2.1919	Removed to Bideford.
549	4.11.1913	Isaac, Lilian Ruby	John	The Dock, W.G.	9.9.1907	Littleham	17.1.1921	Gone to Bideford.
550	12.11.1913	Stevens, Sidney	William	Quay House, W.G.	7.8.1910	None	13.11.1913	Left temporarily. Under 5 yrs.

WEARE GIFFARD CHURCH OF ENGLAND SCHOOL ADMISSION REGISTER, 1905-1945 REGISTER

Admission No	Date of Admission	Full Name of Child	Name of Parent or Guardian	Address	Date of Birth	Name of Last School	Date of Last Attendance at this School	Cause of Leaving and Remarks
551	5.1.1914	Perryman, Daniel Geo:	James	Torridge View, W.G.	17.6.1903	Heavitree Council	23.6.1916	Left. Employed by Mr W. Balsdon in farm service.
552	5.1.1914	Perryman, Harry Roy	James	Torridge View, W.G.	25.10.1906	Heavitree Council	9.12.1920	Exempt by age and attendance. Employed at home.
553	5.1.1914	Perryman, Richard	James	Torridge View, W.G.	24.7.1910	Heavitree Council	1.10.1920	Removed to Monkleigh.
514	1.4.1914	Beer, Nita	Herbert	Weare Giffard	28.1.1908	Weare Giffard	12.4.1922	Exempt by age.
554	12.1.1914	Perryman, Minnie	James	Torridge View, W.G.	22.10.1900	Heavitree Council	21.10.1914	Exempt by age. Working at home.
556	23.2.1914	Isaac, John	John	The Dock, W.G.	23.8.1910	None	30.7.1924	Exempt by age. Employed as garden boy by Dr Armstrong.
557	10.3.1914	Mancy, Frank Vernon	Alfred	The School House, W.G.	1.7.1910	None	18.2.1921	Gone to Bideford Grammar School.
479	5.1.1914	Beer, Doris	Herbert	Weare Giffard	10.1.1906	Huntshaw	8.8.1919	Won Lovering Scholarship. Gone to Edgehill College, Bideford.
558	20.4.1914	Beer, Frederick Ernest	Herbert	Weare Giffard	7.4.1910	None	4.8.1922	Gone to Torrington Cl. School.
550	20.4.1914	Stevens, Sidney	William	Quay House	7.8.1910	Weare Giffard	4.8.1922	Gone to Torrington Cl. School. Drowned in R. Torridge January.
559	6.7.1914	Cooke, Beatrice Dorothy	Frederick G.	Dock	19.9.1908	None	14.4.1916	Removed to Huntshaw
Re-ad 501	6.7.1914	Martin, Frederick	William Martin	Pool Steps	24.4.1907	Woolsery	19.6.1916	Removed to Woolsery temporarily.
560	5.10.1914	Langmead, George	Ernest John	Chope's Bridge	23.1.1901	Monkleigh	20.11.1914	Labour Certificate. Gone to work. Employed by Mr Lake, Beam Farm
561	5.10.1914	Langmead, Fred	Ernest John	Chope's Bridge	16.3.1902	Monkleigh	17.3.1916	Exempt by age. Gone to work. Employed by Mr Martin, Southcott Farm
562	5.10.1914	Langmead, Frank	Ernest John	Chope's Bridge	4.11.1907	Monkleigh	21.12.1921	Exempt by age.
563	5.10.1914	Langmead, Charles	Ernest John	Chope's Bridge	11.2.1909	Monkleigh	30.7.1920	Illness. (Temporarily).
564	12.10.1914	Hill, Percy	Henry	The Dock	4.5.1905	Alverdiscott	24.9.1915	Removed to Fairy Cross.
565	12.10.1914	Hill, Walter	Henry	The Dock	20.12.1906	Alverdiscott	27.9.1915	Removed to Fairy Cross.
566	12.10.1914	Hill, Beatrice	Henry	The Dock	24.11.1908	Alverdiscott	27.9.1915	Removed to Fairy Cross.
567	20.10.1914	Furseman, Wm.	Wm. John	Honeybeam Farm	26.12.1902	Norton Durham	2.3.1916	Exempt by attendance. Employed on farm work by Mrs Jeffery, Honeybeam Farm.
568	4.1.1915	Alcock, Ellie	Richard	New Buildings	20.3.1907	St Paul's, Plymouth	30.4.1915	Returned to Plymouth.
543	21.1.1915	Banbrook, Edna	James	Hillside, W.G.	30.11.1905	Weare Giffard	13.8.1915	Transferred to Hatherleigh temporarily.
545	1.3.1915	Baker, Elsie	John	Myrtle Cottage	5.1.1902	Weare Giffard	3.12.1915	Exempt by attendance. Gone to service.
569	30.3.1915	Squires, Dorothy	Fred	Prospect Place	29.7.1911	None	17.5.1918	Removed to Littleham.
570	12.4.1915	Beer, Dorothy Mary	John	Park Hill	28.1.1911	None	31.3.1925	Exempt by age and attendance.

WEARE GIFFARD CHURCH OF ENGLAND SCHOOL ADMISSION REGISTER, 1905-1945 REGISTER

Admission No.	Date of Admission	Full Name of Child	Name of Parent or Guardian	Address	Date of Birth	Name of Last School	Date of Last Attendance at this School	Cause of Leaving and Remarks
571	12.4.1915	Heale, Henry	Henry	The Dock	16.2.1911	None	21.9.1915	Removed to Fairy Cross.
572	12.4.1915	Jolliffe, Lily Matilda	Reuben	Park Farm	23.9.1910	None	24.5.1917	Removed to Littleham temporarily.
573	12.4.1915	Mancy, Phoebe	Alfred	School House	27.4.1912	None	30.7.1924	Gained County Scholarship. Gone to Edgehill Girls' College, Bideford.
541	31.5.1915	Huxtable, Annie	W^m. Henry	Little Weare	27.3.1909	Weare Giffard	21.12.1915	Left the district. Gone to Bideford.
574	31.5.1915	Huxtable, Florence	W^m. Henry	Little Weare	20.11.1909	None	21.12.1915	Left the district. Gone to Bideford.
575	14.6.1915	Gomer, Florence	William	German Cottage	25.7.1910	None	18.6.1915	Left the district. Gone to St Giles.
576	26.7.1915	Davey, Thomas William	William	Venton Cottage	26.11.1906	Heavitree	29.7.1915	Returned to Exeter. In Weare Giffard on a visit only.
577	11.8.1915	Gerry, Elizabeth	Mrs Clarke	Ivy House	7.11.1904	Wolverhampton Council, Wallsall	11.8.1915	Returned to Wallsall. In Weare Giffard on a visit only.
578	11.8.1915	Squires, Violet	Charles	Prospect Place	5.12.1910	None	11.8.1915	Returned to London. In Weare Giffard on a visit only.
579	13.9.1915	Tucker, Walter Henry	George	Annery Kiln	20.11.1911	None	17.9.1915	Under age.
580	4.10.1915	Edworthy, Elizabeth Ivy	Charles	North Firs	2.10.1910	None	31.10.1924	Exempt by age and attendance. Gone to domestic service.
581	27.10.1915	Cooke, Fred^k W^m.	Frederick G.	The Dock	6.5.1911	None	29.3.1916	Under age. Left the district.
542	22.11.1915	Banbrook, Marie	James	Hillside, W.G.	17.6.1904	Weare Giffard	21.1.1916	Removed to Bideford. Gone to Canada.
543	22.11.1915	Banbrook, Edna	James	Hillside, W.G.	30.11.1905	Hatherleigh	21.1.1916	Removed to Bideford. Gone to Canada.
588	23.1.1916	Tithecott, Melbourne	Mr Williams	Rock Mount, W.G.	23.6.1912	None	4.2.1916	Removed to Barnstaple. In Weare Giffard only on a visit.
589	31.1.1916	Moore, John Pickard	Titus	Riversdale, W.G.	29.8.1910	None	29.7.1921	Gone to Cardiff. Attending a Cardiff secondary school.
576	1.2.1916	Davey, Thos W^m.	William	Little Weare, W.G.	26.11.1906	Heavitree	10.2.1916	Returned to Heavitree. In Weare Giffard only on a visit.
590	9.2.1916	Fowler, Amy Alice	Mrs Rew	The Cottage, W.G.	21.4.1906	Barley Grove, Torrington	14.4.1916	Returned to London. In Weare Giffard only on a visit.
591	14.2.1916	Rew, Ernest	Annie	The Cottage, W.G.	25.8.1905	Barley Grove, Torrington	21.7.1916	Removed to Torrington
491	28.2.1916	Edworthy, Winifred	Charles	North Firs, W.G.	20.6.1904	West Worlington Council	16.4.1917	Removed to Torrington.
592	27.3.1916	Nethercott, Vera	W^m. Henry	The Dock, W.G.	20.5.1904	Little Torrington	17.5.1918	Exempt by age. Gone to work in collar factory.
593	27.3.1916	Nethercott, W^m.	W^m. Henry	The Dock, W.G.	23.12.1907	Little Torrington	5.1.1920	Removed to Monkleigh.
594	27.3.1916	Rookes, Gladys Mary	Eli John	The Dock, W.G.	13.2.1911	St Giles in the Wood	28.3.1923	Gone to Bideford Church Gls School.
595	3.4.1916	Jewell, William	Thomas	Venton Cottage	21.5.1907	Gunstone St.Bideford	29.7.1921	Exempt by age and attendance.

WEARE GIFFARD CHURCH OF ENGLAND SCHOOL ADMISSION REGISTER, 1905-1945 REGISTER

Admission No.	Date of Admission	Full Name of Child	Name of Parent or Guardian	Address	Date of Birth	Name of Last School	Date of Last Attendance at this School	Cause of Leaving and Remarks
596	3.4.1916	Jewell, John	Thomas	Venton Cottage	10.10.1909	Geneva Infts, Bideford	26.9.1921	Removed to Week, nr Torrington
597	1.5.1916	Lake, Edith Mary	Alfred	Huxwill Farm, W.G.	30.11.1910	None	18.3.1919	Gone to Torrington temporarily.
575	1.5.1916	Gorner, Florence	William		25.7.1910	St Giles in the Wood	11.5.1916	Removed to St Giles.
598	1.5.1916	Phyllis Mabel Beer	John	Park Hill, W.G.	13.12.1912	None	22.12.1926	Exempt by age. Living at home.
599	1.5.1916	Woolridge, Thomas	Thomas	Post Office, W.G.	23.1.1910	Milton C.Sch., Eastney	6.6.1916	Returned to Eastney. In Weare Giffard on a visit only.
600	8.5.1916	Scott, Muriel Mary	Samuel	The Dock, W.G.	7.1.1907	Monkleigh	3.7.1916	Removed to Bideford
601	15.5.1916	Williams, Violet	John	Rock Mount, W.G.	23.3.1912	Nil	9.6.1916	Under age.
576	19.6.1916	Davey, Thos Wm.	William	Little Weare	26.11.1906	Heavitree	11.7.1916	Returned to Heavitree. Visitor to W.G.
601	28.6.1916	Williams, Violet	John	Rock Mount	23.3.1912	Weare Giffard	30.6.1916	Returned to Exeter.
602	25.9.1916	Lewis, Bessie	John	Gammaton Cross	9.10.1903	Woolfardisworthy	12.10.1917	Exempt by age.
603	25.9.1916	Martin, Flossie	Mrs Jolliffe	Park Farm	1.9.1903	Westleigh	4.4.1917	Returned to Westleigh.
604	6.11.1916	Chapman, Freda	Alfred	Road Cliff	1.10.1911	None	3.10.1917	Removed to Northam.
579	13.11.1916	Tucker, Walter Henry	George	Amery Kiln	20.11.1911	Weare Giffard	23.12.1925	Exempt by age and attendance.
605	8.1.1917	Tanton, Doris	Alfred	Weare Giffard	5.11.1913	None	19.12.1927	Exempt by age. Gone to domestic service.
501	8.1.1917	Martin, Frederick	William G.	Sunnyside	24.4.1907	Woolsery	9.5.1919	Gone to Woolsery temporarily (ill-health).
606	16.4.1917	Squire, Cora Mabel	Charles	New Buildings	9.5.1912	None	20.12.1917	Removed to Bovey Tracey (temporarily).
607	17.4.1917	Jeffery, Vera	Henry	Honeybeam Farm	23.4.1910	Newton Abbott Cl	4.5.1917	Removed to Huntshaw (temporarily)
608	23.4.1917	Fairhead, Grace	Bertha	New Buildings	19.4.1912	Edingham, Norfolk	30.7.1924	Removed to Brighton
609	30.4.1917	Charnings, Emma	William	Little Weare	21.7.1912	None	1.5.1917	Under age
610	21.5.1917	Beer, Reginald Albert	Herbert Henry	Cliffe Cottage	20.6.1912	None	4.8.1922	Gone to Torrington Cl Boys School
599	4.6.1917	Woolridge, Thomas	Thomas	Post Office, W.G.	23.1.1910	Wimborne Rd C., Eastney	14.12.1917	Illness.
568	4.6.1917	Alcock, Ellie	Richard	Chope's Bridge	20.3.1907	St Boniface's Ch. Sch., Plymouth	22.6.1917	Returned to Plymouth. Visitor to Weare Giffard.

WEARE GIFFARD CHURCH OF ENGLAND SCHOOL ADMISSION REGISTER, 1905-1945 REGISTER

Admission No.	Date of Admission	Full Name of Child	Name of Parent or Guardian	Address	Date of Birth	Name of Last School	Date of Last Attendance at this School	Cause of Leaving and Remarks
611	18.6.1917	Chapman, Evelyn	Edmund	Road Cliff	13.5.1907	St Giles in the Wood	6.7.1917	Returned to St Giles. Visitor to Weare Giffard.
575	18.6.1917	Gomer, Florence	William	German Cottage	25.7.1910	St Giles in the Wood	3.8.1917	Gone to St Giles. Deceased Mar: 16th 1918.
572	20.6.1917	Jolliffe, Lily Matilda	Reuben	Park Farm	23.9.1910	Littleham	14.7.1921	Removed to Langtree.
607	25.6.1917	Jeffery, Vera	Henry	Honeybeam Farm	23.4.1910	Huntshaw	3.8.1917	Removed to Newton Abbott
612	25.6.1917	Edworthy, Mary	Charles	North Firs	18.9.1913	None	25.6.1917	Under age.
601	24.7.1917	Williams, Violet	John	Rock Mount	23.3.1912	St Thomas, Exeter	30.10.1917	Returned to Exeter. Visitor to Weare Giffard.
613	27.9.1917	Squire, Violet Annie	Frank	Prospect Place	8.12.1910	Hersham C.E.	27.9.1917	Returned to Hersham. Visitor to Weare Giffard.
611	1.10.1917	Chapman, Evelyn	Edmund	Road Cliff	13.5.1907	St Giles in the Wood	3.10.1917	Removed to Northam.
614	5.11.1917	Drowley, Albert John	Thomas	New Buildings	31.8.1909	Council School, Bovey Tracey	20.12.1917	Returned to Bovey Tracey. Visitor to W.G.
615	5.11.1917	Drowley, Wm. George	Thomas	New Buildings	18.11.1911	Council School, Bovey Tracey	20.12.1917	Returned to Bovey Tracey. Visitor to W.G.
616	12.11.1917	Pankhurst, Alfred Oliver	Ralph	New Buildings	1.10.1911	None	28.3.1918	Returned to Worthing. Visitor to W.G.
491	19.11.1917	Edworthy, Winifred	Charles	North Firs	20.6.1904	Torrington Council	6.6.1918	Exempt by age. Gone to service.
483	12.12.1917	Start, Gladys	Wm.	Chope's Bridge	1.3.1905	Ford Council Devonport	19.2.1919	Exempt by age. Employed in gloving.
606	28.1.1918	Squire, Cora Mabel	Charles	New Buildings	9.5.1912	Bovey Tracey Cl	30.7.1925	Gone to Bideford Church Girls' School.
576	25.2.1918	Davey, Thos Wm.	William	Little Weare	26.11.1906	Heavitree Parochial	28.3.1918	Returned to Heavitree. Visitor to W.G.
617	4.3.1918	Cox, Leslie	Charles	Marshbrook	13.7.1905	St Giles in the Wood	8.7.1919	Exempt by age. Employed at Mr Lee's farm.
618	4.3.1918	Cox, Frederick	Charles	Marshbrook	15.10.1908	St Giles in the Wood	21.12.1922	Exempt by age.
619	25.3.1918	Busby, Joyce	Jane	2 The Hill Cottages	31.7.1907	Little Ealing Gls. Cl.	29.7.1921	Exempt by age and attendance.

WEARE GIFFARD CHURCH OF ENGLAND SCHOOL ADMISSION REGISTER, 1905-1945 REGISTER

Admission No.	Date of Admission	Full Name of Child	Name of Parent or Guardian	Address	Date of Birth	Name of Last School	Date of Last Attendance at this School	Cause of Leaving and Remarks
620	8.4.1918	Percy Wm. Cox	Charles	Marshbrook	23.11.1906	St Giles in the Wood	9.12.1920	Exempt by age and attendance. Employed by Col. Phelps.
621	8.4.1918	Beer, Marjory Ellen	John	Park Hill	1.11.1914	None.	8.8.1918	Under age.
622	8.4.1918	Wise, Elsie May	John	Chope's Bridge, W.G.	3.7.1913	None	29.7.1926	Gone to Torrington Council School.
623	8.4.1918	Fairhead, Ralph Jeffery	Bertha	New Buildings	14.12.1913	None	31.5.1918	Illness. Under age.
624	8.4.1918	Moore, Doris Gertrude	Wm.	Polkinghome	28.1.1912	None.	20.12.1923	Gone to Edgehill College, Bideford.
609	8.4.1918	Channings, Emma	William	Little Weare	21.7.1912	Weare Giffard C.E.	15.4.1921	Gone to secondary school (Mrs Braund's) Bideford
612	27.5.1918	Edworthy, Mary	Charles	North Firs	18.9.1913	Weare Giffard C.E.	30.7.1924	Gone to Torrington CI Girls' School.
625	27.5.1918	Cox, Mary Ann	Charles	Marshbrook	2.12.1913	None	21.12.1922	Removed to Monkleigh.
546	3.6.1918	Baker, Frances	John	Myrtle Cottage	17.12.1904	Weare Giffard C.E.	18.12.1918	Exempt by age and attendance.
626	3.6.1918	Gilbert, Roy	Mrs Hunter	Chope's Bridge	1.8.1912	Eastney, Hants	8.8.1918	Returned to Eastney. Visitor to W.G.
623	10.6.1918	Fairhead, Ralph Jeffery	Bertha	New Buildings	14.12.1913	Weare Giffard C.E.	4.10.1918	Illness. Under age.
627	25.7.1918	Banbrook, Gertrude	Gertrude	The Hill Cottage	2.12.1911	Lethbridge Road, Swindon	26.7.1918	Returned to Swindon. Visitor to W.G.
628	9.9.1918	Tanton, Wm. Alfred	Alfred	Quay Cottage	30.7.1915	None	7.2.1919	Illness. Under age.
629	2.12.1918	Gilbert, Robert Wm.	Percy	Honeybeam Farm	30.5.1907	Blue Coat, Barnstaple	14.3.1919	Returned to Barnstaple. Visitor to W.G.
623	16.12.1918	Fairhead, Ralph Jeffery	Bertha	New Buildings	14.12.1913	Weare Giffard C.E.	19.12.1919	Gone to Monkleigh.
628	3.3.1919	Tanton, Wm. Alfred	Alfred	Quay Cottage	30.7.1915	Weare Giffard C.E.	2.8.1929	Exempt by age and attendance. Employed as garden boy by Miss Fleming, Annery House. Mother dead, staying at home to help father.
630	25.3.1919	Tyrell, Wm. John	Joseph	Annery Kiln	5.5.1910	Woolsery	6.6.1924	Exempt by age and attendance.
631	25.3.1919	Tyrell, Lily Cory	Joseph	Annery Kiln	16.9.1912	Woolsery	18.5.1923	Gone to Monkleigh.
632	31.3.1919	Rookes, Florence May	Eli	Dock Cottages	6.11.1913	None	1.6.1926	Under T.B. Officer. Gone to Sydney House, Torrington.
621	15.4.1919	Beer, Marjory Ellen	John	Park Hill	1.11.1914	Weare Giffard	1.11.1919	Exempt by age. At home.
633	28.4.1919	Moore, Marjory Ellen	Wm. Heywood Moore	Polkinghome	28.6.1913	None	29.7.1926	Gained Lovering Scholarship for Edgehill Girls' College, Bideford.

WEARE GIFFARD CHURCH OF ENGLAND SCHOOL ADMISSION REGISTER, 1905-1945 REGISTER

Admission No.	Date of Admission	Full Name of Child	Name of Parent or Guardian	Address	Date of Birth	Name of Last School	Date of Last Attendance at this School	Cause of Leaving and Remarks
634	16.6.1919	Jelfs, Barty	James	Myrtle Cottage	1.4.1914	None	26.10.1919	Gone to Dolton (temporarily).
635	15.9.1919	Beer, Elsie Winifred	Herbert	Cliffe Cottage	26.7.1914	None	27.7.1928	Exempt by age.
501	16.9.1919	Martin, Frederick	William	Sunnyside	24.4.1907	Woolsery	29.7.1921	Exempt by age and attendance.
634	17.11.1919	Jelfs, Barty	James	Myrtle Cottage	1.4.1914	Dolton	10.12.1919	Gone to Torrington.
623	8.3.1920	Fairhead, Ralph Jeffery	Bertha	New Buildings	14.12.1913	Monkleigh	23.10.1922	Gone to Monkleigh temporarily.
634	12.4.1920	Jelfs, Barty	William	Myrtle Cottage	1.4.1914	Dolton	25.2.1921	Gone to Dolton (temporarily).
636	12.4.1920	Beer, Eric James	James Charles	Quay Cottage	28.5.1914	Monkleigh	30.7.1925	Gone to Bideford Grammar School. Awarded the Lovering Scholarship.
637	12.4.1920	Beer, Ida Doreen	James Charles	Quay Cottage	29.2.1916	None	29.7.1927	Gained County Scholarship. Gone to Edgehill Girls' College, Bideford.
638	19.4.1920	Mills, Marjory Phyllis	Frederick John	Foodlands, W.G.	12.3.1915	None	23.9.1920	Removed to Woking.
639	10.5.1920	Wheeler, Frances Maud	Wm. Henry	Dock Cottages, W.G.	6.8.1907	Monkleigh	29.7.1921	Exempt by age and attendance. Gone to domestic service.
640	10.5.1920	Wheeler, Reginald John	Wm. Henry	Dock Cottages, W.G.	21.11.1909	Monkleigh	29.9.1921	Removed to Huntshaw.
641	10.5.1920	Wheeler, Frank	Wm. Henry	Dock Cottages, W.G.	27.6.1914	Monkleigh	29.9.1921	Removed to Huntshaw.
642	10.5.1920	Wheeler, George	Wm. Henry	Dock Cottages, W.G.	25.7.1916	Monkleigh	29.9.1921	Removed to Huntshaw.
643	10.5.1920	Drew, George Henry	Walter George	Marshbrook. W.G.	12.12.1908	Huntshaw	23.3.1921	Removed to Beaford.
599	30.8.1920	Woolridge, Thomas	Thomas	Post Office, W.G.	23.1.1910	Weare Giffard	29.7.1921	Gone to Bideford Grammar School.
644	30.8.1920	Henderson, Helen Lucy	Walter	The Dock	23.3.1910	Monkleigh	31.3.1925	Exempt by age and attendance.
645	30.8.1920	Henderson, Winifred	Walter	The Dock, W.G.	24.10.1912	Monkleigh	24.6.1926	Removed to Abbotsham.
563	27.9.1920	Langmead, Charles	Ernest John	Belgium Cottage, W.G.	11.2.1909	Weare Giffard	8.12.1920	Gone to Sydney House, Torrington, for treatment.
646	10.1.1921	Coniam, Percy Wm.	Mrs Harding	New Bldings, W.G.	3.1.1916	Kingsteignton	12.4.1921	Gone to Bideford.
647	14.2.1921	Ackland, Frederick	Mrs Busby	2 The Hill Cottages, W.G.	9.1.1915	Convent, Bridport	26.4.1921	Gone to Eastleigh.
634	14.3.1921	Jelfs, Barty	William	Myrtle Cottage	1.4.1914	Dolton	23.3.1921	Gone to Dolton (temporarily)
648	4.4.1921	Beer, Vera May	John	Park Hill, W.G.	9.2.1917	None	31.3.1931	Exempt by age and attendance. At home.
634	11.4.1921	Jelfs, Barty	William	Myrtle Cottage, W.G.	1.11.1914	Dolton	15.4.1921	Gone to Dolton (temporarily)
634	4.5.1921	Jelfs, Barty	William	Myrtle Cottage, W.G.	1.11.1914	Dolton	16.5.1922	Gone to Dolton. Removed to Dolton.
649	27.6.1921	Stevens, Rose Mary	John	Annery Kiln, W.G.	25.6.1916	Derby Sch., Barnstaple	14.10.1921	Gone to Barnstaple.
588	11.7.1921	Tithecott, Melbourne	Florence	Quay, W.G.	23.6.1912	Pilton, Barnstaple	29.7.1921	Returned to Barnstaple. Visitor to W.G.

WEARE GIFFARD CHURCH OF ENGLAND SCHOOL ADMISSION REGISTER, 1905-1945 REGISTER

Admission No	Date of Admission	Full Name of Child	Name of Parent or Guardian	Address	Date of Birth	Name of Last School	Date of Last Attendance at this School	Cause of Leaving and Remarks
650	11.7.1921	Tithecot, Leslie	Florence	Quay, W.G.	20.2.1914	Pilton, Barnstaple	29.7.1921	Returned to Barnstaple.
651	29.8.1921	Edworthy, Arthur George	Charles	North Furze, W.G.	15.7.1916	Nil	1.8.1930	Exempt by age and attendance. Employed on Mr Martin's farm, Woodhouse, W.G.
652	10.10.1921	Babb, Winifred Mary	W.T. Babb	Venton Cottage, W.G.	21.6.1914	Hartland Council	23.2.1923	Removed to Webbery.
653	8.2.1922	Becklake, Edith Sarah	Elem Becklake	Park Farm, W.G.	26.2.1910	Parkham Council	31.3.1924	Exempt by age. Working at home.
563	1.3.1922	Langmead, Charles	Ernest John	Pool Steps	11.2.1909	Weare Giffard	28.3.1923	Exempt by age and attendance. Employed as garden boy by Col. Phelps.
654	27.3.1922	Squire, Pamela	Mrs J. Squire	Prospect Place, W.G.	6.12.1914	Sunningdale	26.4.1922	Returned to Sunningdale. Visitor to W.G.
655	27.3.1922	Squire, Muriel	Mrs J. Squire	Prospect Place, W.G.	28.2.1916	Sunningdale	26.4.1922	Returned to Sunningdale. Visitor to W.G.
656	28.3.1922	Manning, Cyril	Mary	Marshbrook, W.G.	29.9.1916	Monkleigh	19.6.1925	Gone to Sydney House for treatment.
657	4.4.1922	Mancy, Lucy Joan Mabel	Alfred	School House, W.G.	18.2.1919	Nil	2.8.1929	Gained a Lovering Scholarship. Gone to Edgehill Girls' College, Bideford.
658	4.4.1922	Brown, Dora	Wm John Brown	Salerns Farm, W.G.	26.3.1909	Huntshaw	30.3.1923	Exempt by age and attendance. Gone to farm service.
659	4.4.1922	Braund, Winifred Maria	Wm John Brown	Salerns Farm, W.G.	16.6.1912	Huntshaw	23.3.1925	Removed to Monkleigh.
660	24.4.1922	Moore, Joan Ann	Wm Henry Moore	Polkinghorne, W.G.	14.7.1916	None	4.4.1928	Gone to Edgehill Girls' College, Bideford.
661	1.5.1922	Braund, Edwin Arthur James	Wm. John Brown	Salerns Farm, W.G.	24.12.1908	Huntshaw	21.12.1922	Exempt by age. Working at home on farm.
662	15.5.1922	Edworthy, Harold Henry	Charles	North Furze, W.G.	21.1.1918	None	14.7.1922	Illness. Under age.
663	28.6.1922	Berry, Reginald	Walter	Salerns Farm, W.G.	28.11.1912	Braunton	30.6.1922	Returned to Braunton. Visitor to W.G.
664	26.7.1922	Martin, James Wm.	William	Sunnyside, W.G.	24.5.1918	None	31.7.1931	Gone to Torrington Boys' Council School.
665	4.9.1922	Gilbert, Susan Florence	Alice	Honeybeam Farm, W.G.	20.2.1912	Newton Abbot Cl	31.3.1926	Exempt by age. Employed at home on farm.
666	4.9.1922	Gilbert, Mildred Adelaide	Alice	Honeybeam Farm, W.G.	30.11.1915	Newton Abbot Cl	29.7.1926	Removed to Exmouth.
667	25.9.1922	Gilbert, Gladys Gertrude	Alice	Myrtle Cottage, W.G.	17.3.1914	Newton Abbot Cl	29.7.1926	Removed to Exmouth.
646	25.9.1922	Coniam, Percy Wm.	Mrs Harding	New Bldgs, W.G.	3.1.1916	Bideford, Geneva	2.10.1922	Returned to Bideford. Visitor to W.G.
668	9.10.1922	Brownjohn, Stella	Mrs K. Nutt	Hillside, W.G.	30.8.1915	St Aloysius, Oxford	29.7.1926	Gained Devon County Scholarship. Bideford Edgehill Girls' College.
569	19.10.1922	Squire, Dorothy	Fred	New Bldgs, W.G.	29.7.1911	Tawstock Ch.	6.11.1922	Returned to Tawstock. Visitor to W.G.

WEARE GIFFARD CHURCH OF ENGLAND SCHOOL ADMISSION REGISTER, 1905-1945 REGISTER

Admission No	Date of Admission	Full Name of Child	Name of Parent or Guardian	Address	Date of Birth	Name of Last School	Date of Last Attendance at this School	Cause of Leaving and Remarks
669	19.10.1922	Squire, Charles Thomas	Fred	Prospect Place, W.G.	5.1.1913	Tawstock Ch.	21.12.1922	Returned to Tawstock. Visitor to W.G.
670	19.10.1922	Squire, Frederick Arthur	Fred	Prospect Place, W.G.	30.3.1915	Tawstock Ch.	24.11.1922	Returned to Tawstock. Visitor to W.G.
623	8.1.1923	Fairhead, Ralph Jeffery	B. Brooks	New Buildings	14.12.1913	Monkleigh	31.3.1924	Gone to Torrington Boys' Council Sch.
671	8.1.1923	Gilbert, Marjory Frances	Mrs F. Gilbert	Honeybeam Farm, W.G.	15.10.1917	None	29.10.1931	Exempt by age and attendance. Working at home (farm?).
672	5.3.1923	Wilton, Frank Anthony	Thomas	Cleave Farm, W.G.	25.2.1917	None	2.4.1931	Exempt by age and attendance. Working on father's farm.
673	9.4.1923	Mugford, Ivy	Elijah	Hallspill, W.G.	28.5.1910	Frithelstock	6.6.1924	Exempt by age and attendance. Gone to farm service.
674	9.4.1923	Mugford, Amy	Elijah	Hallspill, W.G.	28.7.1915	Frithelstock	27.7.1923	Staying in Bideford temporarily.
675	9.4.1923	Mugford, George	Elijah	Hallspill, W.G.	15.4.1913	Frithelstock	16.3.1925	Removed to Littleham.
676	9.4.1923	Pearson, Kenneth Alfred	Bessie	Venton Cottage, W.G.	24.1.1918	None	25.11.1924	Removed to Barnstaple.
677	9.4.1923	Becklake, Ernest	Elam	Park Farm, W.G.	18.2.1919	None	31.3.1933	Exempt by age and attendance. Working on father's farm.
662	9.4.1923	Edworthy, Harold	Charles	North Furze, W.G.	21.1.1918	Weare Giffard	16.4.1930	Gone to Torrington Boys' Cl School.
678	17.4.1923	Mugford, Barbara	Elijah	Hallspill, W.G.	28.7.1914	Monkleigh	11.3.1925	Removed to Littleham.
679	20.6.1923	Braunton, Phyllis	Frank	Chope's Bridge, W.G.	28.6.1917	Newton St Petrock	31.7.1931	Exempt by age and attendance. Gone to domestic service.
680	27.8.1923	Beer, Lilian Evelyn	Herbert	Cliffe Cottage, W.G.	31.7.1918	None	27.7.1932	Exempt by age and attendance.
681	29.8.1923	Johnson, Albert	W. J. Squire	2 Dock Cottages, W.G.	7.1.1918	Barry, Jenner Park	14.9.1923	Returned to Barry. Visitor to W.G.
682	29.8.1923	Johnson, John	W. J. Squire	2 Dock Cottages, W.G.	18.12.1919	Barry, Jenner Park	14.9.1923	Returned to Barry. Visitor to W.G.
683	3.9.1923	Williams, Reginald	John	Quay, W.G.	4.11.1914	Exeter, John Stock's	26.9.1923	Returned to Exeter. Visitor to W.G.
674	3.9.1923	Mugford, Amy	Elijah	Hallspill, W.G.	28.7.1915	Geneva, Bideford	13.3.1925	Removed to Littleham.
631	25.9.1923	Tyrell, Lily Cory	Joseph	Annery Kiln	16.9.1912	Monkleigh	29.10.1926	Exempt by age and attendance.
684	15.10.1923	Manning, Ruth Lilian	George	Marshbrook	8.10.1919	None	25.1.1924	Under age.
685	22.10.1923	Braunton, John Thos	John	Chope's Bridge	8.4.1919	None	12.4.1933	Exempt by age and attendance. Gone to employment as garden boy.
686	5.11.1923	Clarke, Albert	Charles	Dock Cottages	20.4.1910	Monkleigh	31.3.1924	Exempt by age and attendance.
687	6.11.1923	Clarke, Dorothy	Charles	Dock Cottages	17.9.1916	Monkleigh	25.9.1924	Removed to Chapelton

WEARE GIFFARD CHURCH OF ENGLAND SCHOOL ADMISSION REGISTER, 1905-1945 REGISTER

Admission No	Date of Admission	Full Name of Child	Name of Parent or Guardian	Address	Date of Birth	Name of Last School	Date of Last Attendance at this School	Cause of Leaving and Remarks
688	7.1.1924	Braunton, Aubrey	Frank	Chope's Bridge	15.12.1920	None	22.12.1932	Gone to Torrington Council School.
689	21.1.1924	Wilcox, William John	William John	Ridd Cottage, Monkleigh	20.10.1918	None	23.5.1924	Gone to Hartland.
690	19.2.1924	Orchard, Virginia	Nathan	Ridd Cottage, Monkleigh	27.9.1915	Beaford Cl.	26.2.1924	Removal to South Molton. Travelling gipsies.
691	28.4.1924	Moore, Wm. Heywood	Wm. Heywood	Polkinghorne, W.G.	18.6.1918	None	2.8.1929	Gone to Bideford Grammar School.
669	8.9.1924	Squire, Charles Thos	Fred	Prospect Place, W.G.	5.1.1913	Tawstock Church	22.12.1926	Exempt by age. Working at home.
692	30.9.1924	Bailey, Joseph Edwin	Richard M.	Dock Cottages, W.G.	18.5.1912	Roborough	23.12.1925	Removed to Northam.
693	30.9.1924	Bailey, Gwendoline Annie	Richard M.	Dock Cottages, W.G.	6.3.1915	Roborough	31.3.1926	Removed to Northam.
694	30.9.1924	Bailey, Winifred Doris	Richard M.	Dock Cottages, W.G.	20.11.1916	Roborough	23.12.1925	Removed to Northam.
695	30.9.1924	Bailey, Victor Douglas	Richard M.	Dock Cottages, W.G.	26.1.1920	Roborough	11.11.1924	Under age.
684	6.10.1924	Manning, Ruth Lilian	George	Marshbrook, W.G.	8.10.1919	Weare Giffard	30.9.1927	Removed to South Molton.
696	5.1.1925	Hearn, Gladys May	Mary	Ridd Cottage, Monkleigh	1.8.1911	Bideford Ch. Girls	31.3.1925	Returned to Bideford.
695	5.1.1925	Bailey, Victor Douglas	Richard M.	Dock Cottages, W.G.	26.1.1920	Weare Giffard	23.12.1925	Removed to Northam.
697	26.1.1925	Stevens, Kathleen Joyce	Charles	Quay, W.G.	24.10.1919	Bideford East the Water Inf.	9.-.1925	Returned to Bideford.
698	23.3.1925	Martin, Ivor Wm.	Mr J. Tyrell	Annery Kiln, W.G.	3.7.1920	Bideford, Geneva	28.1.1927	Removed to Bideford.
699	20.4.1925	Skinner, Wm. Henry	Henry	Saltern's Farm, W.G.	19.4.1913	Braunton Council	21.4.1925	Returned to Braunton. Visitor to W.G.
700	22.4.1925	McKenzie, John Wallace	John	Southcott House, W.G.	12.6.1919	Horsted Keynes, Sussex	2.8.1929	Gained a Lovering Scholarship. Gone to Bideford Grammar School.
701	15.6.1925	Wicks, Kenneth	George	Quay Cottage, W.G.	2.2.1914	Shebbear Council	26.6.1925	Return to home at Sidcup. Visitor to W.G.
702	18.1.1926	Manning, Myrtle	George	Dock Cottage, W.G.	25.7.1921	Nil	30.9.1927	Removed to South Molton.
703	22.2.1926	Becklake, Clara	Elam	Park Farm, W.G.	7.2.1921	Nil	25.3.1935	Exempt by age. Working at home on farm.
704	1.3.1926	Braunton, Vera Maud	Frank	Chope's Bridge, W.G.	26.11.1921	Nil	7.12.1935	Exempt by age. Working at home.
705	1.3.1926	Stevens, Evelyn Beatrice	Alfred	Chope's Bridge, W.G.	10.1.1922	Torrington Council Infts	25.10.1926	Removed to Lovacott.
697	15.3.1926	Stevens, Kathleen Joyce	Charles	The Quay, W.G.	24.10.1919	Bideford (East the Water Infts)	5.5.1926	Return to home at Instow. Visitor to W.G.
706	15.3.1926	Busby, Betty Nesta	Harry	The Hill Cottage, W.G.	7.2.1921	Nil	29.5.1931	Gone to Lynton. Housing shortage in W.G.

WEARE GIFFARD CHURCH OF ENGLAND SCHOOL ADMISSION REGISTER, 1905-1945 REGISTER

Admission No.	Date of Admission	Full Name of Child	Name of Parent or Guardian	Address	Date of Birth	Name of Last School	Date of Last Attendance at this School	Cause of Leaving and Remarks
707	29.3.1926	Braunton, Gwendoline Mary	Frank	Chope's Bridge, W.G.	5.1.1923	Nil	21.1.1927	Under age.
708	3.5.1926	Banbrook, Gertrude Mary	Fred	Hill Cottage, W.G.	2.12.1911	Swindon Lethbridge Road	22.7.1926	Returned to Swindon. Visitor to W.G.
656	12.5.1926	Manning, Cyril	George	The Dock, W.G.	29.9.1916	Weare Giffard C.E.	30.9.1927	Removed to South Molton.
709	6.9.1926	Porter, Edward	William	Annery Lodge, W.G.	4.7.1921	Nil	6.4.1927	Removed to Monkleigh.
707	7.3.1927	Braunton, Gwendoline Mary	Frank	Chope's Bridge, W.G.	5.1.1923	Weare Giffard C.E.	14.7.1927	Under age.
694	4.4.1927	Bailey, Winifred Doris	Richard	The Dock, W.G.	20.11.1916	Northam Ch.	29.7.1927	Returned to Northam. Visitor to W.G.
710	11.4.1927	Edworthy, Dulcie Violet Joy	Charles	North Furze, W.G.	10.4.1922	Nil	11.7.1930	Gone to Exeter.
632	2.5.1927	Rookes, Florence May	Eli	Dock Cottages, W.G.	6.11.1913	Open Air School, Sydney House, Torrington	19.12.1927	Exempt by age and attendance. At home.
711	30.5.1927	Braunton, Alfred John	Percy	Wyatt Cottage, Hallspill	11.9.1913	Westleigh	27.10.1927	Exempt by age and attendance. Gone to work on Mr Grigg's Farm.
712	30.5.1927	Braunton, Hilda May	Percy	Wyatt Cottage, Hallspill	7.2.1917	Westleigh	28.3.1930	Gone to Geneva School, Bideford.
713	30.5.1927	Braunton, John Henry	Percy	Wyatt Cottage, Hallspill	2.5.1922	Westleigh	23.3.1932	Left the district. Removed to Mudiford.
714	8.6.1927	Curtis, Violet May	Albert	Chope's Bridge, W.G.	20.6.1922	None	29.7.1936	Exempt by age and attendance. Gone to domestic service.
698	13.6.1927	Martin, Ivor Wm.	Mr J. Tyrell	Annery Kiln, W.G.	3.7.1920	Bideford, Geneva Infts	14.10.1927	Removed to Bideford.
707	5.9.1927	Braunton, Gwendoline	Frank	Chope's Bridge, W.G.	5.1.1923	Weare Giffard C.E.	22.12.1936	Exempt by age and attendance. Gone to domestic service.
715	28.11.1927	Squire, Phyllis Mary	Arthur	The Dock, W.G.	26.11.1922	Nil	9.12.1927	Gone to Barnstaple.
705	24.1.1928	Stevens, Evelyn Beatrice	Alfred	The Quay, W.G.	10.1.1922	Instow	17.2.1928	Returned to Holmacott Visitor to W.G.
716	15.2.1928	Gorvett, Wm. George	Aubrey	Annery Kiln, W.G.	19.6.1920	Geneva Infts	22.10.1931	Died on November 19th 1931.
697	12.3.1928	Stevens, Kathleen Joyce	Charles	Quay House, W.G.	24.10.1919	Instow	27.7.1928	Returned to Instow temporarily.
717	5.4.1928	Braunton, Kathleen Joyce	Frank	Chope's Bridge, W.G.	15.11.1925	None.	29.6.1928	Under age.
715	11.6.1928	Squire, Phyllis Mary	Arthur	The Dock, W.G.	26.11.1922	Weare Giffard	27.9.1935	Removed to Drewsteignton

WEARE GIFFARD CHURCH OF ENGLAND SCHOOL ADMISSION REGISTER, 1905-1945 REGISTER

Admission No.	Date of Admission	Full Name of Child	Name of Parent or Guardian	Address	Date of Birth	Name of Last School	Date of Last Attendance at this School	Cause of Leaving and Remarks
718	12.6.1928	Squire, Marjorie Ada	Arthur	The Dock. W.G.	19.9.1924	None	27.9.1935	Removed to Drewsteignton.
719	25.6.1928	Day, Frank	Walter	Annery Lodge, Monkleigh	16.7.1920	Southborough, Kent	3.7.1930	Temporarily living with grandparents. Attending Langport School near Tunbridge Wells.
720	25.6.1928	Day, Iris Jean	Walter	Annery Lodge, Monkleigh	8.7.1921	Southborough, Kent	2.8.1933	Gone to Geneva Council School, Bideford.
721	9.7.1928	Williams, Gertrude	Herbert	Cranbury Cottage, W.G.	28.10.1916	Abbey Westminster Millbank L.C.C.	27.7.1928	Returned to Westminster. Visitor to W.G.
722	16.7.1928	Squire, Norman Trevor	James	Prospect Place, W.G.	19.12.1921	Geneva Infts Bideford	27.7.1928	Returned to Bideford. Visitor to W.G.
723	3.9.1928	Dymond, Wm. Douglas	Henry	Chope's Bridge, W.G.	14.9.1917	Torrington Cl Mixed	29.10.1931	Exempt by age and attendance.
724	3.9.1928	Dymond, Hilda Frances	Henry	Chope's Bridge, W.G.	28.6.1916	Torrington Cl Mixed	1.8.1930	Exempt by age and attendance. Gone to domestic service at Beam Farm, Torrington. Died in Hawkmoor Sanatorium Mar. 1937.
725	3.9.1928	Lawrence, Winifred Amy	Albert Edward	Venton Cottage, W.G.	28.6.1923	None	29.10.1931	Left (temporarily). Staying at Little Torrington.
717	12.11.1928	Braunton, Kathleen Joyce	Frank	Chopes' Bridge, W.G.	15.4.1925	Weare Giffard C.E.	5.4.1939	Exempt by age. Employed in domestic service.
726	3.12.1928	Challice, Beryl	William	The Quay, W.G.	17.4.1924	None	7.12.1928	Return to Exeter. Visitor to W.G.
697	14.1.1929	Stevens, Kathleen Joyce	Charles	Quay Cottage, W.G.	24.10.1919	Instow	11.11.1929	Return to Holmacott, Instow.
727	14.1.1929	Shute, Gwendoline Mary Alice	Fred	The Dock Cottage, W.G.	10.6.1925	None	7.3.1930	Removed to Fairy Cross.
728	19.2.1929	May, Thomas Geoffrey	Esther Maud	Roadcliff, W.G.	20.9.1923	Tonypandy Cl	30.4.1929	Removed to Bideford.
729	8.4.1929	Grigg, Eileen Phyllis	James	Netherdowns, W.G.	27.3.1924	None	29.7.1936	Gone to Edgehill Girls' College, Bideford.
730	8.4.1929	Grigg, Mary Rebecca	James	Netherdowns, W.G.	17.4.1925	None	29.7.1937	Gained Lovering Scholarship to Edgehill Girls' College, Bideford.
731	8.4.1929	Tanton, Joyce	Charles	Salterns, W.G.	7.7.1925	None	2.8.1929	Under age and illness (whooping cough).
732	8.4.1929	Beer, Rosalie May	Alfred	Brook Cottage, W.G.	9.4.1925	None	5.4.1939	Exempt by age. Employed in domestic service.
733	8.4.1929	Wooldridge, John Edward	Thomas Ed.	Post Office, W.G.	10.10.1923	None	1.8.1930	Gone to Convent School, Bideford.
734	8.4.1929	Mitchell, Wm. Norman	William	Annery Kiln, W.G.	22.10.1924	None	1.8.1935	Gained Lovering Scholarship. Gone to Bideford Grammar School.
735	25.6.1929	Beer, Harold Richard	John	Bonifants, W.G.	17.12.1925	None	9.11.1934	Left temporarily. On a visit to Taunton.

WEARE GIFFARD CHURCH OF ENGLAND SCHOOL ADMISSION REGISTER, 1905-1945 REGISTER

Admission No	Date of Admission	Full Name of Child	Name of Parent or Guardian	Address	Date of Birth	Name of Last School	Date of Last Attendance at this School	Cause of Leaving and Remarks
736	2.7.1929	Braunton, Joan Madeline	Frank	Chope's Bridge	28.6.1926	None	2.8.1929	Under age.
737	15.7.1929	Parker, Maurice	Frances	Ridd Cottage, Monkleigh	29.5.1923	Somerset Place, Stoke, Devonport	2.8.1929	Returned to Devonport. Visitor to W.G.
722	22.7.1929	Squire, Norman Trevor	James	Prospect Place, W.G.	19.12.1921	Geneva Boys'	2.8.1929	Returned to Bideford. Visitor to W.G.
738	7.10.1929	Husband, Marjory	Alfred	Lower Huxill, W.G.	16.10.1916	Bideford Convent	31.10.1929	Returned to Bideford Convent School.
739	7.10.1929	Husband, Jamie	Alfred	Lower Huxill, W.G.	17.11.1918	Bideford Convent	31.10.1929	Returned to Bideford Convent School.
740	7.10.1929	Husband, Sheila	Alfred	Lower Huxill, W.G.	21.9.1921	Bideford Convent	31.10.1929	Returned to Bideford Convent School.
741	7.10.1929	Husband, Walter	Alfred	Lower Huxill, W.G.	21.11.1923	Bideford Convent	31.10.1929	Returned to Bideford Convent School.
742	6.1.1930	Busby, Eric Donald	Edward	1 Harbour Houses, W.G.	29.12.1924	None	31.10.1935	Gone to Bideford Grammar School. Lovering Scholarship.
736	6.1.1930	Braunton, Joan Madeline	Frank	Chope's Bridge, W.G.	28.6.1926	Weare Giffard		
737	3.2.1930	Parker, Maurice	Frances	Ridd Cottage, Monkleigh	29.5.1923	Somerset Place, Stoke, Devonport	2.6.1931	Returned to Devonport. Visitor to W.G.
743	27.3.1930	Gordon, Edith Mary	Richard	The Dock, W.G.	15.10.1919	Frithelstock	26.10.1933	Exempt by age and attendance.
744	28.4.1930	Cole, Evelyn Florence	Lewis	Venton Cottage, W.G.	3.9.1924	None	27.7.1938	Exempt by age and attendance.
745	28.4.1930	Cole, Olive Gwendoline	Lewis	Venton Cottage, W.G.	6.10.1925	None		
746	28.4.1930	Grigg, Desmond James	James	Netherdowns, W.G.	29.6.1926	None	27.7.1938	Gained Lovering Scholarship. Gone to Bideford Grammar School.
731	28.4.1930	Tanton, Joyce	Charles	Sallerns, W.G.	7.7.1925	Weare Giffard C.E.	20.3.1934	Removed to Chittlehampton.
747	8.9.1930	Lawrence, Richard John	Albert Edward	Venton Cottage, W.G.	27.10.1925	None	29.10.1938	Left temporarily. Staying at Little Torrington.
748	8.9.1930	Gorvett, Ernest	Aubrey	Annery Kiln, W.G.	28.11.1926	None		
719	15.9.1930	Day, Frank	Walter	Annery Lodge	16.7.1920	Langton, nr Tunbridge Wells	31.7.1931	Removed to Tunbridge Wells.
749	5.1.1931	Ball, Bertie Douglas John	Cecil	Pool Steps, W.G.	9.10.1918	Huntshaw Ch:	9.9.1932	Removed to Great Torrington.
750	5.1.1931	Ball, Leslie Cecil George	Cecil	Pool Steps, W.G.	19.10.1919	Huntshaw Ch:	9.9.1932	Removed to Great Torrington.
751	5.1.1931	Ball, Marjorie Mary	Cecil	Pool Steps, W.G.	25.7.1921	Huntshaw Ch:	9.9.1932	Removed to Great Torrington.

WEARE GIFFARD CHURCH OF ENGLAND SCHOOL ADMISSION REGISTER, 1905-1945 REGISTER

Admission No	Date of Admission	Full Name of Child	Name of Parent or Guardian	Address	Date of Birth	Name of Last School	Date of Last Attendance at this School	Cause of Leaving and Remarks
752	5.1.1931	Ball, Reggie Thos.	Cecil	Pool Steps, W.G.	30.3.1923	Huntshaw Ch:	9.9.1932	Removed to Great Torrington.
753	5.1.1931	Ball, Ethel May	Cecil	Pool Steps, W.G.	4.6.1924	Huntshaw Ch:	23.3.1932	Gone to Torrington (temporarily).
754	5.1.1931	Parkhouse, Ivor Claude	William	Vine Cottage, W.G.	6.3.1923	Geneva Cl, Bideford	27.9.1935	Removed to Newton St Cyres.
755	5.1.1931	Beer, Vera May	John	River View, W.G.	7.2.1926	None		Torrington Senior.
756	12.1.1931	Parkhouse, Alec	William	Vine Cottage. W.G.	5.3.1925	Geneva Cl Infts, Bideford	27.9.1935	Removed to Newton St Cyres.
757	20.4.1931	Hoblin, Peggy	John Henry	Annery Kiln, W.G.	20.4.1922	Somerset Place Cl, Devonport	21.5.1931	Return to Devonport. Visitor to W.G.
758	29.6.1931	Moyse, Arthur James	Daisy	Ridd Cottage, Monkleigh	21.2.1921	Littleham Cl	30.10.1931	Removed to Bideford.
759	29.6.1931	Moyse, Eric	Daisy	Ridd Cottage, Monkleigh	15.2.1923	Littleham Cl	30.10.1931	Removed to Bideford.
760	7.9.1931	Gorvett, Ronald Aubrey	Aubrey	Annery Kiln	29.6.1928	None		Torrington Senior.
761	3.11.1931	Brodie, Kathleen	Mrs R. Jeffery	Hallspill House, W.G.	29.8.1923	St Stephen's, W. Kensington	27.7.1932	Returned to Kensington. Visitor to W.G.
706	25.11.1931	Busby, Betty Nesta	Harry	Harbour House, W.G.	7.2.1921	Lynton Council	27.11.1931	Returned to Lynton.
725	14.12.1931	Lawrence, Winifred Amy	Albert Edward	Venton Cottage, W.G.	28.6.1923	Little Torrington Church	29.7.1937	Exempt by age and attendance. Gone to domestic service.
762	4.4.1932	Prouse, Ada Mary	Ernest W^m. Prouse	Annery Kiln, W.G.	20.6.1927	None		Torrington Senior.
763	4.4.1932	Lawrence, W^m. Henry	Albert Edward	Venton Cottage, W.G.	20.4.1927	None	12.4.1933	Gone to Alverdiscott (temporarily).
753	26.4.1932	Ball, Ethel May	Cecil	Pool Steps, W.G.	4.6.1924	Torrington Girls' Council	9.9.1932	Removed to Great Torrington.
764	10.5.1932	Stevens, Lilian	Alfred	Quay Cottage, W.G.	22.12.1925	Instow Council		Torrington Senior.
705	24.5.1932	Stevens, Evelyn Beatrice	Alfred	Quay Cottage, W.G.	10.1.1922	Instow Council	2.8.1934	Awarded Lovering Scholarship to Edgehill Girls' College, Bideford.
765	31.5.1932	Braunton, Beatrice Edith	Frank	Hedgedown Cottage, Chope's Bridge	22.2.1929	None	22.7.1932	Under age.
747	14.12.1932	Lawrence, Richard	Albert Edward	Venton Cottage, W.G.	27.10.1925	Little Torrington Ch.	12.4.1933	Gone to Alverdiscott (temporarily).
766	27.2.1933	Slee, Jean Muriel	Charles	Harbour House, W.G.	5.4.1928	None	21.12.1933	Removed to Bideford.
767	20.3.1933	Cole, Ernest Francis	Lewis	Venton Cottage, W.G.	20.3.1927	None		Torrington Senior.

WEARE GIFFARD CHURCH OF ENGLAND SCHOOL ADMISSION REGISTER, 1905-1945 REGISTER

Admission No	Date of Admission	Full Name of Child	Name of Parent or Guardian	Address	Date of Birth	Name of Last School	Date of Last Attendance at this School	Cause of Leaving and Remarks
768	27.3.1933	Beer, Betty	Alfred	Brook Cottage, W.G.	23.12.1928	None	23.6.1933	Illness. (Under age).
765	27.3.1933	Braunton, Beatrice Edith	Frank	Hedgedown Cottage, W.G.	22.2.1929	Weare Giffard C.E.	1.8.1940	Transferred to Torrington Senior School.
769	4.4.1933	Coad, Peter	Wilfred	Bonifants, W.G.	24.6.1929	None	15.11.1933	Left. Removed to Plymouth.
770	4.4.1933	Oarway, Jean	Roy	Bonifants, W.G.	12.10.1929	None	17.4.1935	Removed to Northam.
771	5.4.1933	Gibbons, Derek John	John Albert	Prospect Place, W.G.	6.5.1928	None	16.2.1934	Left. Removed to Portsmouth.
772	24.4.1933	Vinnicombe, Alfred James	Grace	Little Weare, W.G.	12.9.1921	Chillaton	4.7.1933	Removed to Holsworthy.
747	15.5.1933	Lawrence, Richard	Albert Edward	Venton Cottage, W.G.	27.10.1925	Alverdiscott	23.12.1937	Removed to Monkleigh.
763	15.5.1933	Lawrence, William Hy.	Albert Edward	Venton Cottage, W.F.	20.4.1927	Alverdiscott	23.12.1937	Removed to Monkleigh.
773	11.9.1933	Lawrence, Reginald George	Albert Edward	Venton Cottage, W.G.	10.7.1928	None	23.12.1937	Removed to Monkleigh.
768	8.1.1934	Beer, Betty	Alfred	Brook Cottage, W.G.	23.12.1928	Weare Giffard C.E.		Torrington Senior.
769	29.1.1934	Coad, Peter	Wilfred	Bonifants, W.G.	24.6.1929	Weare Giffard C.E.	1.3.1934	Illness. Under age.
770	9.4.1934	Tucker, Margaret Rose	James	Dock Cottages, W.G.	28.9.1929	None	11.3.1937	Removed to Appledore.
771	9.4.1934	Tucker, Nancy May	James	Dock Cottages, W.G.	28.9.1929	None	11.3.1937	Removed to Appledore.
772	9.4.1934	Cole, Queenie Doreen	Lewis	Venton Cottage, W.G.	25.3.1928	None		
773	22.5.1934	Grigg, Bettine Beryl	James	Neatherdowns Farm, W.G.	29.9.1929	None	1.8.1940	Transferred to Torrington Senior.
774	10.6.1934	Matthews, Merlyn Saskadoc	Kenneth Percy Matthews	North Furze, W.G.	6.10.1925	Plymtree C.E.	23.4.1937	Removal to Instow.
775	10.6.1934	Matthews, Gwendolyn Manadoc	Kenneth Percy Matthews	North Furze, W.G.	10.8.1927	Plymtree C.E.	23.4.1937	Removal to Instow.
769	5.7.1934	Coad, Peter	Wilfred	Bonifants, W.G.	24.6.1929	Weare Gifford C.E.	2.8.1934	Return to Plymouth.
776	10.9.1934	Smith, Joan Audrey	Mrs Helen Sophia Smith	The Rectory, W.G.	10.5.1930	Brenreth School, nr Ashford, Kent	26.11.1935	Removal to Kilmington, Nr Axminster.
777	10.12.1934	Netherway, Dorothy	Eva	Ridd Cottage, W.G.	27.5.1923	Newton St Petrock	30.1.1936	Gone to Princess Elizabeth Orth: Home, Exeter.

WEARE GIFFARD CHURCH OF ENGLAND SCHOOL ADMISSION REGISTER, 1905-1945 REGISTER

Admission No.	Date of Admission	Full Name of Child	Name of Parent or Guardian	Address	Date of Birth	Name of Last School	Date of Last Attendance at this School	Cause of Leaving and Remarks
778	10.12.1934	Netherway, Cecil	Eva	Ridd Cottage, W.G.	3.8.1925	Newton St Petrock		
779	25.2.1935	Pidler, Alan George	Frederick George	Harbour Cottage, W.G.	29.10.1929	None	26.1.1939	Removed to High Bickington, temporarily.
735	12.3.1935	Beer, Harold Richard	John	Bonifants, W.G.	17.12.1925	Rockwell Green, nr Wellington	4.4.1935	Return to Rockwell Green.
769	16.4.1935	Coad, Peter	Wilfred	Bonifants, W.G.	24.6.1929	Camel's Hd, Plymouth	19.7.1935	Return to Plymouth.
780	29.4.1935	Curtis, Albert Howard Hy.	Albert	Downings Cottage, W.G.	18.7.1930	None	30.7.1941	Torrington Senior School.
781	29.4.1935	Lawrence, Gladys May	Albert Edward	Venton Cottage, W.G.	15.6.1930	None	23.12.1937	Removed to Monkleigh.
782	29.4.1935	Martin, Frederick Wm. John	Frederick	Marshbrook, W.G.	8.4.1930	None	24.2.1939	Removed to Bideford, temporarily.
783	30.9.1935	Hedden, Joyce Annie	Albert James	The Barton, W.G.	10.3.1923	Newton St Petrock Cl	24.3.1937	Exempt by age and attendance. Working at home on farm.
784	30.9.1935	Hedden, Mary Edith	Albert James	The Barton, W.G.	13.6.1925	Newton St Petrock Cl		
785	28.10.1935	Coad, Peter	Wilfred	Chopes' Bridge, W.G.	24.6.1929	Camel's Hd, Plymouth	22.7.1938	Return to Plymouth.
786	5.11.1935	Short, Sheila Mary	O.M. Short	Quay, W.G.	29.8.1930	Frithelstock	23.2.1937	On a visit to Newton St Petrock.
735	6.1.1936	Beer, Harold Richard	John	Bonifants, W.G.	17.12.1925	Rockwell Green, Nr Wellington	6.9.1937	Gone to Street, Somerset.
770	27.1.1936	Oatway, Jean	Roy	Bonifants, W.G.	12.10.1929	Northam C.E.	6.2.1936	Return to Northam. Visitor to W.G.
787	3.2.1936	Plows, Loveridge Jack	Thomas William	River View, W.G.	20.3.1922	Northam C.E.	8.4.1936	Exempt by age and attendance.
788	3.2.1936	Plows, Kingsley Gordon	Thomas William	River View, W.G.	21.4.1923	Northam C.E.	22.12.1936	Removed to Stoney Cross, Alverdiscott.
789	3.2.1936	Plows, Lavinia Christine	Thomas William	River View, W.G.	18.12.1924	Northam C.E.	22.12.1936	Removed to Stoney Cross, Alverdiscott.
790	3.2.1936	Plows, Trevor Newton	Thomas William	River View, W.G.	22.6.1927	Northam C.E.	22.12.1936	Removed to Stoney Cross, Alverdiscott.

WEARE GIFFARD CHURCH OF ENGLAND SCHOOL ADMISSION REGISTER, 1905-1945 REGISTER

Admission No	Date of Admission	Full Name of Child	Name of Parent or Guardian	Address	Date of Birth	Name of Last School	Date of Last Attendance at this School	Cause of Leaving and Remarks
791	3.2.1936	Plows, Christopher John	Thomas William	River View, W.G.	12.11.1928	Northam C.E.	22.12.1936	Removed to Stoney Cross, Alverdiscott.
792	20.4.1936	Carter, Kathleen Ruby	George	Roadcliffe, W.G.	17.2.1931	None	30.7.1942	Torrington Senior School.
793	20.4.1936	Grigg, Glenys Linda	James	Neatherdowns, W.G.	18.2.1932	None		Gone to Rockwell Green, nr Wellington.
794	20.4.1936	Coad, Allan James	Wilfred	Chope's Bridge, W.G.	15.9.1931	None	3.2.1938	Gone to a private school at Bournemouth.
795	20.4.1936	Mathews, Mildred Esther	Kenneth Percy	North Furze, W.G.	7.10.1931	None	16.4.1937	Return to Portsmouth. Visitor to W.G.
796	11.5.1936	Gibbons, Iris Beryl	John Albert	Prospect Place, W.G.	22.12.1930	Stamshaw Infts	22.7.1936	Return to Portsmouth. Visitor to W.G.
771	11.5.1936	Gibbons, Derek John	John Albert	Prospect Place, W.G.	6.5.1928	Stamshaw Boys'	23.7.1936	Exempt by age and attendance. Gone to domestic service.
777	7.9.1936	Netherway, Dorothy	Eva	Ridd Cottage, W.G.	27.5.1923	Princess Elizabeth Orthopaedic Hospital, Exeter	29.7.1937	Return to Monkleigh. Visitor to W.G.
797	26.10.1936	Clements, Desmond Reuben	Horace	Osborne House, W.G.	25.8.1928	Monkleigh C.E.	11.12.1936	Gone to Beaford on a visit.
786	10.3.1937	Short, Sheila Mary	O.M. Short	Dock Cottages, W.G.	29.8.1930	Newton St Petrock	14.9.1938	Removed to Monkleigh.
798	5.4.1937	Lawrence, Albert Edward	Albert Edward	Venton Cottage, W.G.	7.11.1931	None	23.12.1937	Gone to Torrington Senior School.
799	18.5.1937	Hunt, Elizabeth Joan	V.M. Hunt	North Furze, W.G.	6.10.1930	Colaton Raleigh	15.8.1941	
800	6.9.1937	Prouse, Wm. George	William	Annery Kiln, W.G.	4.7.1933	None		Gone to Torrington Senior School.
801	6.9.1937	Allin, Mavis Joyce	Owen Allin	Chopes' Bridge, W.G.	7.8.1930	Halsdon House Torrington (Private School)		
802	20.9.1937	Evans, Phyllis Mary French	Hilda	The Dock Cottages, W.G.	7.8.1933	Nil		
770	11.10.1937	Oatway, Jean	Roy	Bonifants, W.G.	12.10.1929	Johnson Terrace Infants, Plymouth	2.12.1937	Return to Bideford. Visitor to W.G.
803	24.11.1937	Redwood, Horace Ayre	D.V. Redwood	The Dock, W.G.	11.8.1931	Ashill, nr. Cullompton	26.11.1937	Return to Ashill. Visitor to W.G.
735	10.1.1938	Beer, Harold Richard	John	Bonifants, W.G.	17.12.1925	Rockwell Green, nr. Wellington	27.7.1938	Gone to Bideford Grammar School.

WEARE GIFFARD CHURCH OF ENGLAND SCHOOL ADMISSION REGISTER, 1905-1945 REGISTER

Admission No.	Date of Admission	Full Name of Child	Name of Parent or Guardian	Address	Date of Birth	Name of Last School	Date of Last Attendance at this School	Cause of Leaving and Remarks
804	7.2.1938	Jewell, Christine Winifred	Arthur	Marshbrook, W.G.	25.12.1927	St Giles in the Wood	30.3.1938	Returned to St Giles in the Wood.
805	24.2.1938	Becklake, Mary	William	Brook Cottage, W.G.	12.3.1930	Alwington C.E.	28.2.1938	Returned to Alwington. Visitor to W.G.
794	8.3.1938	Coad, Allan James	Wilfred	Chopes' Bridge, W.G.	15.9.1931	Rockwell Green, nr. Wellington	27.7.1938	Returned to Plymouth.
806	25.4.1938	Trathen, Ena Nellie	Albert	Venton Cottage, W.G.	24.1.1926	Huntshaw		
807	25.4.1938	Poore, Raymond	Arthur	Annery Lodge, Monkleigh	29.4.1933	Nil	23.9.1938	Gone to Gunnislake, temporarily.
770	20.6.1938	Oatway, Jean	Roy	Bonifants, W.G.	12.10.1929	Donington Church, nr Oxford	24.6.1938	Removed to Plymouth.
808	5.9.1938	Martin, Betty Florence Mary	Frederick	Marshbrook, W.G.	17.7.1934	Nil	24.2.1939	Removed to Bideford, temporarily.
786	3.10.1938	Short, Sheila Mary	O.M. Short	Dock Cottage, W.G.	29.8.1930	Newton St Petrock		
809	24.10.1938	Short, Mary Frances	O.M. Short	Dock Cottage, W.G.	22.4.1930	Frithelstock	22.12.1938	Returned to Frithelstock. Visitor to W.G.
807	22.11.1938	Poore, Raymond	Arthur	Annery Lodge, Monkleigh	29.4.1933	Gunnislake Church	30.11.1938	Removed to Gunnislake.
785	9.1.1939	Coad, Peter	Wilfred	Bonifants, W.G.	24.6.1929	JohnstonTerrace Cl Mixed,	20.1.1939	Returned to Plymouth.
794	9.1.1939	Coad, Allan James	Wilfred	Bonifants, W.G.	15.9.1931	Keyham, Devonport	20.1.1939	Returned to Plymouth
808	3.4.1939	Martin, Betty Florence Mary	Frederick	Marshbrook, W.G.	17.7.1934	Geneva Cl Sch., Bideford		
782	3.4.1939	Martin, Frederick Wm. John	Frederick	Marshbrook, W.G.	8.4.1930	Geneva Cl Sch., Bideford	15.8.1941	Gone to Torrington Senior School.
779	16.4.1939	Pidler, Alan George	Fred. Geo.	Harbour Cottage	29.10.1929	Weare Giffard	1.8.1940	Bideford Grammar School.
810	16.4.1939	Prouse, Phyllis Mabel	Ernest	Annery Kiln, W.G.	9.1.1935	None		
811	16.4.1939	Grigg, William Lancelot	James	Neatherdowns Farm	21.12.1933	None		
812	11.9.1939	Wicks, John	J.N. Wicks	Torridge View	24.6.1933	Sidcup Junior	1.12.1939	Returned to Sidcup.

WEARE GIFFARD CHURCH OF ENGLAND SCHOOL ADMISSION REGISTER, 1905-1945 REGISTER

Admission No.	Date of Admission	Full Name of Child	Name of Parent or Guardian	Address	Date of Birth	Name of Last School	Date of Last Attendance at this School	Cause of Leaving and Remarks
813	11.9.1939	Goulding, Beryl	S. Goulding	Bridge View	31.1.1931	(Peckham Road, Birmingham)	22.9.1939	Returned to Birmingham.
814	11.9.1939	Goulding, Joyce	S. Goulding	Bridge View	31.1.1931	(Birmingham)	22.9.1939	Returned to Birmingham.
815	14.9.1939	Jenner, Peter	Helene Jenner	Carmen, W.G.	10.1.1935	None	10.11.1939	Returned to Carshalton.
816	26.9.1939	Jeffery, Jean Pauline	G.H. Jeffery	Carmen, W.G.	12.7.1930	(St Stephen's, London)	15.12.1939	Returned to London.
817	26.9.1939	Jeffery, Joel	G.H. Jeffery	Carmen, W.G.	8.7.1933	(London)	15.12.1939	Returned to London.
818	2.10.1939	Coad, Allan James	D.M. Coad	Bonifants, W.G.	15.9.1931	(Johnston (Terrace Board School,	5.10.1939	Returned to Plymouth.
819	2.10.1939	Coad, Peter	D.M. Coad	Bonifants, W.G.	24.6.1929	(Plymouth	5.10.1939	Returned to Plymouth.
818	1.11.1939	Coad, Allan James	D.M. Coad	School House, W.G.	15.9.1931	(Johnston (Terrace Board School,	30.7.1942 23.4.1940	Torrington Senior School. Gone away to Glasgow.
819	1.11.1939	Coad, Peter	D.M. Coad	School House, W.G.	24.6.1929	(Plymouth	1.8.1940	Bideford Grammar School.
820	5.2.1940	Tanton, Phyllis Margaret	George Tanton	Hadlow Cottage, Gammaton	28.7.1929	Monkleigh	1.8.1940	Transferred to Torrington S.S.
821	5.2.1940	Tanton, Mary Christine	George Tanton	Hadlow Cottage, Gammaton	15.5.1930	Monkleigh	15.8.1940	Transferred to Torrington S. Sch.
822	1.4.1940	Ford, Irene May	Arthur Ford	Southcott Farm, W.G.	9.10.1934	None		
823	8.6.1940	Gilder, Margaret June	M.N.L. Gilder	Sunset, Landcross	26.6.1931	Salisbury Road, Plymouth	23.6.1942	Gone to Plymouth. County Scholarship.
824	8.6.1940	Oatway, Jean	Roy	Bonifants, W.G.	12.10.1929	Plymouth	1.8.1940	Returned to Plymouth.
825	9.9.1940	Isaacs, Brian Ernest John	John Isaac	Annery Kiln	28.11.1935	Nil		
826	9.9.1940	Taylor, Shirley	Harry Taylor	Rockmount, W.G.	6.8.1935	Nil	28.3.1941	Returned to London.
827	9.9.1940	Huxtable, Marjorie	Thomas Huxtable	Downing Terrace	9.5.1931	Newchurch, I.O.W.	24.1.41	Left for Eastleigh.
816	25.9.1940	Jeffery, Jean	G.H. Jeffery	Hallspill, W.G.	12.7.1930	St Stephen's (London)	26.5.42	Transferred to L.C.C. Register.
817	25.9.1940	Jeffery, Joel	G.H. Jeffery	Hallspill, W.G.	8.7.1933	St Stephen's (London)	26.5.1942	Transferred to L.C.C. Register.

WEARE GIFFARD CHURCH OF ENGLAND SCHOOL ADMISSION REGISTER, 1905-1945 REGISTER

Admission No	Date of Admission	Full Name of Child	Name of Parent or Guardian	Address	Date of Birth	Name of Last School	Date of Last Attendance at this School	Cause of Leaving and Remarks
828	30.9.1940	Huxtable, Greta	Thomas Huxtable	Sunnyside, W.G.	8.4.1932	Newchurch, I.O.W.	16.2.42	Gone to live with mother at Westleigh.
812	8.10.1940	Wicks, John	J.N. Wicks	Dock Cottage, W.G.	24.6.1933	Sidcup, Kent	18.12.1942	Removed to Bideford.
829	11.11.1940	Welbrock, Jean	E.S. Welbrock	Vine Cottage, W.G.	24.6.1931	Calvert Road, London	12.12.1940	Removed to Torrington.
830	11.11.1940	Vanstone, Winifred	c/o Mrs Tallamy	Venn Farm, Woolsery	25.8.1934	Woolsery	19.12.1940	Returned to Woolsery.
831	6.1.1941	Goulding, Diane	c/o Mrs R.E. Samuels	56 Caversham Road, B'ham	16.1.1936	None	20.6.1941	Returned to Birmingham.
832	22.4.1941	Worden, June	R. Worden	Little Weare Barton Cottage	1.4.1931	Newton St Petrock	21.7.1942	Transferred to Torrington Senior School.
833	28.4.1941	Griffin, Joan	James Griffin	Bonifants, W.G.	22.4.1936	None	10.9.1942	Convent School, Bideford.
815	27.6.1941	Jenner, Peter	Helene Jenner	Carmen, W.G.	10.1.1935	Convent, Sutton	7.11.1941	Returned to Carshalton.
834	1.9.1941	Tanton, Linda	Phyllis Tanton	Rockmount, W.G.	4.8.1936	None		
835	1.12.1941	Duncan, Margaret M.	Mrs C. Duncan	c/o Rockmount, W.G.	2.7.1934	Scotland	20.2.1942	Returned to Scotland.
836	5.1.1942	Worden, Thomas Arthur	M. Worden	Little Weare Barton Cott.	27.12.1936	Newton St Petrock	23.12.1942	Removed to Merton.
837	5.1.1942	Worden, Hazel Elizabeth	M. Worden	Little Weare Barton Cott.	27.12.1936	Newton St Petrock	23.12.1942	Removed to Merton.
838	20.4.1942	Tucker, Ernest	S.F. Tucker (Mrs)	Annery Kiln	24.1.1937	None		
839	20.4.1942	Prouse, Albert	William	Annery Kiln	6.6.1937	None		
840	20.4.1942	Grigg, Hilary (Hilene)	James	Netherdowns Farm	15.5.1937	None	7.9.1944	Gone to Stella Maris Convent, Bideford.
817	26.5.1942	Jeffery, Joel	G.H. Jeffery	Ridd Bungalow	8.7.1933	Transferred from L.C.C. Register	17.9.1943	Returned to London.
841	9.6.1942	Stroud, Moreen	Jean Stroud	c/o Ridd Cottage	9.10.1931	Blythe St., Belfast	30.6.1942	Returned to Ireland.
842	9.6.1942	Stroud, Shirley	Jean Stroud	c/o Ridd Cottage	4.10.1935	Workman (J), Belfast	30.6.1942	Returned to Ireland.
843	1.3.1943	Huxham, Donald A.	W. Huxham	Vine Cottage, W.G.	10.7.1934	Homelands Open Air, Torquay	16.4.1943	Returned to Torquay.
844	1.3.1943	Huxham, Jean W.	W. Huxham	Vine Cottage, W.G.	12.4.1937	Homelands Open Air, Torquay	16.4.1943	Returned to Torquay.

WEARE GIFFARD CHURCH OF ENGLAND SCHOOL ADMISSION REGISTER, 1905-1945 REGISTER

Admission No.	Date of Admission	Full Name of Child	Name of Parent or Guardian	Address	Date of Birth	Name of Last School	Date of Last Attendance at this School	Cause of Leaving and Remarks
845	15.3.1943	Long, Eric George	Gertrude Long	Little Weare Barton Cottage	24.9.1934	Roborough	17.9.1943	Left for Roborough.
846	3.5.1943	Vanstone, John	Frank Vanstone	Wyatt Cottage, W.G.	30.3.1938	None		
847	28.6.1943	London, James A.A.	Ivy London	Rockmount, W.G.	23.10.1936	Roding School, Dagenham	30.7.1943	Returned to London.
848	16.8.1943	Lee, Jeffrey	Winifred Lee	La Maisonette, Landcross	15.9.1936	Bideford Church I.		
847	30.8.1943	London, James A.	Ivy London	Rockmount, W.G.	23.10.1936	Roding School, Dagenham		Transferred to L.C.C. Register (Evacuée).
849	11.10.1943	Pidler, June	Frederick Pidler	Harbour Cottage	.6.1938	None		
850	24.4.1944	Allin, Royston Owen	Owen Allin	Bridge Dairy	20.3.1939	None		
851	4.9.1944	Griffin, Robert John	James Griffin	Brook Cottage	21.9.1939	None		
852	4.9.1944	Evans, Vera	Walter Evans	Torridge View	17.7.1939	None		
853	4.9.1944	Prouse, Sylvia Ann	Ernest Prouse	Annery Kiln	7.11.1939	None		
854	20.11.1944	Egan, Gladys Mary	Mrs C. Egan	Yeo Cottage, Monkleigh	29.5.1935	Thornhillhead		
855	8.1.1945	Short, Marg'. Short	Mrs Short	Hallspill, W.G.	19.1.1940	None		

WEAR GIFFORD

CHURCH OF ENGLAND SCHOOL

LOG BOOK

1900 - 1945

WEARE GIFFARD CHURCH OF ENGLAND SCHOOL LOG BOOK
1900 - 1945

1900

May 1st 1900	Staff W. Ashton Jewell, Head Master. Fanny D. Clarke, Assistant. Number of children on Register - 65. **Second Quarter** Commenced the 2nd Quarter of our school year yesterday. Average for 1st Quarter 52.7. A very good attendance today, 57 present.
May 3rd	Torrington Fair is being held to-day, the attendance at school being in consequence very low, only 37 children present out of 65 on Register. A very wet and stormy day. 31 children present this afternoon. Seeing that the attendance is so materially affected by Torrington Fair it would be advisable in the future to close school on such occasions. Owing to so many absentees, Friday afternoon's lessons will be substituted for those of to-day. Needlework and Drawing will therefore be taken on Friday.
May 4th	Average for past week only 50.2 out of 65 on books.
May 7th	Admitted Walter J. Johns. This lad is in his sixth year and has never before attended school. About 2.30 this afternoon two children Thomas and Stanley Matthews were observed by the Master to be showing symptoms of measles. They were at once sent home and their attendance cancelled. A step-sister of these children is already suffering from measles.
May 8th	Only 47 children present this morning. Measles are increasing. Attendance still falling off. 42 children only present this afternoon, leaving 23 absentees. A thunderstorm during the dinner hour is responsible for the absence of a few, but additional cases of illness account for the majority.
May 9th	Attendance still very bad. 42 present. Many of the children have bad colds.
May 10th	Number in attendance now reduced to 38. Much progress at present is out of the question.
May 11th	Average for past week only 44.6.
May 14th	Cold and boisterous weather. Sickness is still prevalent in the parish, the attendance being low. 47 present this morning out of 67 on registers. Readmitted Amy Gorner after an absence of many months through illness. Admitted Elsie Short, bringing the total on books to 67.
May 16th	Weather much warmer. Attendance slightly improved: 49 present this morning, 51 children present this afternoon; a great improvement upon the attendance of last week, although a percentage of 77 is not sufficiently high to be conducive to sound progress.
May 18th	Attendance down again to 42. Several more children ill. Date assured by Lord Roberts for the relief of Baden Powell and his brave defenders in Mafeking. No news of the promised relief, however, has been yet received. Average for past week 46.7.
May 19th	Relief of Mafeking after a resistance of 216 days. Actually relieved on Wednesday 16th.
May 21st	Measles spreading rapidly - only 26 children present this morning. A half holiday will be given this afternoon in honour of Baden Powell, Mafeking's brave defender.

WEARE GIFFARD CHURCH OF ENGLAND SCHOOL LOG BOOK 1900 - 1945

1900

May 22nd	Attendance lower than ever, only 23 present. The school was therefore closed to await the decision of the Medical Officer of Health. Diocesan Inspection fixed for June 18th.
May 23rd	Opened school again this morning, 12 children only present. Closed until Monday. Notices will at once be sent to H.M. Inspectors.
May 24th	School closed by order of Dr Slade King Medical Officer of Health.
June 5th	Re-opened school this morning, the measles having considerably abated. 31 present. Lord Roberts enters Pretoria.
June 6th	Attendance considerably improved. 44 present this morning.
June 8th	Average for past week 41.7. Many children still absent on account of measles. Willie Brooks marked absent this afternoon. A horse chased him while on his way to school.
June 15th	A busy week ending in a futile attempt to make up for time lost during the epidemic of measles. Average improving though now only 52 out of 68 on books.
June 18th	Diocesan Inspection by the Rev. I.F. Powning. 61 children present. The usual half holiday was given in the afternoon.
June 19th	Attendance down again to 50. Measles having abated, strawberry picking is now responsible for many absentees.
June 20th	After the wretched attendance of the past two months it is quite a pleasure to record an attendance of 60 children today. It will, however, take some considerable time to pull up the backward work.
June 21st	In accordance with notice previously given to H.M. Inspectors, there will be a whole day's holiday to-day.
June 22nd	Very fair attendance this morning, 57 present. Average for past week 55.6.
June 25th	Very stormy weather, exceptionally so for June. 56 children present this morning.
June 26th	School opened 15 minutes earlier this afternoon to enable the master to leave in time to attend a meeting at Bideford.
June 28th	The Upper Division were set Writing this morning for the lesson following the Recreation, in error. The lessons in both Divisions were therefore reversed.
June 29th	Many children have been absent this week strawberry picking, reducing the average to 53.7. Such irregularity is most unsatisfactory, and renders work in school doubly hard, as many lessons have to be repeated over and over again for the benefit of irregular attenders. Much progress is therefore impossible.
July 2nd	Commenced school this week with only a fair attendance, 55 present out of 68 on books. The weather, however, is very unlike July, being dark and wet.

WEARE GIFFARD CHURCH OF ENGLAND SCHOOL LOG BOOK
1900 - 1945

1900

REGISTERS CHECKED	Examined the registers and found them correct. Stephen Wade.
July 3rd	Copy of Diocesan Report
	Teacher's Work:- Discipline, Tone etc. Excellent. Scholars on the Books 68. Scholars present at the Inspection Boys 30 Girls 31. The school is classed as Very Good.
	General Remarks:- Long continued epidemic sickness has considerably affected the attendance of the children at this well ordered school and consequently the proportion of those who were able to answer promptly and intelligently on June 18. Some of the scholars in the upper group showed a capital knowledge of the syllabus they had prepared, and were an evidence of the pains and ability bestowed upon their Religious Instruction.
	Hon. Mention:- Fred Squires - Alice Trace - Maude Braunton - Winnie Bright - Ethel Short - Florence Gomer - Charles Parkhouse - George Gomer - Samuel Brownscombe - Minnie Davey.
	Stephen Wade, Correspondent.
July 3rd	A wretched attendance again to-day - 47 children only present.
July 6th	The attendance during the past week has been very irregular, 15 children being absent on an average each day. This is very unsatisfactory: but so long as the powers of compulsory attendance are delegated to an Attendance Committee sitting at Torrington, which knows nothing whatever of the local circumstances connected with each case, so long will matters remain as they are.
July 9th	59 children present this afternoon. A very hot day - summer heat seems to have arrived at last.
July 12th	A heavy thunder-shower occurring just before the closing of morning school, but which was over before the children left, has provided another flimsy excuse for the usually careless and indifferent parents. No less than 23 children absent this afternoon.
July 13th	Average for past week 54. Strawberry picking and hay harvest are almost over now, and it is hoped the attendance will improve.
July 16th	Very bad attendance again this morning. 49 only present.
July 17th /Pens/	Just one half of the first division absent - 12 out of 25 on the register. Work in school under such conditions of irregularity as have existed during the past 3 or 4 months is difficult and discouraging. Supplied two dozen new pens.
July 19th /Heat/	An exceedingly hot day.
July 20th	The past week has been very trying for both teachers and taught, on account of the great heat. The average is still low, in fact just below that of last week.
	Notice has to-day been sent to H.M. Inspectors informing them of a holiday on Thursday next, also of the date fixed for the commencement of summer holidays viz. Aug: 3rd 1900. Average 53.8.
July 23rd	A little better attendance this morning. 58 children present. 61 present this afternoon. Very hot weather.

WEARE GIFFARD CHURCH OF ENGLAND SCHOOL LOG BOOK
1900 - 1945

1900

July 24th	Weather still very hot. Attendance down again.
July 25th	Bideford Regatta being held to-day is responsible for many absentees - only 50 children present. To prevent a further lowering of the attendance school will open this afternoon a half hour earlier, closing at 3.40, so as to enable many children to go to Bideford. They would otherwise absent themselves for the whole day.
July 26th /TREAT/	In accordance with notice previously given to H.M. Inspectors there will be a whole day's holiday on the occasion of the School Treat.
July 27th	Resumed work this morning with a very fair attendance after the holiday excitement of yesterday. The children were driven in brakes to Westward Ho, where they had a splendid time on the sands. Next year the new railway there will probably be opened. In consequence of the Needlework and Drawing being missed yesterday those subjects will be taken this afternoon. Average for past week 54.5.
	End of Second Quarter. Times open 103. Total Attendance 5213. Average 50.6. Measles epidemic reduced the average very much.
July 30th	Third Quarter Commenced this week, and the 3rd Quarter of the school year, with a good attendance. News, of national if not educational interest, received today of the unconditional surrender of the Free State General Prinsloo with 5,000 men to Generals Hunter and Macdonald. King of Italy assassinated on Sunday.

WEARE GIFFARD CHURCH OF ENGLAND SCHOOL LOG BOOK
1900 - 1945

1900

July 31st	Visited the School. G. Hayward.
	1. In case of closure, timely notice on these yellow post cards should be sent 1. To Mr H.Cowie, HMI. 2.To Mr R. Matta. 3. To me.
	2. Form IX and the other Annual Returns should be forwarded within 10 days of the end of the year to the officer who last visited the School.
	3. All Lists of Posting etc. and new Time Tables should be ready for the signature of an officer who will visit the School towards the 6th month of the year.
	4. The notification of Candidates requiring to be examined for Labour Certificate should be made either to Mr Matta or to me.
	5. A back support seems to be needed on the top step of the Infants' Gallery.
	6. The boys' offices need washing out and an early opportunity for washing out or painting out their scribbling on the door of the girls' offices should be taken.
	7. A Thermometer is needed. See p. 87 of book - and the temperature of the rooms as recorded by it should be entered in the Log Book several times in each winter month. A pan holding water should be kept upon the stove when the latter is in use.
	8. The Infants are not yet soundly and suitably instructed. Points needing attention have been fully discussed with the Teachers.
	The Reading course is not fully provided:-
	   1. Loose letters etc. and a card.
	   2. Reading Sheets containing the lessons in Primer i.
	   3. Primer i.
	   4. Primer ii.
	   5. Infants' Readers.
	
	George and Florence Gomer were examined for Labour Certificates.

August 1st	A low attendance again to-day, only 50 children present.
August 2nd	Attendance worse than ever - only 41 present. Wesleyan Sunday School outing to Westward Ho is responsible for several absentees. Close school for the usual Summer Holiday. Four Weeks.
August 6th	Received 25 cwt of coal for school use (29/6 per ton).
September 3rd	Commenced work again after four weeks' holiday, during which time the schoolroom, classroom and offices have been thoroughly cleaned. Admitted Ed Crowley from Monkleigh. 52 children present. George and Florence Gomer who were examined on July 31st by G. Hayward Esq: for Labour Certificates (Stand V) both passed in all subjects. Certificates were accordingly granted them.

WEARE GIFFARD CHURCH OF ENGLAND SCHOOL LOG BOOK
1900 - 1945

1900

September 7th	Only 45 children present this afternoon out of 67 on books. The attendance at this school continues to steadily fall off, many parents exhibiting an absolute indifference as to the education of their children. The local Managers are powerless to enforce attendance. Average for past week 52.6.
September 10th	Commenced this week with an excellent attendance. 58 children present out of 65 on books.
September 12th	During this morning the master was indisposed and was obliged to absent himself from school for a hour (11 to 12), leaving the Assistant in charge. A very good attendance to-day. 59 present.
September 13th	The Assistant, Miss Clarke, was granted leave for this afternoon to visit a dentist. Friday afternoon's lessons will therefore be taken to-day and Needlework, Drawing etc. on Friday.
September 14th	The attendance during the past week has been more satisfactory; the average, 56.5, having been exceeded once previous during the present school year.

Aid Grant	**Aid Grant**
	A grant of Ten pounds 5/- has been recommended under the Vol: Sch: Act 1897, to be applied as under.
	    To maintain Assistant £10 ——
	    Organising Visitor 5/-
	                        Stephen Wade, Correspondent

September 17th	Commenced this week with a good attendance. 57 children present this morning. Notice sent to H.M. Inspectors (3) re a holiday on Wednesday Sep: 26th next on the occasion of the Harvest Thanksgiving.
September 18th	Fine showers have fallen to-day, the first rain for nearly a month.
September 19th *REGISTERS CHECKED*	Examined the registers and found them correct. Stephen Wade.
September 20th	In order to secure the attendance of several children desirous of going to the Chapel Harvest Thanksgiving, and who would have absented themselves to-day for that purpose, school will meet and close this afternoon a half hour earlier. The time of all lessons will be altered accordingly.
September 21st	Average for past week 52.2 - 4 below that of last week. Good progress is being made throughout the school with the exception of the lowest division where there is an unusual number of very dull children.

WEARE GIFFARD CHURCH OF ENGLAND SCHOOL LOG BOOK
1900 - 1945

1900

September 24th	Welcome showers have fallen this morning, but in spite of the rain there is a good attendance (50 present). During the past week eight children have left this school; Matthews with 4 and Gomer with 3 children having removed to Torrington. George and Florence Gomer have left for employment.
September 26th	In accordance with notice sent to H.M. Inspectors on the 17th September school will close for a half holiday this afternoon.
September 28th	Average for past week 50.4.
October 1st	Very fine weather. Admitted Sydney Down who has been attending Monkleigh.
October 2nd	Very small attendance, only 43 children present. Lady Audrey Buller is opening a Grand Military Bazaar at Bideford to-day, and many children have probably absented themselves in order to show their patriotism by going to see her.
October 3rd	A very good attendance this afternoon. 56 children present. Very fine weather.
October 4th	Very wet and stormy, many children absent. Received from the Correspondent, Rev. S. Wade, the following articles for school use. - 1 sweeping brush - 1 bucket - 2 stove brushes - 1 flue brush - ½ doz. small screw eyes for windows - - 4 larger ones for curtains - 2 small fire shovels - 4 doz. Ex. bk. - 1 pkt f-cap envelopes - 1 pkt cheap envelopes for school correspondence. Signed : Stephen Wade, Correspondent.
October 5th	The attendance has been very bad during the past week, the average being 48.9 only, or about 78%.
October 7th	Commenced school this morning with an improved attendance, 54 children present. Very fine spring-like weather.
October 8th	Received from the Religious Instruction Committee of the Exeter Diocesan Conference a grant of five pounds for the school. Stephen Wade, Correspondent.
October 11th	Torrington Fair being held to-day is responsible for an attendance of only 44 children.
October 12th	An excellent attendance this morning, 59 children present. Received from the Rector, Rev. S. Wade, a supply of materials for Needlework:- ½ doz. cards Darning Wool - 4 reels white cotton - 4 doz. linen buttons - Lace, Print, unbleached calico, Flannelette. The master having been called away on urgent business (illness of a relative), school was left in charge of the Assistant from 3.10 p.m. Writing was substituted for History. Average for past week 52.6, an improvement of 4 upon last week.
October 15th	Commenced this week with a good attendance.
October 19th	A good week's work has been done, the attendance having been more regular. Average 53.8.
October 22nd	A very sharp frost. Commenced lighting fires.

WEARE GIFFARD CHURCH OF ENGLAND SCHOOL LOG BOOK
1900 - 1945

1900

October 23rd	Quite mild again to-day. A very good attendance, 55 present. Charles Squire is being employed whilst still under a legal obligation to attend school. The matter will be reported to the Attendance Committee. Attendance down again to 49. Chas: Squire attending for the first time since the 12th October.
October 26th	Average for past week only 50.6. One or two stormy days are responsible for this falling off. With such a fluctuating attendance it is impossible to make any great progress, the same work having to be gone over so many times.
October 30th	A very wet morning causes a low attendance, only 48 children present. Such is the lot of the rural teacher; every wet day throughout the winter practically brings the work of the whole school to a standstill.
November 1st	Very mild but dull and damp weather. Attendance fair. The school cleaner came this morning at 8.30. As it is impossible for her to thoroughly sweep and dust the room by the time school opens - 9 o'clock - the master refused to allow her to commence. She will therefore clean the room this evening.
November 2nd	Although there has been a lot of rain this week the attendance has improved a little, the average for past week being 52.2. To-day ends the 3rd Quarter of our school year. Considering the irregularity and the loss of time incurred by the epidemic of measles very fair progress has been made.
November 5th	A very good attendance this afternoon. 56 present.
November 7th	A very stormy day with torrential rains has brought its usual accompaniment - an exceedingly low attendance, 33 children only being present this morning. Received from Mr Wyatt, Draper, Bideford, one dozen pkts of assorted sewing needles for school use.
November 9th	Owing to very wet weather the average has this week fallen to 48.6 out of 61 on books. Commencing with Monday next school will assemble for the afternoon meeting at 1.40 p.m., closing at 3.45. This will be continued during the winter months to enable scholars living at a distance to reach their homes before darkness sets in. Stephen Wade, Correspondent.
November 13th	Horace Jewell left this afternoon after the first lesson; his attendance was therefore cancelled.
November 16th	Owing to the heavy rains of the past week the river is very much swollen and in some places overflowing into the road, making it impossible for many of the little children to attend school. There are 40 children only in attendance this afternoon in consequence. Average for past week 48.2.
November 19th	Admitted Charles F. Burman. Although somewhat diminutive, this lad is 8 years of age and only just knows the alphabet. He has therefore been placed by the Master with the upper division infants for a while. Samuel Brownscombe living in Huntshaw parish, whose brother is ill with measles, was requested by the Master to absent himself from school for a while, until his brother recovers.

WEARE GIFFARD CHURCH OF ENGLAND SCHOOL LOG BOOK
1900 - 1945

1900

November 23rd	Punished C. Tallamy, C. Parkhouse, J. Stapleton and Sidney Down for a breach of discipline.
November 23rd	A grant of ten pounds and five shillings has been granted under the Vol: Sch: Act 1897 to be applied as under: To maintain assistant £10 : Organising visitor 5/- Stephen Wade, Correspondent.
November 23rd	Examined the registers and found them correct. Stephen Wade. The average for the past week has considerably improved, being 53 out of 62 on registers. This is due, however, not to an awakened interest in the child's education on the parents' part, but to the fact of there being a prospect of the children being photographed. The old, old story - anything but education!
November 29th	A pouring wet day, and so dark that one almost requires a lamp for indoor work. Only 36 children present out of 62. Such is the lot of the rural school, rainy days alone being responsible for lowering the annual average by at least 4, which in a small school is a considerable loss.
November 30th	Average for past week only 49.1.
December 5th FLOOD	The incessant rains of the past 12 or 15 hours have produced that very undesirable effect for Weare Gifford - a flood. There were only 30 children present and as the roads were becoming impassable, school was dismissed at 2.45, the attendances being duly cancelled.
December 6th	The flood of yesterday continued throughout the greater part of to-day, so that it was impossible to keep school.
December 7th	The brightest morning we have had for some considerable time. Opened school again with a very fair attendance. Average for past week 46.8 only out of 62 on books. Such continued bad attendance is extremely detrimental to satisfactory progress.
December 10th	A dry morning is responsible for an improved attendance, 50 children being present.
December 12th	56 children present this afternoon - the highest attendance for some considerable time. Received one box of pens - one box slate pencils, and 1 doz exercise books for school use supplied by Mr Pearse, Bideford.
December 13th	A mild morning - thermometer standing at 64 in school.
December 14th	Average for past week 52.7, the highest for a month.
December 17th	A good attendance this morning. 53 present, probably due to such a fine morning. The master having quite unexpectedly to absent himself this afternoon, school will be closed for a half holiday. There was not sufficient time to give the required intimation of the same, but notice was at once sent to H.M. Inspectors which would reach them early this morning.
December 19th	Closed for the Christmas Holidays. Re-open Monday December 31st 1900. Average for past week 52.
	Holidays: December 19th to December 31st 1900.

WEARE GIFFARD CHURCH OF ENGLAND SCHOOL LOG BOOK 1900 - 1945

	1900
December 31st 1900	Owing to the incessant rain of yesterday the river has overflowed into the road, rendering it impossible for the children to attend. School is closed until Tuesday.

	1901
Tuesday January 1st, 1901	New Year's Day
January 1st 1901	Commenced school after the Xmas holidays with the New Year. To-day is also recognised as the beginning of the Twentieth Century.
January 4th	The attendance has been bad again this week, 48.3 only out of 61 on register. It is time more stringent measures were taken to compel the habitual absentees to attend. Special attention has been paid to individual work with good results. For Proposed Syllabus of Instruction see opposite.
January 7th	Bright frosty weather but still on a fair attendance. 50 present.
January 9th	Attendance worse than ever.
January 10th	Mr Richard Gomer informed the Master of his desire to have his child Nellie Gomer examined for a Labour Certificate.
January 11th	The attendance is still very bad and so far as the local authority is concerned there is no chance of much improvement. Average for past week 46.2 or about 76 per cent only. The attendance officer never visits the school, and when a defaulters' list is sent to the Committee at Torrington a warning only is given to the parent.
January 14th	A little better attendance this morning. 53 children present.
January 16th	In accordance with notice previously sent to H.M. Inspectors a half holiday will be given this afternoon.
January 17th	Friday afternoon's lessons will be substituted for those of this afternoon, needlework being taken tomorrow. Very mild weather probably accounts for an improved attendance. 56 present.
January 18th	The attendance has been very much better during the past week, the average rising from 46.2 to 52.7.
January 21st	Fourteen children absent again this morning.
January 22nd	Several children marked absent through coming late. Second visit under Art. 84(b). R. Matta S.I.

WEARE GIFFARD CHURCH OF ENGLAND SCHOOL LOG BOOK
1900 - 1945

1901

	Death of Her Majesty Queen Victoria. Jan 22nd 1901
January 22nd	Her Majesty Queen Victoria has passed from an earthly throne into the possession of the glory that fadeth not away. She died at Osborne House, Isle of Wight, at half past six on Tuesday morning. May children of our children say, "She wrought the people lasting good"; Her Court was pure: her life serene: God gave her peace: her land reposed. A thousand claims to reverence closed In her as mother, wife, and Queen. "Long live the King!" Stephen Wade, Correspondent
January 25th	Average for past week 48 only. Such continued irregularity is most discouraging.
FLOODS	Sunday January 27th. River in flood again.
January 28th	Commenced this week with a very bad attendance - 45 children only being present.
January 29th	Received from the Rector, Rev. Stephen Wade, three registers and one Summary of Attendance for the year ending January 31st 1902. It will be observed that in the space - "Date at which supplied to Teacher" the printed figures are 189- instead of 190-. This is due to the publishers having in stock a larger number bearing the date 189- than they were able to dispose of during that time. These figures have been erased and the correct ones written upon the registers.
January 31st 1901	The school year ended to-day. School has been opened 410 times. Total number of attendances 20974. Average 51.1. An epidemic of measles and bad attendance during the last quarter is responsible for a smaller average.
February 1st 1901	Commenced the New School Year, using a separate register for the registration of Infants. This is now a very small class, numbering at present only eleven. Removed all children a stage higher.
February 4th	In accordance with notice previously given there will be a half holiday this afternoon.
February 8th	Punished Charles Burman for disobedience and bad language. Average for past week 50.1.
INK	Received a gallon tin of Duckett's Ink Powder for school use.
Labour Certificate Schedule	Received from Rev. S. Wade, Correspondent, the Proficiency Schedule relative to the examination of Nellie Gomer who was examined, and passed in all 3 subjects of Standard V.

WEARE GIFFARD CHURCH OF ENGLAND SCHOOL LOG BOOK
1900 - 1945

1901

February 15th	The weather has been fine during the past week and the attendance shows a slight improvement. Average 50.8.
February 18th	Commenced this week with a good attendance.
February 20th	To-day being Ash Wednesday the secular instruction will commence at 9 o'clock and be continued until 11 a.m., school being then dismissed to allow those who are desirous of attending the service in church to go.
February 21st	The attendance continues to improve, and were it not for two or three bad cases would now be fairly good.
February 22nd	Average for past week 51.4, a distinct advance upon the attendance during any previous week of the present school year.
February 25th	No less than eleven children absent. The master left this afternoon before the closing of school in order to attend a funeral. The Time Table will be deviated from after the first lesson.
February 28th	The attendance has again fallen off, much to the detriment of the new work for the year in all groups.
March 1st	Average for past week 49.5 only, ten children having been absent every time school has opened.
March 4th	Attendance bad this morning.
March 8th	The attendance to-day is disgraceful. 38 children only being present out of 59 on books. The following books etc. have been received for school use:- 1 Cash Book : 1½ doz No. 1 : 1 doz No. 2 : eight No. 4: eight No. 5: and eight No. 6 Royal English Arithmetics: 1 answers to each: 1 doz Midland Sol-fa Tests: 5 Natural History Readers : 1 Evans Drill Book : 5 doz Drawing Books : 5 doz lead pencils : 1 doz rubbers : ½ doz Freehand Books : ½ doz coloured pencils : 3 doz penholders : 1 Useful Knowledge : 1½ doz History West of England : 1 Elementary Physics : 1 Geography for Senior Division : 1 doz each Cottage Cookery and Sick Room Hints : 1 Popular Science : 4 doz Copy Book Primers : ½ doz each Nelson's Metric Arithmetic I, II and III. 1 answers to each : 2 A-Z Coloured Pictures : 1 doz Domestic Economy : 1 Complete Copy : 1 Algebraic Factors : 1 Typical Deductions : 1 Higher History : 1 Evans Punishment Book : 1 Evans Notes St John : 1 each Good Manners and Rules of Health Chart : 2 Scripture Sheets : 1 pkt Drawing Cards : 1 pkt Brown's Needlework : 9 doz Exercise Books : 1 quire blotting paper : ½ ream foolscap : 1 Time Table : 1 each McDougall's Algebra Stages 1 & 2 : 1 Euclid Bk I : 1 Macnamara's Syllabus of Work. The school is being worked under the new syllabus drawn up at the beginning of the school year. The Time Table has also been altered, and written out in pencil, awaiting the approval and signautre of H.M. Inspector.
	Average for past week 44.8 only.

WEARE GIFFARD CHURCH OF ENGLAND SCHOOL LOG BOOK
1900 - 1945

1901

March 13th	A little better attendance today 53 present.
REPORT	Copy of Report from Board of Education
	The School is in excellent order, and the older children are taught with much industry and success. During the coming year English should have careful attention. Copy Books and exercise books need dates and quality marks. The condition of the Infant Class is not so satisfactory: the teacher needs guidance and supervision and should possess a better knowledge of her work. F.D. Clarke is continued under Art. 68 of the code. She must improve if her recognition is to be continued.
	<pre> £ s. d.
Grant on Average Attendance 20/6 (51)   52   5   6
Grant for Drawing   26 at 1/9   2   5   6
Grant for Needlework (101c)   1   5   0
Grant under Article 104   10   0   0
Grant under Article 105   10   0   0
Gross Total of Claim   75 16   0
Final Payment Fee Gt: 6   0   0
81 16   0
Deduct Contribution to Superannuation 3 0   0
Net sum payable   78 16   0</pre>
	Staff
	W. Ashton Jewell - Certificated Master
	Fanny D. Clarke - Assistant (Art 68)
	Stephen Wade, Correspondent
March 15th	Average for past week 49 - a little better.
March 18th	Started this week with a good attendance.
March 21st	In spite of beautiful weather the attendance continues very unsatisfactory.
March 22nd	Average for past week 49.3.
March 25th SNOW COKE etc.	The first fall of snow for the winter is causing the absence of several children this afternoon. Received coal and coke per Jeffrey.

WEARE GIFFARD CHURCH OF ENGLAND SCHOOL LOG BOOK
1900 - 1945

1901

March 26th	The weather is still very cold.
March 28th	A heavy fall of snow prevents all but 27 children from attending this morning. The present master having been appointed to a larger school has placed his resignation in the hands of the Managers.
March 29th	The average for the past week - 41.9 - is due to bad weather and one or two cases of illness. Progress is slow on account of such irregularity.
April 3rd	A much better attendance - 49 present. Miss Clarke, Assistant Mistress, has been granted permission to absent herself from school tomorrow (April 4th): so with the exception of the first lesson for this afternoon, Thursday's lessons will be taken, to avoid the loss of a needlework lesson to the girls.
April 4th	Examined the registers and found them correct. Stephen Wade.
HOLIDAY	Closed school until Wednesday morning April 10th for the Easter Holiday.
April 10th SICKNESS	Opened school this morning after the Easter holiday with only 39 children present, many being absent suffering from severe colds. Sickness is very prevalent in the district just now.
April 12th	The attendance is slowly going down, the average for this week being 41.6. Sickness is very prevalent, and so long as it continues much progress in school work is out of the question.
April 16th	Attendance worse than ever, no less than 21 children absent out of 56 on books. Sickness is the chief cause, but with such irregularity it is impossible to make any sound progress. Special attention will therefore be given to individual effort. Weather still cold and boisterous.
April 19th LOW AVERAGE	In spite of brighter and warmer weather the attendance has fallen off to an alarming extent, there being 29 children only present this afternoon out of 56 on books. The prevailing sickness seems to be quite an epidemic, scarcely a child escaping. Work is now practically at a standstill but special attention will be devoted individually. Sickness has reduced average to 34.7.
April 22nd	Very mild weather. Dispensed with a fire in the large room to-day. Attendance a little better, 43 present.
April 25th	The Master having been called suddenly away to attend the funeral of a relative, school was closed to-day after the morning attendance.
April 26th	The average for the past week (40.7) shows an increase of 6 but the attendance is still very bad. To-day ends the First Quarter of the present school year. School has been opened 114 times. Total number of attendances - 5230. Average for 1st Quarter - 45.8.
April 29th	Commenced this week and the second quarter with 45 children present.
April 30th	Attendance still improving. Gave an examination to Upper Division.

WEARE GIFFARD CHURCH OF ENGLAND SCHOOL LOG BOOK
1900 - 1945

1901

May 2nd	Torrington Fair. In accordance with notice previously sent to H.M. Inspector a whole day's holiday will be given to-day (*vide* page 1.)
May 3rd	A good week's work has been done, due to a greatly improved attendance. Average for past week 45.3, being the highest since March 22nd.
May 6th SLATES	Received from the Rev S. Wade one dozen slates for school use. 47 children present this morning.
May 10th	For the second time this week the attendance has been small, due to the presence of a circus at Bideford. There seems to be a growing tendency on the part of many parents to indulge their children in a day's absence from school in order to visit each and every penny show which appears in the district. Average for past week 45.3.
May 13th	Opened school this week with an increased attendance. Admitted two lads, Archibald Down and Sydney Tucker, from Monkleigh School.
May 14th	A very hot day. School will commence, and close 15 minutes earlier this afternoon. This alteration applies only to to-day. Gave an examination to Lower Division. Group A is very weak but shows a decided improvement in all subjects. Group B shows good progress generally.
May 16th	Very hot weather. The thermometer registered 90° in the sun, and 67° in school at 11.00 a.m. Attendance very fair.
May 17th	Weather still very hot - 102° in the sun. Average for past week 43.9. To-day ends my term of office as Master of the school; but, although having obtained promotion elsewhere, it is with great regret I say good-bye to the many friends I have made here and to this lovely valley, one of nature's gems. The Rev. S. Wade (Rector), the Managers and Parents have all been uniformly kind and considerate to me for which I am deeply grateful. I hope my successor will be as happy in this beautiful village and district as I have been during my 2½ years' sojourn. Stephen Wade, Correspondent.
June 17th	I, John Manaton Tucker (Certificated Master) commenced my duties in this School, although my appointment dates from the 7th June. Since 17th May Mr Clarke has acted as Locum Tenens for a fortnight and a fortnight's holiday has been given. Received from the Rector 18 copies of "Nature Knowledge" for the Senior Division.
June 24th	Holiday this afternoon by permission of Rector to allow Master to attend meeting of teachers at Buckland Brewer.
June 25th	Examined the registers and found them correct. Stephen Wade.
July 9th	Diocesan Inspection this afternoon by Mr Bicknell. No registers marked.
July 23rd	Visited the school. G. Hayward.

WEARE GIFFARD CHURCH OF ENGLAND SCHOOL LOG BOOK 1900 - 1945

1901

August 1st	Registers marked and closed by 9 a.m. this morning to admit of dismissal at 11, in order to assemble for Sunday School Treat (at Westward Ho!) at 1 p.m. Holiday in afternoon. Broke up for three weeks.
August 28th	Commenced school again after Harvest Holidays. Very wet morning and consequently a poor muster.
September 9th	Half holiday in afternoon and likewise on Tuesday morning on account of Public Tea and festivities in connection with Harvest Thanksgiving.
September 16th	Charles Huxtable admitted and put into the Sixth Standard.
September 27th	The average attendance for the present year will be to all appearances at least 6 lower than that of last year owing to so many families having left the village and consequently reducing the number on the books by 10.
October 4th	Copy of Diocesan Report (Date of Inspection 9th July). Teachers' Work, Discipline, Tone, etc.:- Excellent. Scholars on Books 59. Present at Inspection: Boys 21, Girls 28, total 49. The school is classed as Very Good. General Remarks:- Although there have been changes in the Staff during the year, the work of Religious Instruction has evidently received careful and conscientious attention, and the children generally show an intelligent knowledge of the selected portions of Holy Scripture. There is every sign of good influence, with excellent tone and discipline. J.F. Powning, Diocesan Inspector.
October 15th	Visited the school. G. Hayward. 1. There is no syllabus of work for the Infants. 2. The W.C. seats are dirty - very.
October 17th	Examined the registers and found them correct. Stephen Wade, Correspondent.
October 19th	Mrs Roberts re-commenced to sweep school and light the fire, which from the unsatisfactory manner in which these duties were performed, she had notice from the Rector to give up. I spoke to Matthews who attends to the W.C.s to the effect that H.M. Inspector had stated that the above must be emptied more frequently, and that the Rector also desired it to be done. Matthews has consequently agreed for the future to do the work twice a week viz. on Wednesdays and Saturdays between 12 and 2 p.m. Mr Clarke has also been ordered to carry out the alterations reventilating doors for Boys', and ventilation for Girls' closets suggested by H.M. Inspector.
October 21st	Mr Tanton School Attendance Officer called for first time since I came.

WEARE GIFFARD CHURCH OF ENGLAND SCHOOL LOG BOOK
1900 - 1945

1901

October 24th	Very wet and miserable morning and attendance consequently affected, only 40 present.
November 1st AID GRANT	I am desired by the Rector to record the receipt by him of Fifteen Pounds and Five Shillings under the Voluntary Schools Act 1897 to be applied as under:- To maintain the present charge for salaries 10.0.0 For sanitary improvements 5.0.0 Organising Visitor 5.0 15.5.0
November 8th	Miss Fanny Clarke has today (after due notice) given up her post as Infant Mistress, and at their last meeting the Managers unanimously appointed Mrs Tucker (who is qualified under Article 68) in her place.
November 11th	Mrs Tucker commenced her duties as Infant Mistress.
November 12th	As the Master was unable to attend School today through illness, the Rector consented to a holiday being given. A severe gale is raging today and many of the children are drenched.
November 14th	Received 15 cwt. of coals per Mr Jeffery for School use.
November 15th	Fall of snow during the night. Temperature in main room 46° at commencement but not for long. Many of the younger children absent on account of the severity of the weather.
November 27th	Holiday this afternoon as the Master has to attend a meeting at Torrington. The Rector consents on behalf of the Managers and has informed H.M. Inspectors.
November 28th	Scholars assembled at 1 p.m. today to admit of an early dismissal. Routine not strictly followed.
December 9th	Half holiday in afternoon by desire of Rector who has notified same to H.M.I. on account of a sale of Royal Worcester Porcelain held in School Room, proceeds of which are to be devoted to Church purposes.
December 13th	Landwater. So few children assembled and those in a dangerously wet condition that on my informing the Rector he gave orders for the school to be closed.
December 19th	Drawing not taken this afternoon.
December 20th	Broke up for Xmas (1 week).
December 30th	Commenced school again after Xmas holidays. Very few present owing to landwater.
December 31st	10 cwt of coals brought today.

WEARE GIFFARD CHURCH OF ENGLAND SCHOOL LOG BOOK
1900 - 1945

1902

January 14th	Examined the registers and found them correct. Stephen Wade, Correspondent
	Second visit of Inspection. R. Matta S.I.
January 21st	Re-arranged classes bringing up five boys from Infant Class to Group A.
January 30th	10 cwt of coals and 5 cwt of coke brought by Mr Henry Jeffery for school use.
February 7th	Registers marked and closed by 9 a.m. to admit of early dismissal as the Master has to go to Barnstaple on urgent business to which the Rector has consented, and also to a half holiday being given, of which the Rector has given due notice to H.M. Inspector.
February 10th	Sewing for the future will be taken during the whole of Monday and Friday afternoons, and the intervals for recreation will be from 2.50 to 3 p.m.
February 14th	Very good attendance this week. With 55 on the books, there is an average of 50.
February 20th	Mrs Hole, relict of Major Hole, who resided for many years at "Beam" near here, was buried today. As she had been a great benefactress to the poor of the place, the funeral service was choral. A half holiday was consequently given, and notice was sent to H.M. Inspector yesterday, with an explanation why it was impossible to inform him earlier.
February 21st	The average for the week has been 52, very good considering there are only 57 on the books, and a higher average than was reached during last year. Blanche Braund, who (notwithstanding repeated warnings) has not attended since 31st August last, has been reported to School Attendance Officer.

WEARE GIFFARD CHURCH OF ENGLAND SCHOOL LOG BOOK
1900 - 1945

1902

March 3rd

School Report

Discipline is good and the instruction of the elder children is satisfactory.
The instruction of the Infants, though there are some signs of improvement, does not at present reach a creditable level and will need careful attention during the coming year.
E.M. Tucker is recognised under Article 68 of the Code.

	£ s d
Grant on Average Attendance 45 @ 22/-	49.10.0
Grant under Art. 104	10. 0.0
Grant under Art. 105	10. 0.0
Grant Final Fee	3. 7.6
	72.17.6
Deduct contributions to Superannuation	3. 0.0
	69.17.6

Staff
John Manaton Tucker (Certificated Master)
Emma Mary Tucker Assistant Art: 68

Stephen Wade, Correspondent

March 14th Attendance lower this week. Some of the older boys away gardening.

March 18th Received Statement of Accounts from Rector which I at once posted in School Window.

March 21st Violent colds among the children have been general during the past week, and the average has been consequently reduced to 41.8.

March 24th Very rough and stormy day. Attendance very low.

March 24th Examined the registers and found them correct.

March 26th Broke up today by permission of Managers for Easter Holidays. School to re-open on 7th April.

Stephen Wade, Correspondent

April 7th Commenced school again after Easter holidays, and admitted five fresh scholars.

April 18th Many scholars absent through colds this week.

April 25th Usual progress.

May 1st Holiday today on account of Torrington Fair. A holiday is also given tomorrow, as the Master has to go to Barnstaple.

WEARE GIFFARD CHURCH OF ENGLAND SCHOOL LOG BOOK 1900 - 1945

1902

May 26th	Commenced school again, 49 present. Received circular from Mr Routh H.M. Inspector re Physical Exercises.
May 28th	Examined the registers and found them correct. Stephen Wade, Correspondent
June 2nd	On the announcement in the morning paper of the joyful Proclamation of Peace the scholars had the happy tidings communicated to them and withdrew to the playground, where three times three hearty cheers were heartily given, the echo reaching to the Rectory, whereupon the Rector immediately sent Miss Wade to say a day's holiday was to be given.
June 5th	Miss Beresford visited the school.
June 6th	Very wet day and thin attendance.
June 10th	Received notice of Diocesan Examination to be held on 30th June. Notice of same has been sent to H.M. Inspector.
June 13th	Very wet morning and thin attendance, only 33 present.
June 24th	Message of illness of His Majesty. Coronation indefinitely postponed.
June 25th	Broke up until Monday 30th on which date the Diocesan Exam takes place.
June 30th	Diocesan Exam conducted by the Rev. H. Every, Rector of Eastdowne. Half holiday in afternoon.
July 4th	Attendance has been very thin for some time, owing to strawberry picking which is now in full swing.
July 15th	Copy of Diocesan Report (Inspection 30th June). Teacher's Work:- Discipline, Tone, etc.:- Excellent. The School is classed as Very Good. The children answered brightly, and the examination gave evidence of thorough and conscientious work on the part of the teacher. In the higher group thoughtful answers were given especially in the Catechism and Old Testament subjects. The tone and discipline are exceedingly good. Honourable mention:- Minnie Davey, Winnie Bright, Willie Gomer, Ronald Jeffery, Mary Squires, Florence Parkhouse, Fred Squires, Theo Tucker, Nelly Hooper, Charles Stephens, Ada Squires.
July 17th	Choral Festival at Exeter. Holiday given, of which notice has been sent to G.R.R. Wade Esq. H.M.I. by Mrs Wade in the absence of the Rector.
July 22nd	Working by proposed draft of new Time Table.
August 1st	Broke up for Harvest Holidays.

WEARE GIFFARD CHURCH OF ENGLAND SCHOOL LOG BOOK
1900 - 1945

1902

September 8th	Commenced school again after 5 weeks holiday. An extra week was granted in accordance with the desire expressed by His Majesty the King.
September 12th	Holiday - Harvest Thanksgiving and unveiling of stained glass window in Parish Church by Sir Wm. Dowell in memory of late Major and Mrs Hole of Beam.
September 19th	Attendance very thin this afternoon, only 38 present, a Harvest Thanksgiving tea at Mrs Soames' being the cause.
September 24th AID GRANT	The Rector desires me to record the receipt by him of £6 (Aid Grant). This is a much smaller sum than that granted previously, £15-5, and no reason having been assigned for the diminution the Rector is in correspondence the "Powers that be" regarding the same. The Aid Grant of £6 has been apportioned as follows: 1. To maintain the present charge for Salaries £5.0.0 2. Organising Visitor £1.0.0 £6.0.0
October 1st	Holiday this afternoon (of which due notice has been sent to H.M. Inspector by the Rector) to enable the Master to attend a Teachers' Meeting at Appledore.
October 3rd	Visit Art. 84(a) R. Matta S.I. The Infant Registers must show the attendances of infants under five separately. (See par. 11 of the Keeping of School Records) Half holiday in afternoon with consent of Mr Matta and the Rector.
October 7th	Examined the registers and found them correct. Stephen Wade, Correspondent
October 10th	Coals brought by Mr Jeffery.
October 17th	Gave Group A some subtraction tests which were done very well.
October 24th	Capital attendance (comparatively), average 52.1.
October 31st	Gave Group B tests in four simple rules with very good result.
November 11th	Very wet morning, but attendance good, 52 present. Mrs Tucker today tendered her resignation to Managers to take effect in three months time (11th February). Mrs Tucker's domestic duties during the coming year will make it impossible for her to act as Infant Mistress.
November 18th	The cold weather during this week has rendered the attendance of infants rather thin comparatively.
November 24th	Pouring wet morning and attendance consequently thin.

WEARE GIFFARD CHURCH OF ENGLAND SCHOOL LOG BOOK
1900 - 1945

1902

November 28th	Very few children present this morning and those who did brave the elements got very damp. The "Land water" was out to such an extent at noon that the Rector decided to close school for the day.
December 11th	Examined the registers and found them correct. Stephen Wade, Correspondent
	Closed for Christmas Holidays.

1903

January 5th	"Landwater". As no children mustered it was impossible to open school today.
January 6th	Opened school this morning with only eleven present.
January 15th	Very thin attendance owing to severe weather and colds.
January 16th	Visit Art 84a. G.R.R. Routh H.M.I.
January 21st	Mr Routh H.M.I. kindly called again this afternoon at my request to examine the needlework.
January 26th NEEDLEWORK REPORT	Needlework Report from Board of Education received today is as follows:- Board of Education, Whitehall, London S.W. 23rd January 1903 The following is the Report on the Needlework of Wear Gifford National School. School Date - February. No. of Children Summary Mark Girls 15 Good Infants 4 Good Girls Upper Div: In darning the hole in stocking web material, the loops round the hole on the right side should be caught down by the darning threads. The gathers should be stroked and regulated before being set into the band. In a letter from Mr G.R.R. Routh H.M.I. to the Rector the former states that the Needlework Report is quite satisfactory.
January 27th	Very mild morning. Temperature in the open 51°, inside school 58°. Jeffery brought 10 cwt coal and 10 cwt coke.
January 30th	End of school year today. Half holiday this afternoon as there was none after H.M. Inspector's visit.
February 2nd	Doctor Slade King (Medical Officer of Health) and Mr W. Gomer Sanitary Inspector paid the School offices etc. a surprise visit and wished me to record that they found the whole premises in an extremely satisfactory condition.
February 5th	Holiday with Rector's consent as the Master has to attend a meeting of Church Choirmasters at Barnstaple.
February 9th	Temperature in school 58°, in the open 56°. Very mild for the season. Good attendance consequently.
February 12th	Examined the registers and found them correct. Stephen Wade, Correspondent.

WEARE GIFFARD CHURCH OF ENGLAND SCHOOL LOG BOOK 1900 - 1945

1903

February 19th	Holiday given today by consent of the Rector. As the Master had to be absent on urgent private business it was impossible to give the usual formal notice to H.M. Inspector.
February 23rd	Impossible to work strictly in accordance with Time Table pro tem as no Infant Mistress has been appointed in the place of Mrs Tucker.
February 25th	Ash Wednesday. Registers marked and closed by 9 a.m. to admit of children (who so desire) attending Divine Service at 11 a.m.
March 2nd	Pouring wet morning and very thin school.

March 10th	Government Report
	Weare Giffard C.E. School, Devon
	
	Discipline is good, and the children are in most respects well taught. Arithmetic is unintelligent, and should improve. The Infant Class shows improvement during the year, and is in a creditable state.
	
	H.M. Inspector reports that Physical Training is not taught in accordance with an approved scheme. If the 'Model Course' be not adopted for future use, I am to request that an alternative course, equivalent in scope and aim, may be submitted for approval to the Board of Education.
	The staff must be strengthened if a Grant under Article 105 of the Code is to be again claimed next year.
	The population of the School District was returned as 317 at the official census of 1901. The Managers should give exact particulars explaining the difference between their estimates of the population for the last three years and the official estimate.
	
	           £. s. d.
	Grant on average attendance 48 @ 22/- 52.16.0
	Final Fee Grant 6.12.6
	              59. 8.6
	Deduct £3 superannuation allowance 3. 0.0
	Net sum payable 56. 8.6
	School Staff: John Manaton Tucker Certificated
	      Emma Mary Tucker Art 68
	At the Managers' Meeting this evening Mrs Tucker was reappointed Infant Mistress and her salary increased to £35 per annum.

March 11th	10 cwt of coals brought by Mr Jeffery.
March 20th	The weather has been so wet that the attendance has been somewhat irregular especially among the Infants.
March 25th	Gave the children an object lesson on the "Arum Maculatum or Cuckoo Pint" in which they were much interested, the first of a short series of poisonous plants.

WEARE GIFFARD CHURCH OF ENGLAND SCHOOL LOG BOOK
1900 - 1945

1903

April 1st	Continued the lesson of last week, with a splendid specimen in full bloom, and showed the children a specimen of the little gnat or midge (that fertilizes the plant) under my small microscope. They were delighted.
April 7th	A specimen of Borage brought by Blanche Parkhouse.
April 8th	Gave an object lesson on "Tadpoles and their development into Frogs" to the whole School.
April 9th	Broke up for Easter, one week.
April 20th	Commenced school again after Easter holidays. 48 present.
April 22nd	Object lesson on "What happens when a candle burns", 1st part.
April 29th	Second part of last week's lesson.
May 1st	Registers marked and closed by 1 p.m. this afternoon to admit of the children being dismissed at 3 p.m. as the Rector's family required to have the room prepared for a concert this evening.
May 6th	Object lesson on The Honey Bee and its uses (1st part).
May 7th	Holiday (of which notice has been given to H.M. Inspector) for Torrington Fair.
May 19th	E.D. Fear (Sub-Inspector).
May 21st	Holy Thursday. Registers marked and closed by 9 a.m. to admit of some of the children attending Church at 11 a.m.
June 10th	Half holiday in afternoon, as the Master had to attend a meeting at Merton.
June 12th	Postal Order for £1 No. 77279983 sent to Dr Thos. J. Barnardo as the result of the Waif Saturday collection.
June 23rd	Diocesan Examination this afternoon, of which notice has been sent to H.M. Inspector (G.R.R. Routh Esq.). Registers not marked.
July 1st	Choral Festival at Bideford - Holiday. Notice sent as above to H.M. Inspector. I received the Diocesan Report this morning from the Rector and also a congratulatory letter on the result from him and Mrs Wade. Copy of Diocesan Report:- Teacher's Work: Discipline, Tone etc: - Excellent. The School is classed as Very Good. The Rev. J.F. Powning reports:- The children were in excellent order, and have been carefully taught the portion of the Syllabus prepared. Much praise is due to the Head Master for his single handed exertions in giving the Religious Instruction. The classification of "Very Good" is fully deserved. Hon. mentioned:- Charles Stevens, Nellie Hooper, Rosie Start, Elsie Tucker, Winnie Bright, Mary Squires, Frank Courtenay, Herbert Clarke, Fred: Squires, Walter Taylor.

WEARE GIFFARD CHURCH OF ENGLAND SCHOOL LOG BOOK 1900 - 1945

1903

July 7th	Registers marked and closed by 1 p.m. this afternoon to admit of closing at 3 p.m. as the Master has to attend a meeting at Bideford.
July 13th	Visit without notice. G.R.R. Routh.
July 23rd	Half holiday this afternoon on account of Miss Ethel Fry's wedding. Notice has been sent to H.M. Inspector.
July 30th	Broke up for Harvest Holidays, 4 weeks.
July 30th	Examined the registers and found them correct. Stephen Wade, Correspondent.
August 31st	Commenced School again after Harvest Holidays.
September 9th	Had a visit from Mr Sing, the newly appointed Superintendent Attendance Officer for the Devon County Council. He gave a little sound advice to the children on the altered state of affairs respecting the way in which the law would be enforced for the future.
September 10th	Scholars assembled and registers marked by 1 p.m. today to admit of dismissal at 3 p.m.
September 11th	Holiday today as the room is prepared for a similar entertainment to that given last evening. Notice has been sent to H.M. Inspector.
September 17th	Half holiday in afternoon (notice sent to H.M.I.). Master had to attend a Church Conference at Torrington.
September 21st	Registers marked and closed by 1 p.m. this afternoon to admit of dismissal at 3 p.m. to arrange room for Harvest Thanksgiving Tea.
September 30th	The date for the New Authority to take over the School.
October 9th	Had first visit from a new Manager Mr Thomas Wilton.
October 15th	Such high "landwater" that it was impossible to open school, only 10 scholars present, and their feet were very wet. The water was still rising and with the approval of Mrs Wade (in the Rector's absence) I closed school for the day.
October 21st	Sent an order to Mr T. Fry (Correspondent) for 15 cwt of coals which I stated were required at once.
October 22nd	Mr F. Beer, another of the new Managers, visited. Sent a long order off to the County Education Committee for school materials.
October 26th	Examined the registers and found them correct. Stephen Wade, Correspondent.
October 28th	The roads were flooded and quite impassable and as no scholars presented themselves it was impossible to open school.
November 5th	Have only today received the coals which I applied for to the Correspondent on 21st October.
November 20th	Mr Percy Balsdon called and checked registers and found them correct.
December 7th	Sent note to ask Mr T. Fry (Correspondent) to order at once 5 cwt of coals.
December 10th	Coals supplied as above.

WEARE GIFFARD CHURCH OF ENGLAND SCHOOL LOG BOOK 1900 - 1945

1903

December 11th	Had word from Mr Blackmore that his little boy was suffering from scarlet fever. The children are therefore unable to attend school.
December 17th	Heard from Mr Parkhouse that his little girl has the scarlet fever. The children who usually attend are wisely kept away, as it is likely to spread. The Rector on behalf of the Managers wished me to inform H.M. Inspector and Mr J.F. Young, Exeter, that we shall close tomorrow afternoon for Xmas and reassemble on January 4th 1904.

1904

January 4th	Commenced school again after Christmas holidays, two weeks. School very thin on account of so much sickness being prevalent.
January 6th	From the playground today I and several of the scholars about 11 a.m. distinctly heard the explosion of the dynamite Factory at Hayle in Cornwall in which four men were killed. At first we thought it was thunder, but the report was so sharp and sudden that I was curious enough to note the time.
F.J.B January 12th	Registers examined by Mr F.J. Beer (Manager) and found correct. Attendance Officer Mr F.P. Beadon, 24 Castle Street, Torrington.
January 22nd	Mr Beadon (School Attendance Officer) called.
January 25th	Sent today to ask Mr Fry (Correspondent) to order 15 cwt coals immediately.
January 26th	Mr Beadon, School Attendance Officer, visited.
January 27th	Received a Notification from Mr W. Gorner (Sanitary Inspector) to the effect that Mrs Squires has scarlet fever and that her children are not to be allowed to attend school in consequence. Mr T. Fry called and checked registers and found them correct. Inspection – Walter Scutt. The Path leading into the school is greatly in need of paving. Pools of water inches deep collect there on wet days. The boys' offices need doors, and the roof of the girls' offices is not waterproof. A coal house is needed. W.S.
February 1st	As I have not been supplied with new registers etc. it was impossible to open school this morning, it being illegal to copy records from any source. I applied to County Education Committee for them over a week ago and since then to Wheaton publisher. I had a note from latter stating that they had been sent in a parcel to Bideford Station addressed to Mr Fry (our Correspondent) but he states he has not received them, and I have asked him to try to get them so that I can open school by this afternoon. This is a unique experience for me. Mr Beadon S.A.O. called. Registers, Summary and Stock and Stores Book arrived at 2.15, too late for afternoon school, so we have had to close school for the day.

WEARE GIFFARD CHURCH OF ENGLAND SCHOOL LOG BOOK 1900 - 1945

1904

February 3rd	The tide came up so exceptionally high at the Dock this morning that the roads were impassable for the many children from Annery Kiln. Our attendance was consequently low. It improved however in the afternoon.
February 8th	It is my painful duty to record the Death of our Rector, the Rev. Stephen Wade, which took place last evening (Sunday) about 10.30. For about 12 years the reverend gentleman who was greatly beloved has been Rector of Wear Giffard and Chairman and Correspondent of the School, and his signatures will be often noticed in this book. Today is a day of gloom for us all and the greatest sympathy is felt for Mrs Wade and the family. A fearfully rough morning. Not one infant present. I cannot remember such a circumstance before.
February 10th	Holiday this afternoon: our poor Rector's funeral. Received a note from Mr J.L. Sing to the effect that Willie Gomer had failed through "Writing" to qualify himself for a Labour Certificate.
February 27th	Ash Wednesday. Secular work commenced and Registers marked and closed at 9 a.m. so as to allow children belonging to Church to attend Divine Service at 11 as usual. Of course it is optional on the part of the children.
February 28th	Wrote to the Sanitary Inspector (Mr W. Gomer) at the request of Doctor Ackland and asked him to have the drainage of the School House thoroughly examined and also the water analysed.
February 29th	Received Form IX and Duplicate from our Correspondent Mr T. Fry. This ought to have been sent off within seven days of the end of the school year, but I could not get them before. I filled it in as far as I was concerned and sent it up to Mr Fry in time for post.
March 2nd	Mr J. Groves Cooper visited, checked the registers and found them correct.
March 3rd	As my little baby has been very dangerously ill and Doctor Ackland said he feared it was from defective drainage or the drinking water, I applied to the Sanitary Inspector to have the water analysed, and the drains tested, with the result that he met three of the managers (viz: Messrs J. Groves Cooper, R.P. Balsdon and T. Fry) here this morning, and applied the "smoke test" to the drains, with the result that the drain which passes underneath the class room was far from being in a satisfactory state. Many of the Infants have been afflicted with similar disorders and the cause has now been probably discovered.
March 10th	Mr John Clarke called and took measurements for sending in an estimate for a store cupboard.
March 21st	Managers' Meeting at which my new agreement with them was signed. They also agreed to close school from Friday next to April 11th on account of its being necessary to do the drains.
March 25th	Broke up for Easter Holidays (2 weeks).
April 11th	Commenced school again after Easter Holidays

WEARE GIFFARD CHURCH OF ENGLAND SCHOOL LOG BOOK 1900 - 1945

1904

Report	Weare Giffard C.E. School, Devon.
April 12th	Discipline is satisfactory. Instruction is given in a somewhat perfunctory manner, and, though fairly successful in some respects, should aim to a greater extent at the development of the intelligence of the children. In particular Arithmetic still lackes intelligence. Composition for the younger children should receive more attention. Spelling is weak in the first class, and Drawing should improve. The Infants are fairly well taught. The school is expected to improve during the coming year. The playground and approaches to the school are apt to become "impossible" in wet weather and should receive attention. Staff: John Manaton Tucker, Certificated Master Emma Mary Tucker, Art 68 *(no signature)* Correspondent
April 18th	School visited in the morning by E.D. Fear Esq, H.M. Inspector.
April 21st	The Rev. Canon Winterbotham, Budleigh Lodge, Exmouth, (who has been offered the living of this Parish) visited the school.
April 26th	Mrs Tucker absent. She had to go to Bideford on urgent business. Mr R.P. Balsdon called and checked registers and found them correct.
May 5th	Torrington Fair. A holiday is the customary thing in this and neighouring schools. As the date slipped my memory, it was impossible to get the Managers' consent in time to send due warning to H.M. Inspector. In the afternoon however I let the children assemble and had registers marked at 1 p.m. so that they could be dismissed at 3 p.m.
May 12th	Holy Thursday. Registers marked and closed by 9 a.m. to admit of children (who so desire) attending church at 11 a.m.
May 17th	Have had the consent of Messrs T. Fry, T. Wilton and F. Beer for a week's holday at Whitsuntide, and have advised the Education Committee to that effect.
May 30th	Commenced after Whitsuntide holidays.
June 1st	Examination on the work of the first term ended 31st May.
June 10th	Attendance very good this week, although the strawberry season has commenced. This is an improvement on previous years.
June 17th	Sent monthly statement to Mr J. Loftus Sing, Superintendent of Attendance Officers.
June 22nd	The Rev. T. Dunn visited the school. He told me Lord Ebrington had offered him the living of Wear Gifford and he seemed likely to accept it. He is at present acting as Curate at Oakford.
June 23rd	Anniversary Tea at the Wesleyan Chapel this afternoon. Registers marked and closed by 1.15 p.m. to admit of the children being dismissed at 3.15.
F.J. Beer	June 29th

WEARE GIFFARD CHURCH OF ENGLAND SCHOOL LOG BOOK
1900 - 1945

1904

July 4th	Diocesan Exam by Mr Bicknell. No registers marked.
July 6th	Mr Beardsley, Inspector under the County Council, visited the school this morning.
July 15th	Attendance very good this week. All the girls in the lower division made full attendances.
July 27th	Managers' meeting last evening, at which they decided to close for the summer holidays on Friday next, 29th inst. and re-open on August 29th. A Report on the water supply for the School House, in which the Medical Officer of Health (Doctor Slade King) states it to be quite unfit for use, was also considered.
July 28th	Wesleyan Sunday School Treat, outing to Westward Ho! Attendance consequently thin - only 37 present this morning.
July 29th	Broke up for Harvest Holidays (4 weeks).
August 29th	Commenced school again after Harvest Holidays. 52 present.
September 7th	Mr Beadon (Attendance Officer) visited.
September 15th	The Rector (Rev. T. Dunn) visited and brought the Diocesan Report. As the Exam took place on July 4th it must have been in the hands of the late Correspondent (Mr T. Fry) a considerable time. I note it is dated as dispatched from Exeter 1st August. Copy of Diocesan Report Discipline, Tone, etc. :- Excellent. The school is classed as "Very Good". The children are being well instructed and show interest in their work. The Repetition is commendably said throughout. The knowledge of the Biblical subjects in the lower group is a little wanting in depth and fulness, but on the whole the children pass a decidedly creditable examination. Honourable mention: Mabel Squire, Dorothy Tucker, Elsie Tucker, Thomas Huxtable, Walter Johns, Cyril Hooper, Florence Parkhouse, Alice Trace, Fred Squire.
September 26th	Harvest Thanksgiving Tea in the afternoon. School closed for the same, of which notice has been sent to H.M.I. and County Council.
October 6th	Examined Registers and found them correct. T. Dunn
October 11th	Mr Stevens commenced to attend to the school offices.
October 13th	10 cwt of coals and 5 cwt of coke supplied by Mr H. Jeffery. Registers marked and closed by 1.30 this afternoon with the consent of the Rector, as this arrangement saves many children from absenting themselves for the purpose of attending Torrington Fair.
October 14th	Mr A.J. Hammond (19 Castle Street, Torrington), the new School Attendance Officer, visited the school for the first time.

WEARE GIFFARD CHURCH OF ENGLAND SCHOOL LOG BOOK 1900 - 1945

1904

October 25th	Marked and closed Registers by 1.30 p.m. with the Rector's consent, to admit of closing at 3.30 as the Master had to attend a meeting at Bideford.
November 6th	At a Managers' meeting held this evening, it was decided to give a monthly half holiday if the percentage of average attendance reached or exceeded 90. The attendance has been exceptionally good for the last month, second best for the district. It has been decided to have the half holiday on the first Friday afternoon in each month.
December 2nd	After due notice being sent to H.M. Inspector and the Devon County Education Committee by the Rev. T. Dunn (Correspondent), a half holiday is given this afternoon for good attendance. During the month ended 25th November, our school was first on the list with a percentage of average for the month of 96.7. During the previous month we were second. This is most satisfactory considering the scattered state of the parish, and exceptional local influences such as floods which act prejudicially.
December 5th	Received two notices from the Sanitary Inspector (Mr W. Gomer), one in regard to the children of Mrs Denford, and the other respecting the children of Mrs Pengilly, to the effect that they were not to be received into the school for 42 days, or until they were in a fit and proper state to attend, as a member of each family was suffering from an infectious disease.
December 12th	Have today at noon received notice from the Sanitary Inspector (Mr Gomer) that there is an infectious disease in the family of Mrs Start, Dock Cottages, and May and Rose are not to attend for 35 days. They have not attended school by Doctor Macindoe's orders since November 11th and it is very strange that the case has not been notified to the Medical Officer of Health earlier. I wrote to him on Friday last drawing his attention to the case.
December 16th	Broke up for Xmas (2 weeks).

1905

January 2nd	Commenced school again after Xmas holidays.
January 22nd	G.R.R. Routh.
February 1st	Commencement of new school year. Holiday (with consent of H.M.Inspector G.R.R. Routh Esq.) on account of good attendance and Jumble Sale.
February 7th	Children brought some lovely bunches of snowdrops. Mrs Tucker made a beautiful cross and we went up at noon and placed it on the grave of our late dear Rector, who died 12 months ago today.
February 16th	The Rev. Mr Ffiffe of Landcross visited the school with the Rector.

WEARE GIFFARD CHURCH OF ENGLAND SCHOOL LOG BOOK 1900 - 1945

1905

February 27th	Percy Morris Esq: A.R.I.B.A. Architect for the Devon County Education Committee visited the school premises. I sent up for the Rector (who is Correspondent) but found he was away, and Mr Morris asked me to express his regret at not being able to send notice to him of his visit. He said some structural alterations would be required re closets etc. and that a thorough analysis of the water supply would be recommended by him.
March 4th	Usual monthly half holiday for good attendance in the afternoon. The % of average attendance for last month has been over 94.
March 8th	Registers marked and closed by 9.15 this morning and secular work commenced at one in order to enable the children who wish it to attend the morning service at Church at 11.30, it being Ash Wednesday. As it was stormy however the Rector did not wish the children to come.
March 15th	Report (received this morning) : Weare Giffard Church of England School No. 2392 Copy of Report made by H.M.I. Mr G.R.R. Routh after visit of January 23rd 1905: Discipline is satisfactory. Instruction has been vigorously given and the defects noticed in last year's report are considerably less apparent. Continued efforts will be needed to arouse the interest of the children and to encourage them to be more readily responsive. The number of children in the class room is somewhat large, but the infants are orderly and have been fairly well taught. The approaches to the school have been paved during the year. The inside walls of the school have an untidy appearance and might with advantage be plastered. Thos. Dunn, Correspondent. Staff:: John Manaton Tucker, Certificated Master; Emma Mary Tucker, Art. 68
March 21st	Examined the registers and found them correct March 21st 1905. R.F. Balsdon.
March 31st	Sent off monthly record of attendance to Mr J. Loftus Sing. Very good % average indeed for the last four weeks, viz. 97.4, 95.6, 96.2, 95.8.
April 6th	Registers marked and closed this afternoon by 1.15 p.m. with the consent of the Rector and Mr F.J. Beer so as to allow the children to be dismissed earlier for the Wesleyan Tea.
April 7th	Usual monthly half holiday this afternoon.
April 14th	Usual good attendance.
April 20th	Broke up for Easter holidays, one week.
May 1st	Commenced school again after Easter holidays. 57 present out of 61 on books.
May 8th	Mr Hammond (School Attendance Officer) called. Nothing of importance to report to him as the attendance is as usual very good

WEARE GIFFARD CHURCH OF ENGLAND SCHOOL LOG BOOK 1900 - 1945

1905

May 16th	Thomas Huxtable ran away to his home at Umberleigh from his aunt's (Mrs Roberts) here this morning. He came over to dust the school and left it undone. Everything was in a very dusty state. Such matters ought not to be left to a boy.
May 25th	As the Wesleyan Tea takes place this afternoon, the children assembled at 1 p.m. and will be dismissed about 3 p.m. with the consent of the Rector and Mr F.J. Beer.
June 2nd	Usual monthly half holiday this afternoon for good attendance.
June 6th	The Rev. T. Dunn (Rector) checked Registers this morning and found them correct.
June 9th	Broke up for Whitsuntide Holidays (1 week).
June 19th	Commenced school again after Whitsuntide Holidays.
June 27th	Diocesan Examination at 2 p.m., conducted by Rev. J.F. Powning, Vicar of Landkey.
July 3rd	Monthly half holiday given this afternoon instead of on Friday next as there is a meeting of Sunday School Teachers at Huntshaw which (with the Rector's consent) I wish to attend.
July 10th	Diocesan Report (received today) Discipline and tone: Excellent. The School is classed as Very Good. In the Infants' Group the Repetition work was accurately rendered by a good proportion of the children and they had a good though somewhat partial knowledge of their Old and New Testament narratives. In the Upper Group several children showed a praiseworthy grasp of their Biblical subjects, and the classification of "Very Good" is again awarded. Honourably mentioned: Walter Taylor, Alice Trace, Florence Parkhouse, Ada Squire, Fred: Squire, Charles Stevens.
July 19th	School very thin this morning, only 28 present out of 61 on books, owing to Wesleyan Sunday School outing to Westward Ho! With the Rector's consent I only allowed one hour for dinner and so dismissed them at 3 p.m. Mr E.D. Fear H.M. Inspector visited this afternoon.
July 20th	Holiday given today with the consent of three Managers (Rev. T. Dunn, Rector, Messrs Thomas Wilton and Edward Martin) as the Head Teacher is asked to play at the Wedding of Mr Clement Govett at Washfield near Tiverton. The reason for closing earlier on 19th inst. was that the Master had to cycle to Tiverton, and there were so very few present.
July 21st	Mr Beardsley, Devon County Education Committee Inspector, visited this morning.
July 28th	Fair attendance this week, but not up to our usual average.
August 4th	Broke up this afternoon for Harvest Holiday (5 weeks). We reassemble on 11th September. In the interval considerable alterations and repairs ordered to be done by the County Council Architect are to be executed.

WEARE GIFFARD CHURCH OF ENGLAND SCHOOL LOG BOOK 1900 - 1945

1905

September 18th	As the school premises were not finished, a week's extension had to be granted, so that we could not re-commence until today after 6 weeks' holiday. Everyone on the books (58) present. The school premises have been much improved during the holidays. From today afternoon school will commence at 1.45 p.m. and end at 4 p.m., first lesson 15 minutes, second lesson 10 minutes, third lesson 5 minutes earlier than the time originally stated on the Time Table. This arrangement has been made to meet the Code requirements.
September 25th	Mr Hammond, School Attendance Officer, called.
October 11th	The Master is absent this morning (with the consent of the Rector and Mr F. Beer) as he has to attend the Audit at Torrington as Hon: Clerk of the Parish Council. The school will be conducted by Mrs Tucker.
October 16th	Very cold morning. We commenced fires in school.
October 20th	I have examined the Registers and found them correct. J. Groves Cooper.
October 27th	Mr Hammond, School Attendance Officer, visited.
November 3rd	Children sang several rounds very nicely indeed and some of the older boys have learnt the alto parts of some Hymn Tunes.
November 10th	% of average attendance very good for this week, viz: 98.6.
November 13th	On Saturday last the Sanitary Inspector, Mr Richard Gomer, came with a letter stating that the water at my house had been condemned by Doctor Slade King (Medical Officer of Health) as dangerous, and quite unfit for domestic purposes, and forbidding the use of the same.
November 24th	Mr Hammond called today.
December 1st	Record % of average, viz. 99 for this week.
December 4th	Master ill with chill. Could not telegraph yesterday (being Sunday) to H.M. Inspector. Mr Walter Scutt, H.M.I., came to the school and found matters as stated above. After consulting Correspondent, I sent a telegram to H.M. Inspector stating that there would be a recommencement of duties, I hoped, on Wednesday morning.
December 13th	Registers examined and found correct. J. Groves Cooper.
December 21st	Only 46 present out of 61 this morning owing to Bideford Christmas Market.
December 22nd	Broke up at noon for Xmas, one week.

WEARE GIFFARD CHURCH OF ENGLAND SCHOOL LOG BOOK
1900 - 1945

1906

January 1st	New Year's Day. Commenced school again after Xmas holidays. Many absent suffering from colds.
January 2nd	Inspection - Walter Scutt.
January 18th	Very rough and stormy morning, only 46 present.
January 22nd	Mr G.R.R. Routh, H.M.I., visited this morning.
February 2nd	Usual monthly half holiday resumed this afternoon with Rector's consent. Mumps have seriously influenced attendance for last few weeks.
February 15th	For some time the school has been suffering in attendance through mumps. On Monday last the Sanitary Inspector (Mr Gomer) called and said that he had mentioned the case to Doctor Slade King (Medical Officer of Health) and that he had been instructed to tell us that if the attendance fell 50% the school should be closed. As that was the case this morning, only 30 out of 62 being present, and as the Master's wife was suffering from the epidemic, the Rector agreed to closing the school, and is going to communicate with the above Medical officer, and I am sending the ordinary notices to H.M. Inspector and Devon County Education Committee.
March 5th	Commenced school again after closing for mumps. 55 present out of 64 on books.
March 16th	Severe coughs prevail among the children, and make it hard work to make one's voice heard. One case of whooping cough is reported, viz. Hilda Gomer.
March 22nd	The Rector (Rev. T. Dunn) who is also Correspondent went through the Stock and Stores Book with me and checked the items according to the Instructions of the Devon County Education Committee.
March 27th	Mr J. Loftus Sing visited this afternoon and went through the school registers. The attendance was very thin from the above cause, only 45 present out of 65 on the books.
March 28th	Received new Official School Number 510 from Board of Education.
April 11th	Examined the Registers and found them correct. T. Dunn.
April 12th	Broke up for Easter week.
April 23rd	Commenced school again after Easter Holidays. Attendance somewhat improved but still very low. Only 49 present out of 64 on books.
May 3rd	Torrington Fair - Holiday with the consent of the Rector and Mr F.J. Beer.
May 17th	Attendance very thin this afternoon (only 34 present) on account of the Wesleyan Tea. Had we known early enough some arrangement could have been made.

WEARE GIFFARD CHURCH OF ENGLAND SCHOOL LOG BOOK 1900 - 1945

1906

June 1st	Broke up for Whitsun (one week).
June 11th	Commenced school again after Whitsun Holidays.
June 15th	Diocesan Examination by the Rev. Powning. Register not marked for the day.
June 26th	Mr E.D. Fear, H.M Inspector, visited the school this morning. 66 out of 67 present.
July 3rd	Diocesan Report received today, of which the following is a copy:- Discipline and Tone: "Excellent". School classed "Very Good". Three outbreaks of epidemic sickness have affected the attendance and the continuity of work in this school. The thoroughness and readiness of the answering in the head group show that much earnest attention has been paid to the Religious Instruction by the Vicar and Head Teacher. Honourable mention: W. Short, P. Braund, E. Clements, W. Taylor, H. Moore, F. Parkhouse, E. Martin, L. Williams, H. Shute, A. Squire, C. Stevens.
July 6th	Mrs Tucker absent this afternoon with Rector's consent, she having to take her little girl Marjory to be examined by Doctor Ackland. She was leaning over the low rails in front of the school on Tuesday evening last when she lost her balance, and falling over she sustained a severe cut across the forehead and also broke her right arm. The rails are most unsuitable for children, especially young ones.
July 10th	Mrs Tucker absent this afternoon (with Rector's consent) for the same purpose as on 6th inst.
July 18th	Many children away today on account of Bideford Regatta.
July 19th	As it is the annual Wesleyan Sunday School Treat, the Rector and Mr E. Martin consented to the school being closed.
July 26th	Examined the Registers and found them correct. Thos. Dunn.
July 27th	Holiday given today with consent of the Rector and Mr F. Beer on account of Church Sunday School Treat.
August 3rd	Broke up for Harvest Holidays (4 weeks).
September 3rd	Commenced school again after Harvest Holidays. Only 44 present out of 68 on books on account of measles.
September 14th	Attendance thin this week and last owing to an epidemic of measles which is raging.
September 17th	Winnie Dark admitted. Although nearly 11 years of age she is exceedingly backward and really only fit for the Infants' class.

WEARE GIFFARD CHURCH OF ENGLAND SCHOOL LOG BOOK
1900 - 1945

1906

October 4th	With the Rector's consent, I had the scholars assemble this afternoon at 1 p.m. On account of the Wesleyan Harvest Festival they will be dismissed shortly after 3 p.m.
October 22nd	Examined Registers and found them correct. R.F. Balsdon.
October 31st	The Head Teacher is absent this morning by leave of the Managers to attend the District Audit at Torrington as Overseer and Hon. Clerk to the Parish Council.
November 14th	Visited this morning. H. Beardsley.
November 23rd	Examined the Registers and found them correct. J. Groves Cooper.
December 3rd	Very boisterous morning. Many absentees.
December 7th	Very rough week until this morning. Attendances low on average.
December 13th	With the consent of the Rector, I have today sent notices to H.M. Inspector and also to the Devon County Education Committee to the effect that the school will close for Xmas holidays on Friday 21st December and reopen on 7th January 1907.
December 21st	Broke up for Xmas.

1907

January 7th	Commenced school again after Xmas holidays. 61 present out of 65 on books.
January 16th	Visited the school. G.R.R. Routh.
January 25th	Very cold morning with snow falling. The severe weather during the week has had its effect upon the attendance, and several children are absent through sickness.
January 29th	Mr Balsdon visited school in afternoon.

WEARE GIFFARD CHURCH OF ENGLAND SCHOOL LOG BOOK
1900 - 1945

1907

February 7th	Copy of Government Report received on 7th February 1907 made by H.M.I. Mr Routh after his visit on 16th January 1907 The children are orderly, but somewhat apathetic and require encouragement to respond more readily. Sickness has interfered with the year's work, and in the circumstances progress may be considered fair. Reading is too slovenly to be entirely satisfactory and should improve. Arithmetic is decidedly weak; the work done shows little intelligence and many of the exercises are uncorrected. The children have a fair knowledge of History and Geography, and Composition, which was noticeably poor earlier in the year, shows some improvement. For some years the instruction has not been entirely satisfactory in several particulars, which vary from year to year, and it is hoped that a determined effort will now be made to infuse more energy into the teaching, and to raise the general level of the work of the school. The instruction of the infants is given under difficult conditions, but meets with very fair success. The room is too full for satisfactory teaching, and the organisation would be improved if some additional assistance were provided and Standard I were taught with the older scholars in the main room. The premises have recently been much improved. New offices have been built for the boys, the surface of the Playground has been improved, additional ventilation has been provided and the school has been redecorated. Thos. Dunn, 8 February 1907 Staff: John M. Tucker, Certificated Master; Emma M. Tucker, Art. 68
February 14th	Children have made a good start with new work.
February 22nd	Gave children some mental arithmetic at the end of each attendance this week, keeping in those who do not answer readily. I find it a great incentive to make them alert.
February 27th	Gave an Object Lesson on the life of a Frog which the children seemed thoroughly interested in.
March 8th	Half holiday this afternoon (of which due notice has been given to the proper authorities) as school is required for an Inquiry into the Charities of the Parish by Mr Phillimore, one of the Charity Commissioners.
March 13th	Remainder of lesson on Frog life given with same interest evinced on the part of the children.
March 21st	Mr J.L. Sing (Superintendent Attendance Officer) visited about 2 p.m. this afternoon.
March 25th	Holiday (due notice given). School required for Rural District Council Election.
March 28th	Broke up for Easter holidays (1 week).
April 8th	Commenced school again after Easter holidays. Very poor attendance in Infant Class. Only 11 present out of 19 on books.
April 17th	Holiday - Jumble Sale (organised by Miss Beresford) to provide a new American Organ for the school.

WEARE GIFFARD CHURCH OF ENGLAND SCHOOL LOG BOOK
1900 - 1945

1907

April 24th	Mr Start, gardener at Weare Hall, brought a note from the Rector (Rev. T. Dunn) desiring me to deliver up the Harmonium to him (Mr Start) and stating that the Managers had requested it.
April 30th	Examined the Registers and found them correct. T. Dunn.
May 2nd	Holiday (as usual) for Torrington Fair. The Rector and Mr F.J. Beer granted permission. Miss Davey commenced her duties as Monitress yesterday (1st inst.).
May 10th	So many scholars are suffering from colds that the attendance for the week has been thin.
May 17th	Broke up for Whitsuntide (1 week).
May 27th	Commenced school again after a week's holiday. Good attendance, 66 present out of 67 on books.
June 6th	Attendance very thin this afternoon on account of the Wesleyan Tea. Only 42 present out of 68 on books.
June 10th	Attendance Officer called.
June 21st	Diocesan Examination this afternoon by the Rev. H.R. Evers, Diocesan Inspector. There were 65 scholars present out of 68 on the books. The absentees were all prevented from attending through illness.
June 24th	Received Diocesan Report this morning of which the following is a copy:- Teacher's work: Tone and Discipline - Excellent. The school is classed as "Very Good". General remarks:- The children were in excellent order, and the Hymn was nicely sung. The Infants' class knew the memory work fairly well, but more should be made of the Biblical narratives, and pictures might be used to advantage in the class. The monitress, who is partly responsible for their religious teaching, does not appear to be receiving any instruction. In the senior class, a good proportion of the children answered well. Honourable mention:- Percy Tucker, Mabel Gomer, Laura Williams, Charles Stevens, Frank Slee, Arthur Squire, Arthur Stapleton, Harry Shute, Percy Blackmore, Reginald Wise, James Grigg, Maud Mountjoy, Ethel Martin, May Braunton.
July 3rd	Mrs Tucker was absent from school today through illness. I spoke with the Rector about it in the morning.
July 4th	Such very stormy weather at noon today that only 48 scholars presented themselves this afternoon. I find it much better to take Arithmetic for Boys for the first lesson on Thursday afternoon and Drawing for the second lesson instead of Boys' and Girls' Drawing being taken together as per Time Table. The above alteration will therefore be observed for the future.
July 8th	Mr Thomas Wilton (one of the Managers) visited the school this morning at 11 a.m. and remained until 11.30.
July 19th	Mr E.D. Fear (Barrister at Law), H.M. Inspector, visited the school at 9.15 a.m. and remained the whole of the morning, and visited again in the afternoon.

WEARE GIFFARD CHURCH OF ENGLAND SCHOOL LOG BOOK
1900 - 1945

1907

July 26th	Examined Registers and found them correct. Thomas Wilton.
July 31st	Holiday on account of the School Treats of both Church and Wesleyans. This is a good arrangement, as it prevents breaking in to two days.
August 9th	Broke up today for the Harvest Holidays (four weeks). The attendance has been very poor this week, owing to Bank Holiday, and many children having gone for their holidays. The earlier date August 2nd would apparently have been more suitable for us.
September 9th	Commenced school again after Harvest Holidays.
September 19th	Many children absent this afternoon on account of the Wesleyan Harvest Thanksgiving Tea. Only 47 children present out of 69 on the books.
September 25th	Holiday - Church Harvest Tea. Notices of holiday have been duly sent to H.M. Inspector, and the Secretary of the Devon County Education Committee.
October 4th	Willie Isaac has gone to Lyme Regis pro tem. so he has been taken off the Register temporarily.
October 10th	A very wet morning, and also Torrington Fair, both of which causes have had a bad effect on the attendance. A new Time Table, which has been approved by the Managers and sent for the approval of the Devon Education Committee, has been returned for alteration as the minimum time for secular instruction is short (by five minutes) of the time required by the bye-law of the above Authority. At a meeting of the Managers last evening I was asked to amend the Time Table by deducting five minutes from the time allowed on the Time Table for Recreation and again submit it to the County Authority.
October 18th	Very good average this week, though the weather during the month has been most unsettled.
October 25th	Attendance Officer called today.
November 5th	Mr J. Loftus Sing, Superintendent of Attendance Officers, visited the school today about 3 p.m.
November 6th	Absent (with the consent of the Rector) this morning as I have to attend the Government Audit, at Torrington, as one of the Overseers, and as Hon. Clerk of the Parish Council. The school will be in charge of Mrs Tucker. I have notified the fact to H.M. Inspector and the Devon County Education Committee.
November 11th	Examined the Registers and found them correct. J.W.C. Hutchinson, Lt. Col.

WEARE GIFFARD CHURCH OF ENGLAND SCHOOL LOG BOOK
1900 - 1945

1907

November 18th	At the request of Mr J.F. Young for the Devon County Education Committee, the registers were marked and closed by 9.15 a.m. to admit of the children being dismissed at 11.15 a.m. as a meeting in connection with the Educational part of John Lovering's Charity has been arranged to take place at the school at the above time. As it was a very wet morning, only 60 children were present out of 69 on the books. The following were present:- Representing Weare Giffard:- The Rev. T. Dunn (Rector) and J. Groves Cooper, Esq., Trustees, and Messrs F.J. Beer (Chairman of Weare Giffard Parish Council) and J.M. Tucker (Hon. Clerk to the same). Representing the Devon County Education Committee:- Messrs H.P. Hiern, C.C., Hugh Stuckley, C.C., G. Norman, C.C., and J.F. Young M.A. Secretary. Representing Torrington:- Messrs P. Stapleton (Mayor) and G.M. Doe (Solicitor).
November 26th	Very wet morning, and many of the infants absent. Only 58 present out of 68 on books.
November 27th	The school was this morning so flooded, through a drain which passed from the school yard under the road, that I consulted the Rector, who decided to close school for the day. The Sanitary Inspector Mr R. Gomer also considered it would be attended with great risks to have the children in the room where the stench was most objectionable, even if it had been possible to open school.
December 5th	The Torridge was so flooded this morning, and so few children were present - 40, nearly all of whom had wetted their feet by wading through the water - that at the Rector's request (who feared, as the water was still rising, that the roads would soon become impassable) I dismissed the scholars for the day.
December 12th	The Torridge was again so flooded this morning that the Rector asked me to watch the state of the river, and if it got dangerously high I was to dismiss the children. I kept them until 12 o'clock but it had risen so fast by that time and the roads were so flooded that I told them not to return for afternoon school.
December 20th	Broke up for Xmas holidays - 2 weeks.

1908

January 6th	Commenced school again after Xmas Holidays. 64 present out of 67 on books.
January 16th	A very wet morning, and thin attendance. Only 56 present out of 67 on books.
January 24th	Severe colds have interfered with the attendance this week.
February 4th	Mr E.D. Fear, H.M. Inspector of Schools, visited at 9 a.m. and remained during the morning.

WEARE GIFFARD CHURCH OF ENGLAND SCHOOL LOG BOOK 1900 - 1945

1908

February 11th	Seven children made every possible attendance during the past year, viz.: Theo: Tucker, Percy Tucker, Charles Stevens, Ernest Clements, Olive Moore and Marjory Tucker. The school was opened 423 times, and the average for the year showed an increase of 6 on that of the previous year. The year ended on 31st January.
February 17th	Very wet morning, and poor muster. Only 51 present out of 67 on books.
February 27th	Attendance Officer called.
March 2nd	Sent Time Tables and Schemes of Work for approval and signature of H.M. Inspector.
March 11th	The Rector (Rev. T. Dunn) distributed 7 Certificates for <u>Perfect</u> and 7 for <u>Regular</u> attendance to the above children.
March 16th	Mr J. Hawkins, our new Attendance Officer, called for the first time. All the children on the books (67) were present.
March 17th	Ada Squire has been granted a Certificate of Exemption (by her attendances) and brought it for me to see.
March 26th	Mr Rd. Gorner (Sanitary Inspector) visited and inspected the offices etc. and expressed himself as quite satisfied with their condition.
April 3rd	Very good attendance this week : % = 96.2.
April 8th	Sent notice to H.M. Inspector, and Mr J.F. Young, re Easter Holidays (1 week).
April 16th	Broke up for Easter - 1 week.
April 27th	Commenced school again. Irene and Edwin Chamings admitted, making the number on books 64, out of which 63 are present this morning.
April 28th	Very wet morning, only 52 present.
April 29th	Examined Registers and found them correct. Thos. Dunn.
May 7th	Holiday - Torrington Fair. Due notice has been sent to H.M. Inspector and the D.C. Education Committee.
May 15th	Examined Registers and found them correct. J. W.C. Hutchinson, Lt. Col.
May 22nd	Just been notified that the attendance at our school during the last month was the best in the Bideford district - 97%.
June 3rd	With the permission of the Rector, the Master, as Hon. Clerk to the Parish Council, is attending the Government Audit at Torrington. The school is left pro tem. in charge of Mrs Tucker. Notices have been sent to H.M. Inspector and the Devon Education Committee. First periodical Examination this week. Time Table not strictly followed.
June 5th	Broke up for Whitsuntide Holidays (1 week) this afternoon. Owing to several cases of sickness our usual good attendance has been somewhat interfered with this week.

WEARE GIFFARD CHURCH OF ENGLAND SCHOOL LOG BOOK
1900 - 1945

1908

June 15th	Commenced school again after Whitsun Holidays. 58 present out of 64 on books, 5 out of 6 are absent through sickness.
June 26th	Many children are still absent through chicken pox, so our % of average is consequently low comparatively.
July 2nd	Very low attendance this afternoon (only 45 present out of 65 on books) owing to the Wesleyan Sunday School Tea which takes place at 4 p.m.
July 3rd	The Rector (the Rev. T. Dunn) visited the school.
July 10th	Visited. H. Beardsley.
July 14th	Visit of Inspection - J.H. Greet.
July 16th Alteration in Time Table	Holiday given with consent of the Managers on account of Church Sunday School Treat. Object Lessons given for the future to Lower Group on Fridays 2.50 to 3.25 p.m.
July 20th	Diocesan Examination at 2 p.m., conducted by the Rev. Cecil A. Curgenven, Diocesan Inspector. There were 59 children present out of 63 on the books.
July 29th	Wesleyan Sunday School Treat to Westward Ho! Holiday given (as it would take away at least 30 children) with the consent of the Rector and Mr F.I. Beer.
July 31st	Diocesan Report received today of which the following is a copy:- Discipline, Tone, etc. "Excellent". The school is classed as "Very Good". General remarks:- The children in both Groups showed a thorough knowledge of the Subjects in the Old Testament Syllabus. In the Upper Division the Catechism was rather weak, but the repetition was most praiseworthy. <u>Note</u>: Owing to the difficulty experienced in small schools of taking children in different Standards together, it might be well to examine the Upper Group on the Biblical Syllabus of Standard III, but in that case the Communion Service 1909, the Confirmation Service, and the whole of the Catechism should be taken. Honourable mention: Jack Edworthy, James Squires, Percy Blackmore, William Hammett, Hilda Gomer, Gwennie Wise, Charles Stevens, Frank Slee, Maud Mountjoy, Blanche Parkhouse, Theo. Tucker, Dorothy Tucker. Broke up today for Harvest Holidays (4 weeks). We reassemble on 31st August.
August 31st	Commenced school again after Harvest Holidays. 58 present out of 64 on the books. Sent notices to H.M. Inspector and D.C.E. Committee re holiday on 9th September (Harvest Festival).
September 1st	Such a very rough morning that only 35 were present out of 64.

WEARE GIFFARD CHURCH OF ENGLAND SCHOOL LOG BOOK
1900 - 1945

1908

September 9th	Holiday - Church Harvest Festival.
September 10th	Notices sent to the authorities respecting the closing of the school for "Jumble Sale" on 21st September.
September 18th	Miss Davey, Monitress, absent today (with the consent of the Rector) to attend Barnstaple Fair.
September 21st	Holiday today as the school is required for a "Jumble Sale".
October 2nd	% of average for week 89.2. Sickness has had a bad effect on the attendance.
October 7th	Attendance Officer called today.
October 16th	Examined the Registers and found them correct. Thos. Dunn.
October 23rd	% of average this week 95.4, the highest since May 29th last.
October 30th	Gave the children an Examination, the second of the periodical ones.
November 5th	Spoke to the children about Gunpowder Plot.
November 13th	Holiday (of which due notice has been given to H.M.I. and D.C.E. Committee) to admit of the school stove being refixed on more substantial material than wood.
November 27th	Examined the Registers and found them correct. J.W.C. Hutchinson, Lt. Col.
December 11th	Many of the younger children absent through severe colds.
December 18th	Broke up for Christmas - 2 weeks.

1909

January 4th	Commenced school again after Christmas holidays.
January 14th	*
January 28th	Giving children the last of their three periodical Examinations, routine not strictly followed.
January 29th	Last "school day" of school year. The average during the last year has been 59.5, about two less than last year. Ten of the scholars have made perfect attendances (an increase of three on that of last year) and seven (the same number as last year) have made regular attendances (98%).
February 1st	First day of the new school year. Arranged children in their new classes. We have but 61 on books instead of 68 as on the corresponding date last year, owing to the depopulation of the parish, which according to the latest "local" census has decreased by 35 (from 315 to 280).

WEARE GIFFARD CHURCH OF ENGLAND SCHOOL LOG BOOK 1900 - 1945

1909

February 10th	Attendance Officer visited.
February 15th	Have requested Miss Davey (Monitress) to send all cases requiring Corporal Punishment to me.
February 16th	Received back Schemes of Work (for the current school year) which have been sent for the approval of G.R.R. Routh Esq., H.M.I. They have both been approved.
February 24th	Visited the school. Thomas Wilton.
March 2nd	Half holiday this afternoon (of which due notice has been given) as the Lord Bishop of Exeter is holding a confirmation at 2 p.m. and there is a Consecration of the addition to the churchyard at 3 p.m. Colonel Perowne and Mr Burridge from Crediton visited the school and heard the children sing.
March 3rd	Such a heavy fall of snow occurred during the night that it lowered the attendance very materially. Only 45 present this morning out of 61 on books. A little better in the afternoon when there were 53 present.
March 17th	A fall of snow again during the night was the cause of a poorer muster this morning - 55 present out of 62.
March 23rd	The Head Teacher, Mr J.M. Tucker, has been absent from school through severe illness since Friday March 19th 1909. T. Dunn, Correspondent
April 23rd	I took temporary charge of this school Monday April 19th in consequence of the sad death of the late master Mr Tucker. J.A. Attwooll. The attendance has been very good.
April 30th	This week ends the first quarter in the school year. Average attendance for the quarter 56.5.
May 7th	Admitted this week four new scholars.
May 14th	Mrs Tucker's time expires this afternoon. Another supplementary teacher has been appointed to take her place, to commence work on Monday.
May 21st	The attendance this week has fallen off considerably in consequence of many of the children having severe colds. Average attendance 57. Percentage 85.
May 28th	The school will be closed Monday and Tuesday (Whitsuntide).
June 4th	Commenced school Wednesday. Several children are still suffering from colds.
June 11th	Miss Pettican the infant teacher was absent Monday and Tuesday. The scholars, especially the girls, are making good progress, and take an interest in their work.

WEARE GIFFARD CHURCH OF ENGLAND SCHOOL LOG BOOK
1900 - 1945

1909

June 18th	On Thursday afternoon the Bishop of Crediton, the Rev. T. Dunn and Mr Cooper visited the school. After talking to the children and asking them questions we sang several school songs.
June 25th	Special attention has been paid this week to reading, arithmetic, history and geography. Holiday given on account of Church Sunday School treat (Wednesday).
July 2nd	Began school Friday afternoon 1.30 and closed half an hour earlier than the usual time, owing to having to go to Exeter.
July 9th	Attendance Officer visited the school this week as usual, and found a better attendance. A few scholars still absent through sickness.
July 16th	There were only 43 scholars present Wednesday morning in consequence of Bideford Regatta. Mr Wilton, one of the Managers, visited the school and thought it would be advisable to close in the afternoon.
July 21st	Visited. H. Beardsley.
July 23rd	On Wednesday morning H. Beardsley Esq., the County Council Inspector, visited the school, and Thursday afternoon Mr G. Bicknell, the Diocesan Inspector, but not for the purpose of inspection. There will be no examination this year in consequence of the unsettled state of the school.
July 29th	My time expires as temporary teacher of this school. Mr Beer, one of the Managers, present when we closed and gave a short address to the scholars. J.A. Attwooll.
August 30th	I commenced my duties as Head Teacher of this school on Monday August 30th. Rev. T. Dunn and Mr Groves Cooper visited the school during the morning. Admitted two new scholars. Number on books - 59 Number present - 37 Florence L. Wyatt, Certificated Mistress
September 1st	A visit from the Attendance Officer who brought new Duplicate Registers. Rev. T. Dunn brought Form 75, also communication from C.E. Authority confirming the appointment of the Head Teacher (F.L. Wyatt) and Miss Davy as Supplementary Teacher. Another Supplementary Teacher is to be advertised for. Miss Gomer is acting as Monitress pro tem.
September 6th	A Meeting of the School Managers held in the schoolroom at 4 p.m. the Bishop of Crediton and Mr G. Bicknell came from Exeter to attend. I was called in to sign my agreement. The visitors expressed their approval of the repairs which have been carried out in the school and schoolhouse.
September 10th	Several of the children were allowed to leave school a few minutes earlier this afternoon to attend a Harvest Thanksgiving tea at the Chapel.

WEARE GIFFARD CHURCH OF ENGLAND SCHOOL LOG BOOK
1900 - 1945

1909

September 27th	Mr Routh (H.M.I.) visited the school this afternoon and remained until 3 p.m. The boys were at map drawing and girls at needlework. The Inspector does not consider map drawing of much importance except as part of Geography lesson. He advised the Head Teacher to draw up a new time table; he also recommended use of continuous story readers for upper division. Mr Routh considered the boys noisy and disorderly.
September 27th	A meeting of the Managers was held in the school room this afternoon at 4 p.m. to appoint a Supplementary Teacher. Miss Baker from Lustleigh came for an interview and is appointed subject to the approval of the County Council.
September 29th	A holiday all day today on account of the Church Harvest Tea and Concert in the school room. Due notice has been sent by Rev. T. Dunn to H.M. Inspector and to the Secretary of the Devon Education Authority.
October 4th	Received five hundredweight of coal and ten hundredweight of coke for school use.
October 13th	Visited the school. Examined the Registers and found them correct. Thos. Wilton.
October 13th	Visited the school, and saw the children at work. M. Maude Cooper.
October 14th	The attendance of this school is the highest in the district for the last month. Miss Baker commenced duty here as a Supplementary Teacher on Monday October 12th. She is at present in charge of the Lower Division, Standards I, II, III.
October 15th	The Managers have supplied the following articles for school use:- 1 doz yards of towelling to make 4 towels, 1 doormat, 1 watercan, 2 lbs Sunlight soap.
October 18th	Medical inspection. 15 children examined.
October 19th	Miss Baker received permission from Mr Dunn to be absent from school for two days, Monday and Tuesday, to attend a funeral.
October 20th	Rev. T. Dunn opened school this morning, took the Scripture lesson and spoke very seriously to some of the boys who have been particularly disobedient and troublesome.
October 21st	Received from the Medical Inspector notices to be sent to the parents of the following: Thomas Slee, Fred. Bissett, Mary Slee, Gladys Joliffe, Winnifred Edworthy.
October 27th	The Torridge was so flooded this morning that only 21 were present out of 59 - 3 Infants and 16 older scholars. On the advice of the Rector I dismissed the children and closed school for the day.
October 29th	Examined the Registers and found them correct and the school in order. J. Groves Cooper.
November 11th	We have received notice that our school is again the highest in the district for attendance this month.
November 12th	Rev. T. Dunn paid a visit to the school this morning.

WEARE GIFFARD CHURCH OF ENGLAND SCHOOL LOG BOOK 1900 - 1945

1909

November 15th	The Managers have given permission for school to be opened at 1.30 p.m. and closed at 3.45 p.m. during the winter months to allow children who live a long distance from school to get home earlier.
November 23rd	Visited. H. Beardsley.
November 23rd	Mr H. Beardsley paid a visit to the school this afternoon. He expressed himself as well pleased with the writing throughout the school and with the Arithmetic of the upper standards. He recommended that continuous Story Readers be requisitioned for the first class.
December 2nd	Visited the school and found all in order and signed the Registers. J. Groves Cooper, Manager.
December 2nd	The stormy weather this week has caused many absences among the Infants; in the Upper Department the attendance has remained remarkably good.
December 3rd	The Torridge was so flooded again this morning that only 14 boys and 1 girl had arrived at 9.30. On the advice of the Rector I dismissed the children and closed school for the day.
December 4th	Dr Slade King visited the school. He complained of the dust in the school room and the quantity of dead leaves lying in the yards.
December 13th	During this week classes are having examinations in work of the Term.
December 17th	A meeting of the Managers was held in the school room at 4 o'clock.
December 20th	Mr Fear, H.M. Inspector, paid a visit to the school this morning, arriving at 9.15. He remained during the morning. Mr Loftus Sing, Attendance Superintendent, examined registers this afternoon. He informs me that a separate register is necessary for Infants under five; also that 3 infants' attendances have been classed with "under fives" after passing their fifth birthday. This will necessitate an alteration in the summary.
December 21st	Rev. T. Dunn, who is leaving Weare Giffard, came in to say a few words to the children and to wish them "Good bye". Notice has been sent to H.M. Inspector and to the County Council that this school will be closed from December 21st to January 10th for Christmas Holidays. Received 15 cwt of coal for school use. Broke up for Xmas Holidays.

1910

January 10th	Commenced school again after Xmas Holiday. Very wet morning. 50 present out of 55. Miss Baker absent with a cold.
January 13th	Visited the school. Found all in order and examined the Registers and signed them. J. Groves Cooper.
January 14th	The Managers have supplied the following for school use: 1 cinder sifter; 1 coal scuttle; 1 pair of steps (Jones Patent); 2 check dusters.

WEARE GIFFARD CHURCH OF ENGLAND SCHOOL LOG BOOK
1900 - 1945

1910

January 17th	Miss Baker returned this morning after a week's absence through illness.
January 24th	The Torridge again flooded this morning. Only 14 children present out of 55, so dismissed them and closed school for the day.
January 27th	Mr Balsdon signed the new registers this afternoon.
January 28th	The rough weather and bad condition of the roads has considerably reduced the average attendance of Infants this week. Miss Baker absent this afternoon.
February 1st	This is the first day of a new School Year. Arranged children in their new classes. Number on registers 55.
February 7th	Now that the days are lengthening we shall open and close school in the afternoon at the usual time according to the Time Table, viz. 1.45 and 4 p.m.
February 10th	Have given Miss Davy permission to be absent this morning. Half holiday this afternoon on account of Sunday School Tea. Due notice has been sent to the Devon Education Committee and to H.M. Inspector.
February 10th	Examined the Registers and found them correct. R.F. Balsdon.
February 15th	Owing to the high tide and heavy rain the road was flooded this morning from about 9.30 a.m. to 1.30 p.m. This considerably affected the attendance in the afternoon, only 39 being present out of 57.
February 24th	Miss Baker (Supplementary Assistant) has today sent notice to the Managers to resign her appointment on March 24th.
February 25th	Two children, Ethel and Winnie Edworthy, have been absent all the month, owing to condition of the roads. This and the very small attendance on the afternoon of February 15th has considerably reduced the percentage for the month.
March 1st	A new Time Table has been drawn up for the Upper Department; it has been examined at the D.C.E. Office, signed by the Managers and by Mr Routh, H.M.I. The number lesson for Infants on Tuesday and Thursday afternoons will be discontinued, and the time given to 2 Observation Lessons each week.
March 8th	Opened school at 1.30 this afternoon in order to close at 3.45 to enable Head Teacher to go to Bideford after school.
March 11th	The percentage of attendance this week is very low (88%). Three children absent all week through illness, and two others (mentioned above) owing to condition of roads.
March 18th	The attendance this week has greatly improved (97.1%).
March 21st	Signed the Registers and found all present. M. Maude Cooper.
March 24th	School closed this afternoon for Easter Holidays and will reopen on April 4th. Notice has been sent to H.M. Inspector and to D.C.Education Office.

WEARE GIFFARD CHURCH OF ENGLAND SCHOOL LOG BOOK
1900 - 1945

1910

March 26th	As Schoolroom is required on April 4th for Council Election, school will reopen on Tuesday April 5th.
April 5th	Reopened school after Easter Holidays. 2 boys left; admitted 2 new scholars. 50 present out of 56. Miss Northcott commenced her duties here as Supplementary Teacher. She is taking charge of the Lower Division, Standards I, II, III.
April 6th	The Rector (Rev. Rickards) visited the school this morning and took the Scripture lesson.
April 14th	Miss Northcott signed her agreement at the Managers' Meeting.
April 15th	The Rector presented Attendance Certificates to the scholars this morning. 5 for Perfect Attendance, 14 for Regular Attendance.
April 18th	Miss Davey has today commenced a fortnight's training at Torrington Council Infant School.
May 3rd	Examined the Registers and found them correct. Clifford Rickards, Manager.
May 5th	A Holiday has been given today for Torrington Fair. Notice was sent last week to H.M. Inspector and also to D.C.E. Comittee. I am at present relieving Miss Northcott of Standard III to give her more time to devote to Standards I and II.
May 9th	His Majesty King Edward VII died at Buckingham Palace on Friday May 6th.
May 13th	H.M. Inspector Mr Routh accompanied by Mr Morley visited the school this afternoon, arriving about 2.10 and remaining till 3.10. Broke up this afternoon for Whitsuntide Holiday (1 week). Notice has been sent to H.M. Inspector and to D.E. Committee.
May 23rd	Opened school this morning after Whitsun Holiday. 54 present out of 57.
May 25th	A Holiday this afternoon as Schoolroom is required for a Jumble Sale. Notice has been given.
May 28th	Received a letter from Mr Baxter, respecting candidates for Lovering Scholarship.
June 7th	Have allowed Miss Davie to leave at 10.30 this morning to go to Torrington on business. I have received 3 doz. Hymn Books for School use.
June 10th	A very wet morning; several of the scholars (Infants) who come a long distance are absent. 45 present out of 51 on registers. Average for the week only 51.5 and percentage 90.3.
June 17th	Miss Davie has received notice from the Board of Education that she has been approved for her capacity in Teaching and accordingly recognised as a Supplementary Teacher of Infants.
June 22nd	School will open on Thursday afternoon (23rd) at 1 p.m. and close at 3 p.m. on account of Wesleyan Anniversary Tea. Notice of this arrangement has been sent to the parents.

WEARE GIFFARD CHURCH OF ENGLAND SCHOOL LOG BOOK
1900 - 1945

1910

June 23rd	There were 18 absent this afternoon to attend Anniversary Tea although the above alteration was made purposely to accommodate them. Only 38 present out of 56.
June 24th	The very low attendance yesterday afternoon brings down our week average to 50.9 and percentage only 90.8.
July 5th	The Rector has received notice that the Diocesan Inspection will be held here on Thursday July 21st at 2 p.m. Notice has been sent to D.E. Office and to H.M. Inspector.
July 18th	Miss Davey's Form of Agreement has today been returned from the Devon Education Office.
July 20th	Checked the Registers and found them correct. Clifford Rickards, Manager.
July 21st	Diocesan Inspection by Mr G. Bicknell. No Registers marked. There were 54 present out of 57 on the books; 3 children absent through illness.
July 23rd	Mr Baxter (Headmaster of Bideford Boys' School) held an Examination in the Schoolroom in connection with the Scholarship awarded by the Lovering Education Foundation. There were 6 candidates.
July 27th	A Holiday to be given on account of the Wesleyan Sunday School Outing.
July 29th	Closed school this afternoon for summer Holidays (4 weeks). Examined the Registers and found them correct. J. Groves Cooper.
August 3rd	Weare Giffard Cottage Garden Show was held today. 16 girls entered for the Needlework Section, the following obtained Prizes:- Rosie Start, Annie Pengilly, Beatrice Hammett, Ethel Short, Olive Moore, Marian Banbrook, Ethel Martin, Bertha Parkhouse. Several boys and girls gained prizes for collections of wild flowers. John Edworthy destroyed the largest number of queen wasps.
August 13th	A Meeting of the School Managers today.

WEARE GIFFARD CHURCH OF ENGLAND SCHOOL LOG BOOK 1900 - 1945

1910

August 19th	Diocesan Report received today. (Inspection July 31st by Mr G.S.S. Bicknell). Scholars on books - 57 Present - 54 (Boys 28, Girls 26) The following is a copy of report:- Teacher's Work, Discipline, Tone, etc.: Excellent. The School is classed as Excellent. |	Infants	Stds I-III	IV-VII | |---|---|---|---| | Catechism	-	V.G.	V.G. | | N. Testament	V.G.	V.G.	E. | | O. Testament	V.G.	V.G.	E. | | P. Prayers and Collects	E.	E.	E. | | Rep. Scrip. & Hymns	E.	E.	E. | | Written Work	-	G. to E.	V.G.-E.| | Prayer Book	-	G.	G. | There is a very marked improvement in the tone and discipline of this school; the children are bright and responsive, and evidently animated with a desire to show their knowledge of subjects in which they have been interested. The Biblical subjects are specially well known and the Repetition in each group calls for special commendation. The following deserve honourable mention:- Infants: Miriam Squire; Mary Slee; Horace Clements Stds I & II: Alice Parsons; Ethel Edworthy; Frederick Bissett; Walter Fisher Stds III & IV: James Squire; Olive Moore; John Beer; John Edworthy Stds V, VI, VII: Frances Martin; Ernest Clements; Rosie Starr; Mabel Squire; Alfred Stevens; William Parkhouse
August 29th	Commenced school this morning after Summer Holidays. 53 present out of 57 on the books. Miss Northcott was absent this morning and arrived at 2.20 p.m. this afternoon. Have today received 3 doz. Prayer Books for school use; also 2 tins of Sanitas, 6 lbs of Carbolic Soap.
August 31st	There are 11 scholars absent this morning on account of Bideford Regatta. The Rector has advised a half holiday to be given this afternoon in consequence.
September 8th	Visited the School and gave to the children who were commended by the Diocesan Inspector certificates of merit. Afterwards I checked the Registers.
September 12th	We have received notice that a Medical Inspection will be held here on Friday (16th). Notice has been sent to parents of 14 children

WEARE GIFFARD CHURCH OF ENGLAND SCHOOL LOG BOOK
1900 - 1945

1910

September 13th	The Managers have supplied 15 cwt of coal and 10 cwt of coke for school use.
September 16th	Medical Inspection. 13 children examined.
September 20th	Received notice from Medical Inspector that Florence Beer is suffering from adenoids. I have sent notice and advice to Mrs Beer.
September 27th	Miss Davie is absent all day today as Mrs Davie is ill.
September 29th	A holiday this afternoon on account of Harvest Festival and Tea. Notice has been sent to D.E. Committee and to H.M. Inspector.
September 30th	Opened school at 1.30, omitted play and closed at 3.30 p.m. in order to be in time to catch 5.27 train from Bideford.
October 3rd	The following children have had their names taken off the registers, they and their parents having left the village:- Alice and Bertha Parsons; Frederick Bissett; Mabel Beer.
October 4th	Admitted 3 new scholars.
October 11th	Very wet afternoon; only 49 present out of 60.
October 14th	Owing to the very stormy weather this week the attendance is very low. 60 scholars on books. Average 53.4. Percentage 89. Miss Northcott was allowed to leave at 2.45 this afternoon as she is going home for the week-end.
October 17th	Miss Northcott is absent this morning.
October 26th	The Rector (Rev. C. Rickards) tested the Registers this morning.
October 28th	During the winter months, afternoon school will commence at 1.30 and close at 3.40, starting on Monday next, October 31st.
November 4th	Considering the rough weather this week the attendance has been very fair. The older children attend very well; absences have been chiefly among infants who come from long distances. A new broom, 2 new sweeping brushes supplied for school use.
November 11th	The schoolroom was scrubbed today. It was previously done on August 24th last.
November 22nd	A half holiday today on account of a Children's Tea in the schoolroom, given by Mrs Beresford who is leaving the village.
November 30th	Examined the Registers and found them correct. 14 absent out of 61 on the books. J. Groves Cooper.
December 2nd	Have sent duplicate Registers to the Attendance Superintendent. also Stock and Stores Account, to the Devon Education Office as requested.
December 9th	A very wet and rough morning. Only 12 Infants present out of 21 on the books.
December 13th	After the heavy rain, the Torridge rose rapidly during the day so that by 1.30 p.m. the road was partly flooded; this considerably affected the afternoon attendance, only 46 being present out of 56.

WEARE GIFFARD CHURCH OF ENGLAND SCHOOL LOG BOOK
1900 - 1945

1910

December 16th	School was not opened this afternoon; at 1.30 p.m. the road was under water for some distance and the Torridge still rising. On the advice of the Rev. C. Rickards the children were sent home. The rough weather this week has considerably affected the attendance. Average 53.6. Percentage 89.3.
December 21st	Closed school this afternoon for Xmas Holidays. Attendance improved this week. Average 54.1. Percentage 93.2. The Managers, teachers, and scholars this morning presented me with a beautiful hand bag. The Rev. C. Rickards made the presentation, and, in a very kind speech, on behalf of the Managers and parents expressed great appreciation of my work here and regret at my resignation. He was seconded in his address by Mr Groves Cooper.
December 28th	The Sunday School children and choir greatly enjoyed a Tea and Christmas Tree provided and arranged by the Rector and Mrs Rickards, Captain and Mrs Vaughan, Mrs P. Balsdon, Miss Groves Cooper, Mrs Hutchinson and other ladies and gentlemen of the village.
December 31st	Today ends my term of office as Head Mistress of this school. I am returning to Exeter, but cannot help a feeling of regret at parting with some of the nicest children I have ever taught, and the many kind friends I have made among the parents and Managers. I shall ever remember the extreme kindness and consideration shown to my mother and myself by the Rector and Mrs Rickards, Mr and Miss Groves Cooper, Mr Wilton, Mr F. Beer, Mr Balsdon and many others in the parish of Weare Giffard, and in return can only wish this School and the Scholars every success in the future. Florence L. Wyatt, Certificated Mistress.

1911

January 9th	I have today commenced duty in this school (Emily G. Sobey). The Rev. C. Rickards visited the school. Three children have left, one over-age, one infant (3) until the summer, and are to go to Torrington. Attendance 52 out of 56. The school has been scrubbed during the Xmas Holiday.
January 13th	Average attendance 52.8. Percentage 90.1. Several children have been absent, owing to small illnesses.
January 16th	Mary Squires has left - being 14 years of age. The Rev. C. Rickards visited this morning. Two children absent today, both sick.
January 20th	Today the children were weighed for the annual Medical Report. The majority of children had gained considerably since the last record of weight was made. Average attendance 53.7. Percentage 95.8.
January 23rd	Alfred Stevens has left, being 14 years of age. Four children are absent today through sickness. This afternoon the height of children was taken. A Managers' Meeting was held in the schoolroom this evening. I signed my agreement.

WEARE GIFFARD CHURCH OF ENGLAND SCHOOL LOG BOOK 1900 - 1945

1911

January 26th	James Squires has been sent home as his mother sent to say he has Ringworm. It would not have been discovered had she not have informed me. I have advised her to have medical advice immediately.
January 27th	Average attendance 49.3. Percentage 89.6.
February 2nd	Today the Attendance Officer visited, also the Rector in the afternoon.
February 3rd	Average attendance 51.5. Percentage 93.6.
February 9th	Attendance Officer visited this morning. We have started a School "Log" to be kept by the top Boy in the school, now Ernest Clements. Gardens would have been made but I find the playground unsuitable.
February 10th	Average attendance 50.4. Percentage 93.3. Frances Martin has left, being 14 years of age.
February 16th	Mrs Rickards visited the school and examined the drawing and needlework, also heard several songs.
February 17th	Average attendance 51.5. Percentage 95.3.
February 20th	The Rector visited this morning. The Stock Book has been returned from Exeter and has to be made up. The Rector signed the Attendance Certificates. Miss Northcott is absent this morning, returning from a week end at Christow. Attendance very bad, several children suffering from colds.
February 22nd	May Braunton has been sent home as she is suffering from mumps. Thomas Wilton is absent, also reported suffering from mumps.
February 23rd	Thomas Wilton returned to school as his was only a cold.
February 24th	Average attendance 47.3. Percentage 87.5.
February 27th	Miss Davey is absent this morning as her mother is very ill. Several children are absent through bad colds.
February 28th	I have received a letter from Miss Davey, stating that her mother is very ill and asking for permission to remain at home a day or two longer. I have reported the matter to the Rector, who approves of this on behalf of the Managers.
March 3rd	Miss Davey still absent, her mother having passed away last evening. The attendance this week has been very bad, so many children absent suffering from severe colds. Average attendance 46.7. Percentage 86.4. Captain King and his Lieutenant visited the school this afternoon to hear the children sing. They are travelling through the county in the Church Army Van holding mission services.
March 6th	Miss Davey returned to school this morning.

WEARE GIFFARD CHURCH OF ENGLAND SCHOOL LOG BOOK
1900 - 1945

1911

March 8th	The Rector visited school this morning.
March 9th	Mr Wilton, a School Manager, came this afternoon.
March 10th	Miss Davey is absent today, having to go to Barnstaple on legal business. Average attendance 50.8. Percentage 95.8.
March 13th	Miss Davey is present this morning. Attendance good though three children are absent, suffering from bad colds.
March 16th	Mr Bright, H.M.I., visited the school this morning. 51 children present out of 53.
March 17th	Horace Clements absent, suffering from a very bad sore throat. Average attendance 50. Percentage 94.3.
March 23rd	Examined the Registers and found them correct and the school in good order. J. Groves Cooper. Mr Groves Cooper visited the school and saw the children's writing and drawing books. He also heard the Infants sing some of their Nursery Rhymes.
March 24th	Average attendance 49.2. Percentage 92.8.
March 29th	Mr Hawkins visited school. Four children, the family of Squires, have left the school, having removed to Instow, leaving now 49 on books.
March 31st	Average attendance 45.8. Percentage 93.4.
April 7th	Average attendance 45.3. Percentage 92.4.
April 14th	Average attendance 46.1. Percentage 94.1. Today the school closes for the Easter Holiday.
April 24th	School re-opened this morning. Three children admitted. Miss Northcott is absent, ill.
April 25th	I have received a Medical Certificate from Miss Northcott. I have sent it to Rev. C. Rickards for transmission to the County Authority.
April 27th	Average attendance . Percentage 98.5 A Holiday is being given tomorrow, Friday, on account of the School Concert.
May 1st	Miss Northcott returned to school this afternoon.
May 5th	Attendance has suffered this week through children being absent to go to Torrington Fair. Average attendance 48.9. Percentage 94.
May 8th	Rose Start has left school, being over-age. I am extremely sorry to lose so bright and well-behaved a scholar.

WEARE GIFFARD CHURCH OF ENGLAND SCHOOL LOG BOOK 1900 - 1945

1911

May 9th	Visited. H. Beardsley.
May 12th	Average attendance 50. Percentage 98. I dismissed school 15 minutes earlier, as the percentage was 98, for the second time in a month.
May 17th	Mr Hawkins visited. Reported that last month our school was second for the District on Attendance.
May 18th	Notice has been sent to H.M.I. and to the Secretary of D.E.C. regarding the Date of the Scripture Examination.
May 19th	Average attendance 50.5. Percentage 99.
May 22nd	Alfred Beer has left - gone to Torrington, I believe. There has been no communication to me on the subject. I am writing to the Head Master at Torrington to ascertain the reason.
May 24th	Empire Day. National Anthem sung.
May 26th	Average attendance 49.6. Percentage 99.2.
June 2nd	Average attendance 49.2. Percentage 98.4. Have closed for Whitsun Holiday. Managers hold a meeting in the school tomorrow.
June 12th	School re-opened this morning after Holiday.
June 13th	Medical Examination this afternoon. Dr Goulden visited. Several children examined. All passed the examination without remark.
June 16th	Walter Fisher absent all the week. Reported to Mr Hawkins, Attendance Officer. Average attendance 47.7. Percentage 95.4.
June 20th	School closed today for Coronation Holiday. Average attendance 48.2. Percentage 96.5.
June 22nd	Coronation of Their Majesties, George V and Mary III.
June 26th	New child admitted. Rector visited the school.
June 30th	Miss Northcott has left the school today, resigning on Marriage. Miss Groves Cooper, on behalf of the Managers, Staff, and Scholars, presented her with a set of silver Tea-Knives, and a silver inkstand. The Rector made a few suitable remarks, and the children showed great appreciation of their Teacher.
July 7th	Average attendance 50.6. Percentage 99.2.
July 10th	John Edworthy has left to go to Torrington School.

WEARE GIFFARD CHURCH OF ENGLAND SCHOOL LOG BOOK 1900 - 1945

1911

July 14th	Five children are absent today. Gone to a Sunday School Treat. Average attendance 47.9. Percentage 95.8.
July 17th	Today I have received the Scripture Report. The following is a Copy:-

	Infants	Group I, II, III
Knowledge of:		
Catechism	-	V.G.
Prayer Book	-	V.G.
New Testament	E	V.G.
Old Testament	E	V.G.
Written Work	-	V.G.
Repetition of:		
Catechism	-	V.G.
Private Prayers and Collects	-	V.G.
Holy Scripture	E	V.G.
Hymns	-	V.G.

The Infant Division did excellently and were nice, bright children, and knew their Bible stories very well indeed, and deserve great praise. In the Upper Division there seemed to be something lacking. No doubt this division will greatly improve as time goes on, and the new Head Teacher has had more time. The answering was in the hands of a few children, and many did not answer at all. I would suggest that the Bible should be taught so as to be of more practical use to the children, that lessons to be applied to the daily lives of the children should have special mention. I feel sure that this school will do very much better in the future. There is an excellent, and orderly, tone about the school.
Discipline, Tone : - Excellent. The school is classed as Very Good.
Inspector: The Rev. E. Bramwell, Exeter Diocesan Inspector.
The following deserve Honourable Mention: Marion Banbrook, Olive Moore, Reginald Wise, John Edworthy, Ernest Clements, Bertha Parkhouse, Gwennie Wise, Hilda Gomer, Walter Fisher, Thomas Wilton, Horace Clements.
Infants: Florence Gilbert, Winnie Edworthy, Miriam Squire, Mollie Slee, Alice Gilbert, Mary Westlake, Willie Tucker.

July 21st	Average attendance 47.2. Percentage 96.3.
July 22nd	22 children are absent all day, owing to the Wesleyan Treat at Westward Ho!

WEARE GIFFARD CHURCH OF ENGLAND SCHOOL LOG BOOK
1900 - 1945

1911

July 28th	Average attendance 42.3. Percentage 86.3. The attendance this week has been spoilt entirely by the absence of those who attended the Treat. I wish to record, however, that the children came well the following day, none remaining home, except Lilian Colvill, who is not well. I consider this very creditable to parents and children. School closed today for Midsummer Holiday.
September 4th	School re-opened today. Ernest Clements and May Braunton have left, the former to go to Bideford for 12 months, the latter left altogether, being over-age.
September 8th	Average attendance 48.1. Percentage 98.1. Mrs Hammett commenced duty on Monday as Assistant Mistress in this school - Supplementary. I have removed Miss Davey to take Standards I, II, III for the present at any rate.
September 11th	Mollie Slee and Cora Slee have left as the family are removing to Bovey Tracey. I am very sorry to lose such bright, nice little girls. Kindergarten material received this morning from Messrs. Rudd. (15.6 average no. on books.)
September 12th	This morning I received the Result of the Examination for the Lovering Scholarship. Mr Kelly of Langtree was the Examiner. Max: No. of Marks 300. Result: Olive Moore 202, James Grigg 201, Reginald Wise 200, Ernest Clements 171, Ethel Short 106. The Scholarship, tenable at Edge Hill College, Bideford, therefore goes to Olive Moore.
September 15th	Average attendance 46.8. Percentage 99.5. We have missed 100% by 2 attendances, Walter Fisher being absent to go to Barnstaple Fair.
September 18th	Visited the school and found the Registers had just been tested by one of the Managers and everything was in order. J.Groves Cooper.
September 22nd	Average attendance 43.4. Percentage 92.3. Olive Moore has left, having commenced attendance at Edge Hill College.
September 26th	Today I have commenced examining the whole school.

WEARE GIFFARD CHURCH OF ENGLAND SCHOOL LOG BOOK
1900 - 1945

1911

September 28th	This morning I have examined the Infants, in reading. I left Miss Davey in charge of the two Upper Divisions to take an Object Lesson. The order was excellent.
September 29th	Average attendance 45. Percentage 97.8.
October 2nd	Requisition received from Messrs Arnold and entered in Stock Book.
October 6th	Miss Davey went at 2.30 this afternoon to catch a train. Average attendance 45.7. Percentage 99.2.
October 9th	Miss Davey is absent this morning as she could not well return from Plympton yesterday (Sunday).
October 13th	Average attendance 44.5. Percentage 96.7.
October 17th	Mr Sing, Attendance Superintendent, visited the school - looked at Registers, Admission Register, etc.
October 18th	Mr Bright, H.M.I., visited the school this morning. All the children were present.
October 20th	The Rector visited this morning. Average attendance 46.7. Percentage 99.3.
October 23rd	Doris Chamings absent, suffering from Ringworm. William Hammett gone to Torrington School, no reason assigned. I presume it is owing to being reproved for bad behaviour. He was improving in his work, and on this score I am sorry he has gone.
October 24th	William Hammett it appears has not left. He has postponed his departure till the Spring.
October 27th	Average attendance 44.6. Percentage 94.8.
November 1st	Rector visited, bringing Copy of Report of H.M.I. Appended is the Copy:- Devon County Authority, Wear Gifford C. of E. School, No. 510. Inspected on 18th October 1911. Report by H.M.I. Mr G.R.R. Routh. Mixed. The school is in good order, and the children are active, industrious, and attentive. Methods of instruction have been modified and improved, and considerable progress is seen, especially in Arithmetic, in the written Composition of the highest Class, and in Nature Study. The younger children are still backward in writing their thoughts, and the whole school needs more practice in expressing them orally. Some of the Handwriting needs improvement. The Infants are kindly taught and their progress is very fair, but some changes of method, especially in Reading, would be advantageous.

WEARE GIFFARD CHURCH OF ENGLAND SCHOOL LOG BOOK
1900 - 1945

1911

November 3rd	Average attendance 45.4. Percentage 96.5.
November 10th	Average attendance 46.7. Percentage 99.3.
November 13th	Mrs Rickards and Miss Carter visited school this morning. They expressed themselves highly pleased with the Needlework and Drawing. The Infants sang to them, also, which greatly interested them.
November 17th	Average attendance 46.3. Percentage 98.5.
November 24th	Average attendance 44.4. Percentage 94.4.
November 29th	The children have made a collection this week for Dr Barnardo's Homes. £1.3.6 has been forwarded to the Homes.
December 1st	Average attendance 44.4. Percentage 96.5.
December 7th	Torridge in flood. As so many children have to pass dangerous spots, I considered it wise to close school at 2.15. Consequently, I cancelled the attendances.
December 8th	Average attendance 44.2. Percentage 96.1.
December 11th	This week I am conducting an Examination throughout the school.
December 12th	Managers' Meeting. School closes Wednesday December 20th till January 8th 1912 for Xmas Holiday.
December 15th	Two little girls admitted this week from Frithelstock Parish. Average attendance 44.2. Percentage 92.
December 18th	Torridge rising rapidly again. Therefore school commenced at 1.15 and ended at 3.30.
December 20th	Average attendance 44.3. Percentage 92.3. Xmas Holiday commences today.

1912

January 8th	School re-opened. 3 children admitted from Allspill.
January 10th	Rector visited.
January 11th	Miss Davey absent this morning, ill. Ethel Martin has gone into Bideford Hospital, therefore I have removed her name from the books, temporarily. Miss Davey came this afternoon.
January 12th	Average attendance 47.4. Percentage 94.8.

WEARE GIFFARD CHURCH OF ENGLAND SCHOOL LOG BOOK
1900 - 1945

1912

January 15th	Mrs Hammett is absent, as her mother has met with an accident, and she is unable to leave her. She has informed the Chairman of Managers as well as myself. The Rector visited, and tested the Registers, this morning.
January 16th	The Managers have written to Mr Young asking that a Temporary Monitress may be appointed while Mrs Hammett is absent.
January 19th	Average attendance 48.2. Percentage 96.4.
January 22nd	Marion Banbrook with the approval of the Devon County Committee is acting as Monitress during the absence of Mrs Hammett.
January 26th	Average attendance 48.9. Percentage 97.8.
February 2nd	Am sending away to County Office for Attendance Certificates, 3 Perfect, 18 98%. Average attendance Percentage 96.2.
February 9th	Average attendance 47.8. Percentage 95.6.
February 16th	Average attendance 49.8. Percentage 97.6.
February 19th	Nita Beer reported suffering from Measles. Have therefore excluded the whole family. Doris Chamings excluded for Ringworm.
February 21st	Examined the registers and found them correct, 4 absent out of 52, on account of measles. The school is very much improved in tone. M. Maude Cooper.
February 23rd	Average attendance 47.3. Percentage 90.9.
March 1st	Average attendance 46. Percentage 88.4.
March 5th	Land waters are up: consequently several children are compelled to be at home, part of the road being impassable. I have discovered that Gladys Joliffe has measles. I have sent her home. There are only 33 children present. 11.20 a.m. I have cancelled the Marks, and sent the children home for the day as the roads are rapidly becoming impossible.
March 7th	Today I have received the Requisition (Stationery, etc.) from Messrs. Arnold. Have entered same in Stock Book.
March 8th	Average attendance 45.1. Percentage 86.7.
March 15th	Average 50.4. Percentage 95. New scholar admitted: Bruce Lake.
March 22nd	Average attendance 46.6. Percentage 87.9. Influenza colds account for this poor average. Bella Brimmacombe is leaving today. Family removed to Westleigh.
March 26th	Four children admitted - family from Littleham named Huxtable. Average 51. Percentage 91.

WEARE GIFFARD CHURCH OF ENGLAND SCHOOL LOG BOOK
1900 - 1945

1912

April 1st	This week I am conducting the Quarterly Examination in the two upper classes. Therefore Time Table is not being strictly followed.
April 4th	Average 54.3. Percentage 95.3. School closed this afternoon for Easter Holiday.
April 15th	School reopened. Two admissions, one a girl completing her attendances till the age of 14 (a week and 2 days), the other a little boy who has been extremely delicate and has been kept home until over school age.
April 17th	Today I am giving a lesson on the Solar Eclipse and taking First Class out in Playground to watch it.
April 19th	Average attendance 56.8. Percentage 96.2.
April 26th	Today I have received the Needlework Requisition: no more needlework material will be required this year as there is sufficient for the year, i.e. until February 1913. Average 56.4. Percentage 95.5.
May 3rd	Average attendance 55.5. Percentage 94. Yesterday school closed - Torrington Fair.
May 6th	Annie Pengilly has left having reached age of 14.
May 10th	Average 54.2. Percentage 93.4. Three children absent, others in family suffering from measles.
May 17th	Average attendance 51.1. Percentage 89.6. Bad attendance due to prevalence of influenza colds and coughs.
May 22nd	Very bad attendance still. Several children ill in bed, suffering from severe influenza colds - worst attendance I have seen in the school. Five children are also absent this afternoon to attend an Anniversary Tea at Gammaton. Altogether this will be a record for bad attendance.
May 24th	Today being Empire Day the children are singing patriotic songs and saluting the flag, those who are Boy Scouts attending in uniform. School closes today until June 3rd - Whitsun Holiday. Average attendance 48.9. Percentage 85.7. Worst attendance for more than 12 months - influenza colds.
June 3rd	School reopened. Leslie J. Beer, Infant, admitted. 54 present, 58 on books. Reginald Wise attended the Examination for County Scholarships on Saturday June 1st.
June 7th	Average attendance 54.7. Percentage 94.3.
June 13th	Miss Davey has received permission from the Managers to be absent this afternoon to attend a Garden Fete. Several children are absent owing to the Chapel Anniversary Tea.
June 20th	The Managers have given Miss Davey permission to be absent today as she is attending the Annual Meeting of G.F.S. at Ilfracombe.
June 21st	Average attendance 54.5. Percentage 93.9.

WEARE GIFFARD CHURCH OF ENGLAND SCHOOL LOG BOOK
1900 - 1945

1912

June 24th	Miss Davey is absent, ill, so I am taking both divisions. Managers' Meeting on Saturday 22nd. Holidays were decided on: August 2nd - September 2nd.
June 25th	Miss Davey is in school today. Scripture Examination this afternoon, so Registers will not be marked for afternoon session.
June 28th	Average attendance 57.8. Percentage 99.8.
July 2nd	Visited this morning. H. Beardsley.
July 3rd	So many children were absent this afternoon, in consequence of the Historic Pageant, that the Managers deemed it advisable to close the school.
July 5th	Average attendance 52.8. Percentage 91.1. Five children absent this week suffering from chicken pox.
July 11th	Another case of chicken pox.
July 12th	Average attendance 50.7. Percentage 87.4.
July 17th	Attendance very bad. More cases of chicken pox.
July 19th	Average attendance 46.8. Percentage 80.6.
July 26th	Average attendance 47.7. Percentage 83.6. Nita Beer's name removed from books, as she is under 5, and the distance is too great for her to attend school.
July 30th	Managers' Meeting last evening. They decided that the school should close tomorrow, Wednesday, for the Chapel outing.
August 2nd	Average attendance 40.8. Percentage 71.7. School closes today. Midsummer Holiday 4 weeks.
September 2nd	School reopened. Reggie Wise left, gone to Grammar School, having won Lovering Scholarship. James Squire left, gone to Torrington. Thomas Huxtable has been sent home as he has a ringworm.
September 3rd	Rector visited the school.
September 6th	Average attendance 47.8. Percentage 88.5.
September 9th	I was absent from school today by permission of the Managers.
September 13th	Average attendance 48.1. Percentage 89.

WEARE GIFFARD CHURCH OF ENGLAND SCHOOL LOG BOOK
1900 - 1945

1912

September 16th	I sent James Squire home as his father had not answered the letter I sent him regarding insolent behaviour on the boy's part. I am writing to the Managers regarding the matter.
September 17th	Managers met yesterday. I reported the action I had taken with regard to James Squires.
September 20th	Average attendance 46.3. Percentage 87.3.
September 27th	Average attendance 48.3. Percentage 92.8.
September 30th	Today I resign charge of this school. Emily G. Sobey.
October 1st	I have taken temporary charge of this school today. Clara Saunders.
October 3rd	Half holiday for the Church Harvest Festival.
October 23rd	Checked the Registers and found them correct. Clifford Rickards (Manager).
October 28th	The school could not be carried on today, on account of the Torridge being flooded.
November 4th	I (Thirza W. Mancy) have this day begun my duties as Head Teacher of this school. Medical Inspection during the morning. The Doctor examined nineteen children, and several parents were present. Mrs Rickards and Miss Groves Cooper visited during the morning. 10 cwt of coal was received for school use.
November 6th	Attendance Officer visited.
November 8th	Emily Huxtable found to be suffering from ringworm, and excluded in consequence. Average attendance for the week 48.1. 52 on books, percentage 92.5.
November 11th	Attendance Officer visited.
November 15th	Average for the week 45.4. Percentage 87.3.
November 22nd	Attendance Officer called, and reported that Frederick Martin is ill with measles. The absence of several children suffering from colds has affected the attendance. Average attendance 44.3. Percentage 86.8. Afternoon school will commence at 1.30 p.m. for the witer months, closing at 3.45 p.m., to allow children living at a distance to reach home before dark.
November 26th	A very stormy day. Very poor attendance, many of the absentees reported suffering from colds.
December 2nd	The Rector, the Rev. C. Rickards, visited this morning.
December 9th	Attendance Officer visited.
December 20th	Closed school this afternoon for Christmas holidays.

WEARE GIFFARD CHURCH OF ENGLAND SCHOOL LOG BOOK 1900 - 1945

1913

January 6th	Reopened school this morning after Christmas Holiday, with an attendance of 51. Admitted four children.
January 10th	Attendance Officer visited.
January 17th	Average attendance for the week 49. % 90.7.
January 20th	A very stormy morning. Only 44 children present.
January 24th	Visited. H. Beardsley.
February 3rd	The Rector visited, and checked the registers.
February ?19th?	The Rector and Mrs Rickards visited and presented attendance certificates to eight scholars, John Pengilly, Louis Pengilly, Wm. Gilbert, Alice Gilbert, Bertha Parkhouse, Richard Moore, Gladys Joliffe, and Horace Clements.
February 28th	Attendance Officer visited.
March 5th	Received supplies of school stationery from Messrs. Arnold & Co., without an invoice, so am writing to the contractors about the matter.
March 10th	Received invoice for school stationery.
March 12th	The Sanitary Inspector, Mr R. Gomer, visited and inspected the premises. He took samples of the school water supply.
March 21st	Closed school this afternoon for Easter holiday.
March 31st	School reopened with an attendance of 50. Admitted two new scholars, and removed the names of four children who have left: three have moved to another district, and James Squire has gone to Torrington Boys' School.
April 4th	The Attendance Officer visited. Average for the week 49.6, being 99.2%.
April 16th	A very wet morning. Only 33 children present out of 50 on books.
April 21st	Found Gladys Joliffe suffering from ringworm and have sent her home.
April 23rd	Several children reported to be suffering from whooping cough.
April 24th	Only 24 present out of 50 on books this morning.
April 30th	Very poor attendance this morning. 32 only present. Ten children excluded through whooping cough. The Rector visited, and checked the registers.
May 1st	School closed for the day (Torrington Fair).

WEARE GIFFARD CHURCH OF ENGLAND SCHOOL LOG BOOK
1900 - 1945

1913

May 2nd	Three further cases of whooping cough reported. Lilian Colvill found to have ringworm, and consequently excluded. Average for the week 33.5, only 67%.
May 8th	A very stormy morning, consequently the attendance is very low, only 19 children present. On the advice of the Rector the school was closed for the afternoon.
May 9th	School closed for Whitsuntide holiday. Average for the week 29.7, the lowest recorded for some time.
May 19th	Re-opened school with an attendance of 35. Re-admitted William and Florence Gilbert, who have returned from Yarnscombe. As only 3 Infants and Standard I are in attendance, the remaining 9 being excluded with whooping cough, Miss Davey is in charge of Standards II and III, giving the monitor Marion Banbrook time for private study. Average for the week 33.6, being only 64.6%.
May 27th	Miss Cassell, H.M.I., visited during the morning.
May 30th	Miss Davey, who is emigrating to the United States, left the school this afternoon. Mrs Rickards on behalf of the Managers, Staff, Scholars and friends presented her with a gold bracelet and silver inkstand as a token of esteem in which she is held. The Rector made a few suitable remarks and the children showed great appreciation of their teacher. Mr Groves Cooper was present, and heard the children sing.
June 2nd	The School Attendance Superintendent, J. Loftus Sing Esq., visited. The monitress, Marion Banbrook, took charge of Infants and Standard I today, as no assistant has yet been appointed in place of Miss Davey.
June 3rd	Miss L. Ellis, on supply, commenced duties this morning.
June 6th	Attendance for the week much improved, though a wet day on Friday prevented several who come from a distance from being present. Many who have been excluded through whooping cough are now back to school.
June 13th	Attendance improved this week. 44.8 average, 89.6%.
June 24th	Diocesan Inspection this afternoon. Registers not marked in consequence.
June 25th	School closed - whole day's holiday.
June 26th	Afternoon session commenced half an hour earlier on account of the Chapel Anniversary tea.
June 30th	Checked the Registers and found them correct and the school in good order. J. Groves Cooper.
July 3rd	Charles Huxtable found to have ringworm and is consequently excluded.

WEARE GIFFARD CHURCH OF ENGLAND SCHOOL LOG BOOK
1900 - 1945

1913

July 6th	The Rector visited bringing the Diocesan Inspector's report. Appended is a copy:- Date of Examination: June 24th 1913.
Knowledge of	Infants Groups I, II, III Catechism F. to G. Prayer Book F. to G. New Testament E. G. Old Testament V.G. F. to V.G.
Repetition of	Catechism V.G. Private Prayers & Collects E. E. Holy Scripture E. V.G. Hymns E. E. The Infants seemed to be very bright and attentive, having learnt a good number of Hymns, Prayers, Texts, and showing also a good knowledge of the stories from the Old and New Testament. The work of the Seniors is a little uncertain, but a few of them have derived some useful lessons of Faith and Life from a careful study of the Old Testament. More attention might be given to the explanation of words in the Hymns and passages of Scripture. Discipline and Tone : Very Good. Scholars on Books: 52 Scholars present at Inspection : 51 The School is classed as Very Good. Inspector: The Rev. C.A. Curgenven.
July 15th	The average attendance for the week is 52.8, being 96% - the best recorded for some time.
July 23rd	School closed for the day, on account of the Chapel outing to Westward Ho!
July 25th	Terminal examination this week. Time Table not strictly followed in consequence. Florence Gilbert absent through sickness since Wednesday. Thomas and William Wilton and Fred: Martin away ill all the week.
August 1st	School closed today for Summer holiday (4 weeks).
September 1st	Re-opened school with an attendance of 50 children.
September 10th	Only 43 children in attendance this afternoon. Harvest Festival at Gurmeston Moor

WEARE GIFFARD CHURCH OF ENGLAND SCHOOL LOG BOOK
1900 - 1945

1913

September 16th	The Medical Inspector visited (Dr W. Horton Date) and examined 10 children during the morning. Two parents were present.
September 19th	Several children absent, gone to Barnstaple Fair, much reducing the average for the week.
September 24th	School closed this afternoon for Harvest Thanksgiving Festivities.
October 3rd	Several children absent during the week suffering from colds. Bruce Lake has rheumatc fever. Average for the week has fallen to 46.7, being 84.9%.
October 10th	Average for the week has slightly improved, being 47.2 or 87.4%. The name of Edwin Chamings, who has gone to Bideford Grammar School, has been removed from the registers.
October 17th	Attendance much improved this week, 50.2 or 92.9%.
October 22nd	The Rector, the Rev. C. Rickards, visited.
November 13th	W. Bright, H.M.I., visited this morning: 52 children present.
November 21st	A very wet day: only 43 out of 54 children present. Otherwise the attendance for the remainder of the week was very good.
December 2nd	The Rector visited, and checked the registers.
December 19th	School closed this afternoon for Christmas Holidays (two weeks). Received notice from Mr J. Loftus Sing that Doris Beer was to be admitted.

1914

January 5th	Re-opened school this morning. Only 40 children present. Admitted four new scholars, three named Perryman from Heavitree, and Doris Beer from Huntshaw. Mr R. Gomer has notified me that Elsie, Frances, John, and Alfred Baker are suffering from Scarlet Fever.
January 9th	Attendance for the week 44.4, being only 77.8%. Several children have been absent all the week, reported suffering from colds and influenza.
January 15th	10 cwt coke and 8 cwt coal received for school use.
January 16th	The Rector visited, and notified that he had received notice from W. Young, the Education Secretary, that the Board of Education recommended that Miss Lilian Ellis should receive a fortnight's training at Great Torrington Infants' Council School, commencing on Monday February 2nd. The attendance has slightly improved during the week, being 47.6 average attendance or 83.5%.

WEARE GIFFARD CHURCH OF ENGLAND SCHOOL LOG BOOK
1900 - 1945

1914

February 2nd	Miss Ellis today commenced a fortnight's training at Torrington Council Infants' School. In consequence Marion Banbrook is taking charge of the Infants and Standard I during their teacher's absence.
February 5th	Visited. H. Beardsley.
February 12th	Mr R. Gomer, Sanitary Inspector, visited and reported that the Baker family were now free from infection and should return to school on Monday next, February 16th. A wet and stormy afternoon, only 42 children present out of a possible 56.
February 20th	The Rev. C. Rickards visited, and checked the registers. The attendance has slightly improved this week, being 51.9 average or 92.6%.
March 2nd	The monitress, Marion Banbrook, is absent from duty this morning. Her mother sent a note in the afternoon saying she was ill.
March 5th	Marion Banbrook returned to duty this morning. Miss L. Ellis, Supplementary Teacher, absent this afternoon suffering from an abscess in her face.
March 6th	Miss Ellis still away ill. During her absence the Infants and Standard I Division are in charge of the monitress. The attendance during the week has much improved, especially amongst the infants. Average for the week 52.2 or 91.5%.
March 9th	The school could not be carried on today on account of the Torridge being flooded. At 9.30 only 4 children were present, and on the advice of the Rector school was closed for the day. Miss Ellis returned to duty.
March 10th	William Charnings found to have ringworm, and is consequently excluded. Marion Banbrook is again absent from duty this morning.
March 11th	Received a notification from Mr R. Gomer that Jessie Jeffery has Scarlet Fever. As he advises the exclusion of children under 5 years for 14 days, five children are consequently excluded for that period, on the Sanitary Inspector's responsibility.
March 12th	The Torridge again in flood. By 12 o'clock the roads were becoming impassable, and it was deemed advisable to close school for the rest of the day on the advice of the Rector.
March 16th	The monitress, Marion Banbrook, resumed work this morning. Only 37 children present this morning out of a possible 57.
March 20th	Much sickness prevails among the children, consequently the average for the week has fallen to 43.2, being only 75.7%.
March 27th	The names of Wilfred, Henrietta and Ellen Shute have been removed from the register as they have removed to Bideford. Many children have been away ill during the week, further reducing the average to 39.8, 72.2%, the lowest recorded this quarter.

WEARE GIFFARD CHURCH OF ENGLAND SCHOOL LOG BOOK
1900 - 1945

1914

April 3rd	The average attendance is still very low, being only 39.6 or 72%. Many children still absent with colds etc. Admitted Nita Beer, over 6 years of age. This child has attended no school since leaving Weare Giffard school in July 1912.
April 9th	School closed this afternoon for Easter Holidays, until April 20th.
April 20th	School re-opened this morning: 51 present. Admitted two new scholars, both infants.
May 5th	Received notice from the Sanitary Inspector that Elsie Braddon is ill with Scarlet Fever and is excluded for 42 days.
May 7th	School closed for the day. Torrington Fair.
May 8th	The Rector visited, bringing notice of Diocesan Inspection to be held on Thursday, June 18th, at 10 a.m.
May 10th	Removed the name of Annie Huxtable from the registers by permission of the Attendance Committee: though over five years of age, on account of distance and delicate health she is to be exempt for twelve months.
May 13th	Miss Ellis is absent suffering from sore throat and neuralgia. Marion Banbrook, the monitress, is in charge of Infants and Standard I.
May 14th	Miss Ellis still absent.
May 15th	Miss Ellis returned to duty this morning. The monitress, M. Banbrook, is absent this morning.
May 22nd	Mr W. Bright, H.M.I., visited during the afternoon session.
May 27th	Attendance very poor this morning, and further reduced this afternoon owing to Anniversary Tea at Gammaton Moor.
May 28th	Mr R. Gomer, the Sanitary Inspector, visited and inspected the premises. He notified that Doris and Nita Beer were suffering with Scarlet Fever. The whole family of five scholars are consequently excluded. Seven children are now excluded owing to epidemic sickness. The Rector visited and notified that the Managers had decided that the school should close immediately and that the Whitsuntide holiday should be prolonged until June 15th. This had been decided upon the advice of the Sanitary Inspector, in view of the number of cases of Scarlet Fever. Closed school for Whitsuntide holiday until June 15th.
July 6th	School re-opened at 9 a.m. - 49 present, also Miss Ellis (Infants Teacher) and myself (Thomas A. Wing), temporarily head teacher owing to illness of the permanent head teacher, Mrs Mancy. The monitress is absent. The monitress, Miss Banbrook, is present this afternoon.
July 17th	Clifford Rickards.
July 22nd	The school closed this afternoon (Wednesday) till Friday, owing to chapel treat tomorrow.
August 5th	School closed this afternoon for local flower show.

WEARE GIFFARD CHURCH OF ENGLAND SCHOOL LOG BOOK 1900 - 1945

1914

August 6th	School closed after school this afternoon for summer holidays till September 7th. After spending five pleasant weeks in Weare Giffard, and receiving every help from Managers and Teachers, I sever reluctantly my connection with this school. Thomas A. Wing.
September 7th	Re-opened school this morning after the summer holidays. 54 children present out of 57 on books. Miss Ellis unable to be present today, so the Infants have been in charge of the monitress, M. Banbrook. I have received the report on the result of the examination for the Lovering Scholarship held in the school room on Saturday, August 8th. There were five candidates, and Mr Kelly, of Langtree, was the examiner. He reports that he found the quality of all the work much above the average of that of candidates who were examined by him in previous years at Weare Giffard. Maximum number of marks 300. Hilda Gomer 285 Gwendoline Wise 250 Bertha Parkhouse 212 John Banbrook 185 Richard Moore 185. The trustees have decided to award two scholarships, tenable for three years, at Edgehill College, Bideford, to Hilda Gomer and Gwendoline Wise.
September 8th	Miss Ellis resumed duty this morning.
September 18th	The attendance this week has not been quite so good as last week. Average 51.9 or 94%.
September 25th	Attendance this week the best recorded for over two years, being 53.5 or 97.2%.
October 5th	The monitress, Marion Banbrook, has been absent all day, ill. Admitted four boys named Langmead, who have removed into the district from Monkleigh.
October 6th	The monitress resumed duty this morning.
October 19th	Received notice from Dr E.J. Slade-King, M.O.H., that William Tucker, Charles Tucker and Rex Smith were to be excluded from school for 21 days, having been in contact with a fatal case of diphtheria at Annery Kiln Cottage.
November 13th	Attendance this week much improved, being 60.2 or 97%.
November 23rd	The monitress, Marion Banbrook, has been absent all day suffering from sore throat.
November 30th	The monitress returned to duty this morning after a week's absence.
December 7th	The School Medical Inspector, Dr W. Horton Date, visited and examined 24 children during the morning. Miss Cunningham, the School Nurse, was present, and several parents attended. Two children, Alfred and William Chamings, are excluded on account of ringworm.

WEARE GIFFARD CHURCH OF ENGLAND SCHOOL LOG BOOK 1900 - 1945

1914

December 11th	Received notice from Dr W. Horton Date that William Chamings is not to be exluded further, as his ringworm is negative. Mrs Rickards and Miss Walton visited and saw the children at work, afterwards hearing their songs. Clifford Rickards, Chairman.
December 18th	Closed school this afternoon for Christmas holiday, two weeks.

1915

January 4th	Reopened school after Christmas holiday with an attendance of 58. The monitress, Marion Banbrook, absent all day.
January 12th	H. Jervis.
January 25th	Alfred Chamings, now medically certified to be free from ringworm, attended school this morning.
January 29th	Attendance for the week much improved, being 58.6 or 97.6%.
February 12th	The attendance during the week has been badly affected by influenza colds among the children.
February 19th	The attendance has been seriously affected this week by influenza colds among the children. Out of 57 on books only 37.9 or 66.4% have been present.
March 10th	Miss Ellis absent all day, ill. The Infants have been today in charge of the monitress, Marion Banbrook.
March 11th	Miss Ellis still absent. The monitress is also absent and has not notified me the reason. As I am working the school single-handed, time table not strictly adhered to.
March 12th	Miss Ellis ill with pneumonia. Monitress still absent. School worked as yesterday.
March 15th	Marion Banbrook returned to duty. This week she has been in charge of the Infants. Three children have been excluded with whooping cough.
April 1st	Closed school this afternoon for Easter holiday.
April 12th	Re-opened school this morning after Easterholiday with an attendance of 57. Admitted four new scholars. As Miss Ellis is still unfit for duty, the Infant Class is in charge of the Monitress, M.Banbrook.
April 15th	Mr Butler, H.M.I., visited during afternoon session.
April 20th	Seven children are excluded owing to chicken pox.
April 26th	Miss Ellis returned to duty.
April 30th	Chicken pox on the increase, 18 children being excluded.

WEARE GIFFARD CHURCH OF ENGLAND SCHOOL LOG BOOK 1900 - 1945

1915

May 6th	Miss Davies, Organizing Inspectress, D.C.E.C., visited during the morning.
May 7th	The weekly average has fallen to 40.3 or 66%, chiefly owing to chicken pox epidemic.
May 13th	The School Medical Inspector, Dr J.H. Lightbody, inspected 20 children during the morning. Several parents were present.
May 21st	School closed this afternoon for Whitsun holiday of one week.
May 31st	Re-opened school this morning with an attendance of 61. The monitress, M. Banbrook, absent without notice. M. Banbrook present in the afternoon.
June 4th	Attendance for the week greatly improved, being 59.6 or 94.6%.
June 18th	School closed this afternoon for a fortnight to enable the children to help with the hay harvest and strawberry picking, owing to scarcity of labour caused by the war.
July 5th	Re-opened school this morning with an attendance of 56. The monitress, Marion Banbrook, absent all day.
July 6th	M. Banbrook still absent.
July 13th	The Rector informed me that M. Banbrook had resigned her post as monitress.
July 22nd	School closed for the day for the Chapel Outing to Westward Ho!
July 31st	The examination of candidates for the Lovering Scholarship took place in the school room this morning at 10 a.m. Mr Kelly was the examiner.
August 2nd	A very stormy morning. As only 25 children were present out of a possible 65, it was deemed advisable to abandon the school meeintg.
August 6th	Percentage for the week 85%, Average 55.
August 13th	School closed this afternoon for the summer holiday, 4 weeks.
September 13th	Re-opened school with an attendance of 58. The result of the examination for the Lovering Scholarship has been received. Two candidates sat, whose marks are as follows (possible 300):- Marie Banbrook 164 Richard Moore 130. The Trustees have elected Marie Banbrook to the scholarship, tenable for three years, at Edgehill College, Bideford

WEARE GIFFARD CHURCH OF ENGLAND SCHOOL LOG BOOK
1900 - 1945

1915

September 20th	Bertha Parkhouse commenced duty as temporary monitress.
October 1st	Several children are absent this week suffering with severe colds. The average has fallen to 45.4 or 79.6% for the week.
October 6th	A bad attendance this afternoon. Several children absent on account of the Chapel Harvest Tea at Gammaton Moor. Only 40 present in school.
October 8th	The average attendance this week shows a slight improvement, being 47.3 or 86.8%. Winifred Edworthy's name has been removed as she is going to reside at West Worlington with her grandmother. This is the eleventh name removed from the roll since September 13th.
October 18th	Miss Ellis absent suffering from cold and sore throat.
October 21st	As Miss Ellis is still unfit for duty and the new temporary monitress is the only help I have, the time table cannot be strictly adhered to. Today, being Trafalgar Day, the whole school were assembled for the last half hour during morning session, to have a lesson on The British Navy, concluding with the National Anthems of the Allies.
November 1st	Miss Ellis, owing to ill-health, has sent in her resignation the Managers. The doctor orders her a month's rest.
November 12th	Dr Lightbody visited the school this morning at 9 a.m., remaining about twenty minutes to examine the children whom he inspected on his visit of May 13th. Miss R. Start commenced duty this morning as Supplementary Assistant.
November 15th	Found Daniel Perryman has ringworm, and have excluded him.
November 17th	The Monitress, B. Parkhouse, absent all day by permission of the Managers.
November 19th	Miss Cunningham, the School Nurse, visited this morning and examined the girls.
November 24th	Called the Registers and found them correct. Clifford Rickards.
December 3rd	A wet stormy morning. Only 43 children present out of a possible 57.
December 13th	Owing to the choir boys being required for the funeral of Mrs Balsdon, Sen., the Managers requested that afternoon school should commence at 1 p.m. All lessons were consequently taken half an hour earlier than usual.
December 21st	Closed school this afternoon for Christmas holidays, until January 10th 1916.

1916

January 10th	Re-opened school this morning. 47 children present.
January 13th	Six of the elder girls today began a course of cookery lessons, the class being held at Road Cliff by Miss E. Pycroft with the sanction of the Devon County Education Committee.

WEARE GIFFARD CHURCH OF ENGLAND SCHOOL LOG BOOK
1900 - 1945

1916

January 19th	W. Butler Esq., H.M.I., visited the school and remained during morning session. I excluded Wm. Tucker as he is apparently suffering with measles.
January 20th	A heavy thunderstorm just before nine this morning reduced the attendance this morning, only 34 children being present, out of 52 on books.
February 10th	As the Torridge was in flood and the roads were becoming impassable, it was impossible to open school this afternoon. Consequently the school meeting was abandoned.
February 24th	A heavy fall of snow has lowered the attendance today, only 40 children being present out of a possible 53. The cookery class could not be held today. Miss Pycroft has notified the authorities and hopes to be able to take the lessons next Thursday as usual. Visit of inspection. H. Jervis (Inspector D.C.E.C.)
March 3rd	Snowstorms and inclement weather have affected the attendance this week and several children have been absent all the week with colds. Average 43.4 or 80% out of a possible 54. Miss R.M. Start terminated her engagement as temporary supplementary assistant today after three months' satisfactory service.
March 6th	Miss Hilda Lindsay late of Poltimore School commenced duty today as a supplementary teacher.
April 20th	School closed after afternoon session for Easter holiday till May 1st.
May 1st	Reopened school this morning with an attendance of 50. Four new scholars admitted.
May 12th	Average for the week 50.5 or 93.5, a slight improvement on the attendance for the previous week.
May 17th	Winifred Edworthy has ringworm and is consequently excluded.
May 24th	Today being Empire Day a short lecture was given by the head teacher and the children sang patriotic songs and saluted the flag instead of the usual lessons from 11 to 12. The Rector and Mr Groves Cooper who had intended addressing the children were prevented by indisposition from doing so. A half holiday was given in the afternoon.
June 8th	Dr Lightbody, School Medical Inspector, visited at 2 p.m. and examined twenty seven children. The School Nurse Miss Cunningham assisted the doctor and several parents were present. The Rector, the Rev C. Rickards, and Miss Carter also visited during the examination.
June 9th	School closed this afternoon for Whitsun holiday of one week.

WEARE GIFFARD CHURCH OF ENGLAND SCHOOL LOG BOOK
1900 - 1945

1916

July 5th	Mistress absent this afternoon by permission of the Managers.
July 20th	Diocesan Inspection. 50 children present. Holiday given in the afternoon.
July 21st	Two cases of whooping cough reported this week by the parents of Lily Jolliffe and Dorothy Squires.
July 27th	School closed today for Wesleyan Outing to Westward Ho!
August 11th	School closed this afternoon for Harvest Holidays, 6 weeks.
September 25th	School reopened this morning with an attendance of 42. Two new scholars admitted.
September 29th	Miss Castelle, H.M.I., visited, and remained during the morning session. Richard Moore has left to attend Bideford Grammar School, having been awarded the Lovering Scholarship.
October 2nd	Slight alterations in the Time Table will in future be made to allow girls to have 1 hour's drawing weekly instead of half an hour only. Drawing will be taken in all standards from 2 to 3 p.m. on Thursday afternoons. Composition will be taken instead of History on Wednesday mornings from 11.30 to 12, and History will take the place of Moral Instruction on Wednesday afternoons from 3.40 to 4.10, the last half hour's lesson.
November 17th	A very stormy day has interfered with the attendance. Lilian Isaac has returned to school after being absent owing to debility since August.
December 14th	Wintry weather and the slippery state of the roads have interfered with the attendance today, only 40 children out a possible 50 being present.
December 19th	Owing doubtless to the slippery state of the roads, only 18 children out of a possible 50 were present. On the advice of the Rector therefore the school meeting was abandoned and registers not marked. The 18 children were retained in school during the morning, until the roads had thawed enough to enable them to reach their homes in safety.
December 20th	Only 13 children attended this morning. School was therefore closed until January 8th for the Christmas holiday on the Rector's advice. The bad weather conditions are as yesterday.

1917

January 8th	Reopened school after Christmas holiday. Two new scholars admitted.
January 26th	Bitterly cold wintry weather has this week interfered with the attendance, the average for the week being only 46.7 out of a possible 52.

WEARE GIFFARD CHURCH OF ENGLAND SCHOOL LOG BOOK
1900 - 1945

1917

February 9th	Attendance has been seriously affected this week by continued severity of the weather. Average attendance only 42.1 for the week, being only 80%.
February 16th	Attendance has this week slightly improved to an average of 46.7.
February 21st	Checked the Attendance Register and found it correct. Several children were absent owing to illness. Clifford Rickards.
February 22nd	Miss Lindsay absent suffering with a sore throat.
February 23rd	Miss Lindsay resumed duty.
March 1st	Miss Lindsay absent all day with a bad cold.
March 6th	Received a medical certificate regarding Ivy Edworthy, who is not fit to attend school for the present.
March 7th	Dorothy Hammett is medically certified as unfit to attend school until further notice.
March 8th	Leonard Beer is again in attendance. This boy has been absent since August last, undergoing medical treatment.
March 9th	A heavy fall of snow resulted in an attendance of only 18 children. Consequently on the advice of the Rector, as many of the children were wet-footed, the school meeting was abandoned.
March 22nd	I came to the school and heard the children recite and sing and was very pleased and I think there was great improvement. M. Maude Cooper.
April 2nd	Wintry weather has today interfered with the attendance. 38 children present out of a possible 51.
April 5th	School closed after afternoon session for Easter Holiday till April 16th.
April 16th	School re-opened this morning after Easter holiday. 42 children present. Miss Lindsay absent owing to illness.
April 18th	Miss Lindsey returned to duty.
April 19th	W. Butler Esq. H.M.I. visited during the morning session.
May 2nd	Miss Lindsay absent this afternoon by permission of the Managers.
May 11th	Attendance this week the best recorded for some time, being 46.6 or 97%.
May 25th	School closed this morning for Whitsuntide holiday till June 4th.
June 4th	Reopened school after Whitsuntide holiday with an attendance of 48. Admitted 2 new scholars.
June 11th	I have discovered that William Nethercott has ringworm, and have sent him home.

WEARE GIFFARD CHURCH OF ENGLAND SCHOOL LOG BOOK 1900 - 1945

1917

June 18th	Miss Lindsay absent this morning by permission of the Managers.
June 27th	School closed this afternoon for the Children's Pageant at Bideford.
July 3rd	J. Loftus Sing Esq., Superintendent of Attendance, visited and examined the registers this morning.
July 11th	Diocesan Inspection by the Rev. E.F. Hall. 44 children present. Holiday given in the afternoon. Wm. and Alfred Channings are excluded as a sister has measles.
July 27th	Diocesan Report received today, of which the following is a copy:- Date of Inspection: July 11th 1917. Scholars on the Books - 51 Present at Inspection - 44 Infants' Class Hymns and Texts had been intelligently memorised in connection with the Bible stories. This class showed, by a bright and happy response, a keen interest in and a good knowledge of the Bible stories. These had evidently been presented in a manner likely to appeal to the little ones. If it is possible to provide a small selection of large Bible pictures, it would be of much value. The use of "Child Songs" in addition to Hymns A. & M. would be welcomed. Senior Class (Stds II to VI) A capital class, keen and alert. The Church's teaching had been well grasped and the knowledge of the Catechism was particularly good. The Bible narrative had been carefully used in illustration and the general character of the work showed promise. Written work:- Good, intelligent papers. Repetition:- Well known and understood. Discipline and Tone:- A quiet, reverent tone gave character to the work. Present at Inspection: The Rector. (Signed) E.F. Hall, Diocesan Inspector.
August 3rd	School closed this afternoon for Summer holiday till September 11th.
September 17th	The harvest holiday was extended another four days, owing to the lateness of the corn harvest and consequently school was re-opened with morning with an attendance of 48.
October 4th	The weather has affected the attendance this morning, 13 children being absent.
October 22nd	Doris Beer found to be suffering with ringworm, and sent home.
October 26th	Miss Lindsay absent from duty today by permission of the Managers.
November 2nd	Several children have been absent during the week, with influenza colds, reducing the average attendance to 42 or 89.1%.
November 16th	Charles Langmead excluded, with running sores breaking out on his face.

WEARE GIFFARD CHURCH OF ENGLAND SCHOOL LOG BOOK 1900 - 1945

1917

November 30th	Dr Lightbody, School Medical Inspector, visited and examined eighteen children. Several parents were present.
December 3rd	W. Butler, Esq., H.M.I., visited, and remained during the morning.
December 7th	Miss Lindsay tendered her resignation as assistant mistress.
December 20th	School closed this afternoon for Christmas holidays until Jan. 8th. The Rev. C. Rickards visited and said good-bye to the children.

1918

January 8th	School re-opened this morning with an attendance of 44. As no assistant has yet come to take Miss Lindsay's place, the monitress is taking the infants temporarily. The school floor was scrubbed yestereday, January 7th. Mr J. Daubeny, the new School Correspondent in place of the Rev. C. Rickards, visited.
January 16th	School could not be carried on today, as the Torridge is in flood, and the land-waters, the highest for many years, made the roads impassable.
January 17th	A very wintry morning. Only 39 children present. By 2.45 p.m. the river had again risen so high and the road were becoming impassable that I was compelled to cancel the attendance marks for the afternoon and send the children home.
February 19th	Miss G.L. Banbrook commenced duty as Supplementary Teacher.
March 1st	Attendance this week has been very good, being 48.8 average attendance or 99.6%.
March 8th	Received notice from the Sanitary Inspector, Mr R. Gomer, that the boys of the Cox family are to be excluded on account of a case of measles in the home. These boys were only admitted to the school on Monday the 4th March from St Giles-in-the-Wood.
March 15th	Attendance this week the worst recorded for some time, being only 42.6 average or 83.5%. Several children absent all week with severe colds.
March 22nd	The Rector, the Rev. H.O. Cavalier, visited and checked the registers.
April 10th	H.O. Cavalier.
April 17th	H.O. Cavalier.
April 22nd	Instead of the usual history lessons this afternoon the children were taken to the church, where the Rector, the Rev. H.O. Cavalier, gave them a very interesting account of all points of historical interest.
May 1st	Received a medical certificate from Dr Toye, to the effect that Frances Baker is not in a fit state to attend school, unless half-time could be arranged.

WEARE GIFFARD CHURCH OF ENGLAND SCHOOL LOG BOOK
1900 - 1945

1918

May 3rd	The School Nurse visited, and examined all the children. She was much pleased with their clean condition.
May 9th	Instead of the usual Scripture lesson, the children went to church from 9 a.m. to 9.30 a.m. and a holiday was given in the afternoon.
May 16th	Received a medical certificate from Dr Pridham to the effect that Frederick Martin is unfit to attend school.
May 17th	Closed school this afternoon for Whitsun Holiday of one week.
May 27th	Re-opened school with an attendance of 51 out of a possible 55. The monitress, Bertha Parkhouse, was absent all day by permission of the Managers to attend her sister's wedding.
May 29th	H.O. Cavalier.
June 5th	Received a note from Mrs Moore, Polkinghorne, to the effect that her boy George has measles. He and his sister are consequently excluded.
June 10th	Only 42 present this morning out of a possible 57.
June 12th	Several more cases of measles are reported, and the attendance this afternoon fell to 30.
June 13th	Measles still increasing. Only 21 present this afternoon. The Rector, the Rev. H.O. Cavalier, visited and as he had received no reply from the Medical offier of Health with regard to closing the school.
June 14th	Attendance only 22, being only 37% or 63% absent. The Rector called, and as he had received no reply from Dr Slade-King, thought it advisable to close the school, especially as measles were excluding the children of the school house.
July 8th	Re-opened school this morning, with an attendance of 18 out of a possible 56.
July 12th	Average for the week 18.3 or 32.6%. This low percentage of attendance is the result of measles, which are still very prevalent. Owing to a case of diphtheria in the family, William and Walter Tucker are excluded.
July 23rd	Diocesan Inspection. 43 children were present. Miss R.F. Pennell was the examiner.
July 25th	W. Butler, Esq., H.M.I., visited and remained during the afternoon session.
July 26th	A very wet morning, only 32 children present. Several children absent with influenza.
July 29th	Attendance still affected by illness among the children. Further cases of influenza reported this morning; only 35 children present. J. Loftus Sing, Esq., Superintendent of Attendance, visited, and examined the registers.

WEARE GIFFARD CHURCH OF ENGLAND SCHOOL LOG BOOK 1900 - 1945

1918

July 31st	Diocesan Report received this morning, of which the following is a copy:- Date of Inspection: July 23rd 1918. Scholars present:- 43 No. on Books: - 56 General character of the work:- The Infants made a good response and knew their stories well; also their verses and hymns in connexion. It is a great gain that some of Nelson's Wall-pictures and Carey Bonner's Child Songs have been introduced. The Upper Group were keen and responsive. Evidently the progress that was made last year has been well maintained in the school, in spite of a good deal of sickness. Written work was carefully done. (Signed) Rosalie F. Pennell, Diocesan Inspector (Countersigned) Harold O. Cavalier, Correspondent.
August 8th	School closed after afternoon school for summer holiday of four weeks, to re-open on September 9th. Attendance for the week slightly improved to 76.2%. For the past month it has been the worst recorded for some years.
September 9th	School re-opened this morning with an attendance of 50.
September 30th	The river being in flood, and roads impassable, it was impossible to open school today.
October 1st	The Rector, the Rev. H.O. Cavalier, visited.
October 4th	Attendance this week has fallen to 90%, several boys being kept at home to work.
October 11th	Several children absent today suffering from influenza.
October 14th	Owing to the prevalence of influenza, Dr G. Adkins orders the school to be closed from October 14th to October 28th.
October 28th	As the serious influenza epidemic continues, Dr Adkins, the County Medical Officer of Health, order the further closure of the school till November 4th.
November 4th	School re-opened this morning with an attendance of 43.
November 5th	Mistress absent this afternoon, by permission of the managers. Miss Banbrook in charge.
November 15th	Visited. H. Beardsley.
November 22nd	Attendance this week far from good. Several children absent with colds.
December 2nd	Mrs Edworthy called to inform me that owing to the bad state of the lane by which her children pass, she refuses to send her three children, Frank, Joy and Mary, until the road is repaired. For this reason they have been absent all week.
December 19th	School closed this afternoon for Christmas holiday of a fortnight.

WEARE GIFFARD CHURCH OF ENGLAND SCHOOL LOG BOOK
1900 - 1945

1919

January 6th	School re-opened this morning after the Christmas holiday with an attendance of 49.
January 15th	Miss Banbrook absent, ill with cold and toothache.
January 16th	Miss Banbrook still absent.
January 17th	Miss Banbrook still absent. The attendance this week has been badly affected by colds, several children being absent. Average only 43.1 or 82%.
January 21st	Miss Banbrook resumed duty.
January 24th	Average for the week the worst recorded for some time, being only 37 or 72.5%.
February 14th	The School Nurse visited, and examined the girls. Notices sent to six parents with regard to cleanliness.
February 17th	Attendance very poor this morning, only 33 children present out of a possible 50. Absences chiefly due to colds.
March 3rd	Owing to the illness of the Head Teacher, Miss R.M. Luscombe, Uncertificated Teacher, commenced duties as Temporary Supply Teacher at this school on March 3rd.
March 5th	The Monitress, B. Parkhouse, is absent this afternoon, owing to illness.
March 6th	Miss Parkhouse resumed duty.
March 15th	Miss R.M. Luscombe terminated her duties here as temporary head teacher.
March 17th	I (T.W. Mancy) resumed duty after being absent through illness since February 18th
March 26th	The Rector, the Rev. H.O. Cavalier, visited and gave the usual Scripture lesson.
April 7th	School closed for the day, on account of the room being required for the Rural District Council Election.
April 14th	W. Butler, Esq., H.M.I., visited and remained during morning session.
April 17th	The Rector, the Rev. H.O. Cavalier, visited and gave a Scripture lesson. School closed this afternoon for the usual Easter holiday for one week.
April 28th	School re-opened this morning, after the Easter Holiday. Jessie Jeffery's mother called to inform me that Jessie is ordered by Dr Toye not to attend school for a month, owing to general debility.
May 12th	Fred Martin is ordered by his doctor, Dr Pridham, not to attend school for a few days. This boy has heart trouble.
May 29th	Instead of the usual Scripture lesson, this morning the children attended service in church from 9 a.m. to 9.40 (Ascension Day). Received notice, from the Rector, of the Diocesan Inspection to be held on June 26th at 9.30 a.m.

WEARE GIFFARD CHURCH OF ENGLAND SCHOOL LOG BOOK
1900 - 1945

1919

June 6th	Closed school this afternoon for Whitsun holiday of one week.
June 16th	Re-opened school this morning with an attendance of 47. Leslie Cox kept at home by parents, reported to be suffering with ringworm.
June 26th	Diocesan Inspection this morning at 9.30 a.m. Miss R.F. Pennell was the examiner. 47 children were present. Mrs Balsdon, one of the Managers, visited during the inspection.
June 30th	The Rector visited, bringing the report of the Diocesan Inspection which reads as follows:- Scholars on books: 50 Scholars present at inspection: Boys 24, Girls 23. Date of Inspection: June 26th 1919. Discipline and tone: Very satisfactory. General character of the work: Absence through sickness has much hindered the work amongst the Infants and their knowledge of Bible stories has suffered a good deal. Their little hymns were well known. The Upper Group knew their work, and responded well in the main, though they too have been affected by sickness. Prayers and hymns were reverently said and sung. (Signed) Rosalie F. Pennell, Diocesan Inspector. H.O. Cavalier
July 19th	Peace Celebration. Festivities were held in the schoolroom and Rectory Meadow. A procession of the school-children through the village commenced at 2 p.m. On their return, the flag was saluted (flying from the new flagstaff erected in the school yard by Mr A.M. Mancy, made from a tree given by Earl Fortescue). After a thanksgiving service in church, tea and sports were much enjoyed. During the afternoon, souvenir beakers were presented to all children of school age and under.
July 28th	W.P. Hiem, Esq., Chairman of the Devon County Education Committee, visited this morning.
July 31st	School closed for the day for Chapel Outing to Westward Ho!
August 8th	School closed this afternoon for the usual four weeks harvest holiday.
September 15th	Re-opened school this morning with an attendance of 49 out of a possible 50, after five weeks' holiday, the additional week being granted in celebration of peace. Doris Beer has been awarded the Lovering Scholarship, tenable for three years at Edgehill College, Bideford.
September 18th	Miss Castell, H.M.I., visited during the afternoon session.
September 19th	Miss J.D. Davies, Devon County Inspectress, visited, and inspected the needlework, during the afternoon.
September 19th	Roy Perryman has ringworm, and is consequently excluded.
September 29th	Dr W.J. Harper, School Medical Inspector, examined about thirty children at 2 p.m. this afternoon. Several parents were present

WEARE GIFFARD CHURCH OF ENGLAND SCHOOL LOG BOOK
1900 - 1945

1919

September 30th	Mrs Balsdon visited and checked the registers.
October 31st	Attendance this week seriously affected by colds. Doris and Marjory Moore, and Emma Chamings are excluded for impetigo.
November 6th	The monitress, Miss B.E. Parkhouse, absent today with a severe chill.
November 11th	Miss Parkhouse resumed duty. Today, Armistice Day, was observed in the school. In accordance with the King's desire, the children assembled after play at 11 o'clock, and after the names of those belonging to the village who had fallen in the Great War had been read out by the Rev. and Venerable Archdeacon Gilmore, two minutes' absolute silence was kept, in remembrance of the Glorious Dead.
November 20th	School closed for the day to allow of room being used for sale of work.
December 19th	School closed this afternoon for Christmas holiday, 2 weeks.

1920

January 5th	Re-opened school this morning after Christmas holiday. 47 out of 48 scholars present.
January 9th	The Rector, the Rev. H.O. Cavalier, visited and gave the Scripture lesson.
January 12th	The flooded state of the roads affected the attendance today.
January 14th	The School Nurse visited, and examined the girls.
February 6th	Registers signed. H.O. Cavalier.
March 29th	Owing to the serious illness of her mother and brother, the head mistress, with the approval of the Rector, is absent, and the school is left in charge of Miss Banbrook.
March 30th	The managers having decided that the school should close at once for the Easter holiday, the school was dismissed at 10 a.m. and the attendances registered were cancelled.
April 12th	School re-opened this morning after Easter holiday, with an attendance of 47. Three scholars were newly admitted. William Wilton is absent, reported suffering from ringworm.
April 29th	The school dentist visited, and examined and treated the teeth of 15 children, between the ages of 6 and 8 years. Several parents were present, and no objections were made.
April 30th	Attendance this week much improved. Average attendance 49 or 96%.

WEARE GIFFARD CHURCH OF ENGLAND SCHOOL LOG BOOK
1900 - 1945

1920

May 14th	The monitress, Bertha Parkhouse, was absent all day ill.
May 17th	Miss Parkhouse resumed duty.
May 21st	Closed school for Whitsun holiday, after afternoon session, for one week.
May 31st	Reopened school after Whitsuntide holiday.
June 13th	School flag flown at half-mast today on account of the funeral of Leslie John Beer (formerly a scholar of this school) who died on June 11th 1920 after a lingering illness. J. Loftus Sing, Esq., visited and examined the registers.
June 18th	Attendance for this week averages 55.1 or 98.3%. The Rev. H.O. Cavalier visited, and gave the usual Scripture lesson.
June 23rd	School closed for this afternoon, a half holiday being given for the Strawberry Tea and Fête in aid of School Funds for outside painting, etc.
July 12th	Diocesan Inspection this afternoon at 2.15 p.m. by Mr H. Hawkins, Diocesan Inspector. 55 out of a possible 56 were present, and the Rector, the Rev. H.O. Cavalier, remained during the examination.
July 21st	The Rector visited and gave a Scripture lesson. He had received a report from the Diocesan Inspector, a copy of which is as follows: Date of Inspection: July 12th 1920. Scholars on Books: 56. Scholars present at Inspection : 28 boys, 27 girls. The Book of Child Songs had been effectively used in the Infants Group. The children were attentive and several answered readily and accurately. The class as a whole, however, lacks life and an effort should be made to make the children more responsive, by giving greater attention to the expressive side of the work. In the Upper Group some painstaking teaching has been given, and the children were very attentive and appreciative. They showed interest and had been taught to think and to apply their knowledge to the needs of everyday life. The elder children gave some intelligent answers and they easily followed the various lines of thought. The Commandments and the Baptismal Covenant were well known and understood. A reverent atmosphere prevailed in the school. (Signed) Herbert H. Hawkins, Diocesan Inspector. H.O. Cavalier, July 21, 1920.
Diocesan Report	
July 22nd	Dr Walter Harper, the School Medical Inspector, visited at 10.15 a.m. and examined 15 children. Four parents were present.
July 23rd	The attendance has fallen this week to an average of 51.6 or only 92.1%. Three or four children are absent through illness.

WEARE GIFFARD CHURCH OF ENGLAND SCHOOL LOG BOOK
1900 - 1945

1920

July 28th	A half holiday was given this afternoon for a fete at Monkleigh, in aid of the District Nursing Association.
July 30th	The Rector, the Rev. H.O. Cavalier, visited and gave a Scripture lesson. School closed after afternoon session for summer holiday of four weeks.
August 30th	School re-opened this morning after the summer holiday with an attendance of 52. Three new scholars wee admitted. Thomas Woolridge, after being excluded for nearly three years owing to tubercular lung trouble, is now allowed by his medical attendant to attend school. The Lovering Scholarship has been awarded by the Trustees this year to Jessie Jeffery, who obtained a very good report from the examiner, Mr S. Kelly.
September 6th	J.J. Draper, Esq., H.M.I., visited and remained during the morning session.
September 8th	A whole day's holiday was given today for Sunday School and Choir Outing to Bideford Regatta.
September 16th	The School Medical Inspector, Dr W. Harper, visited, and examined the cases referred at his last visit. Ralph Fairhead, for ringworm of scalp, and Mary Ann Cox, for impetigo, are excluded. Charles Langmead, who is now under the care of the Tuberculosis Officer, is also excluded from School attendance.
September 28th	Frank Edworthy was run over by a motor car, and had to be sent home before afternoon school. The accident apparently happened through the boy riding to school on a bicycle having no brakes.
November 3rd	Ralph Fairhead again excluded for ringworm of scalp.
November 12th	Frank Wheeler and George Wheeler, of the Infant Class, are excluded, the elder boy having chicken-pox.
November 15th	More cases of chicken-pox are reported, the following children now being excluded by their parents: Frank George, Reginald and Frances Wheeler, Alfred and Doris Tanton, Reginald and Elsie Beer, Ralph and Grace Fairhead, Mary Edworthy.
November 16th	Florence Rookes this morning is reported to have chicken-pox. Mr Richard Gomer, Sanitary Inspector, visited re epidemic of chicken-pox.
November 29th	More cases of chicken-pox are reported by parents this morning. 18 children out of a total of 54 are excluded, or 33 1/3%. 14 out of 18 Infants are excluded.
December 3rd	Four more cases of chicken-pox reported this morning, making a total of 22 or 40%.
December 9th	Received notice from the Correspondent that he had received notice from Mr J.F.Young that by order of the Medical Officer of Health, Dr E.J. Slade King, the school is to be closed until after the Christmas Holiday.

WEARE GIFFARD CHURCH OF ENGLAND SCHOOL LOG BOOK 1900 - 1945

1921

January 10th	Re-opened School with an attendance of 51, only 1 child being absent.
January 12th	W. Butler, Esq., H.M.I, visited during the afternoon.
January 19th	The Rector, the Rev. H.O. Cavalier, who is leaving the parish, visited during the afternoon to say good bye to the children.
February 10th	W. Bright, Esq, the Correspondent, visited, with the report of His Majesty's Inspector. The following is a copy of the report:- Board of Education: Local Education Authority, Devon. School: Weare Giffard C. of E. No. 510. E.C. 699/21 Reg. No. Inspected on January 12th 1921. Report by H.M.I. Mr J.J. Draper. Mixed:- the satisfactory discipline and good habits of the children mentioned in the last report are well maintained under the present Head Teacher. The work is carefully planned, and while the general progress has recently been somewhat retarded by the effects of epidemic sickness, there is ample evidence of methodical teaching and the cheerful co-operation of the children. The Infants are suitably managed and trained and they are clearly happy in their school life. William Bright, Correspondent.
February 25th	The attendance this week is a record one, being 51 or 100%. Mrs Balsdon visited and checked the registers.
March 9th	The Committee's Regulations as to Scholarships and Free Places was read to the elder children this morning, and they were told to inform their parents, who may apply to the Head Teacher for further information if required.
March 23rd	School closed after afternoon session for Easter holiday, to resume work on April 4th.
April 4th	School re-opened this morning with all scholars (50) present.
April 5th	Miss Banbrook absent this morning owing to her mother's illness.
April 11th	Miss Banbrook still absent. The school dentist visited and examined 23 children. Several parents were present. There was only one objection to treatment.
April 13th	School closed by permission of the managers to allow the Head Teacher to take her son to Exeter for an operation.
April 20th	Miss Banbrook still absent. The monitress Miss B. Parkhouse is helping with the Infant class.
April 29th	Miss Banbrook resumed duty.
May 3rd	Mistress absent today, by permission of the managers, to go to Exeter on private business.
May 13th	School closed after afternoon session for Whitsuntide Holiday of one week.

WEARE GIFFARD CHURCH OF ENGLAND SCHOOL LOG BOOK
1900 - 1945

1921

May 23rd	Re-opened school this morning after Whitsun Holiday. 45 present out of a possible 48.
June 3rd	Attendance for the week much below the average for several months past, owing to illness of four scholars.
June 16th	A half holiday was granted by the managers this afternoon for a Strawberry Tea and Fete at the Rectory.
June 17th	The Sanitary Inspector, Mr R. Gomer, visited.
June 23rd	A whole holiday was granted today in commemoration of the recent visit of H.R.H. The Prince of Wales to Devonshire.
July 7th	School closed today for the Chapel Outing to Westward Ho!
July 15th	Diocesan Inspection this morning at 10 a.m. Mr H.H. Hawkins was the examiner.
July 19th	Mr W. Bright, Correspondent, brought the report of the Diocesan Inspection, of which the following is a copy:
Diocesan Report	Date of Inspection: July 15th 1921 No. of Scholars on Books 51 No. of Scholars Present 49. Present at Inspection: The Rector. Systematic work has been done during the year and the children showed that they had been carefully instructed. They answered brightly and seemed to be quite happy in their work. Attention and interest were good , and a quiet, reverent atmosphere prevailed. (signed) H.H. Hawkins, Diocesan Inspector. W. Bright, Correspondent.
July 26th	Mrs Balsdon visited, and checked the registers.
July 29th	School closed for summer holiday of four weeks, August 1st to August 26th.
August 29th	School reopened this morning with 41 scholars present. Marjory Moore is excluded with impetigo of face.
August 31st	A whole holiday granted for Bideford Regatta.
September 1st	Dr Harper, School Medical Inspector, visited this morning, and examined the children referred for treatment.
September 29th	The school nurse visited and examined four scholars referred on her last visit. They were found to be quite clean. Barty Jelfs fell against the school wall during the play interval about 2.40, and received a nasty wound in her forehead about an inch long. As a stitch seemed necessary, and the child's mother was away from home, I sent her to Torrington, to the doctor, in charge of Miss Banbrook. Miss Parkhouse took charge of the Infant Class during the last half hour.
October 27th	Barty Jelfs again in attendance, after being absent, owing to the injury to her head, for a month.

WEARE GIFFARD CHURCH OF ENGLAND SCHOOL LOG BOOK
1900 - 1945

1921

November 17th	The School Nurse visited, and examined four girls, whom she saw on September 29th. One, again, received a warning notice. The others were found to be quite clean.
November 30th	The Rev. R.H. Moyses visited and checked the registers.
December 21st	School closed, after afternoon session, for Christmas holiday, to re-open on January 9th.

1922

January 9th	Re-opened school this morning with 34 scholars in attendance. Miss Parkhouse, who has been ill during the holiday is not yet allowed by her doctor to resume duty.
January 11th	I have excluded Grace Fairhead, who is apparently suffering with impetigo.
January 16th	A rough and stormy morning. Only 22 children present.
January 19th	The School Nurse visited and examined all the children.
January 20th	Owing to influenza and severe colds among the scholars the attendance has been seriously affected, the weekly average being 20.4 or only 56%, the last three days, only 19 children were present out of 36 on books, 17 children being absent ill.
January 23rd	Miss Parkhouse resumed duty.
January 27th	The attendance has improved, though several children have been absent with colds and influenza.
February 8th	The School Medical Inspector, Dr W. Harper, visited and examined nine children. The School Nurse was present, and several parents came.
February 17th	Attendance for the week a record one, being 37 or 100%.
February 28th	Today being the wedding day of HRH The Princess Mary and Viscount Lascelles, a whole holiday was given, by the desire of His Majesty the King. The children of the Weare Giffard Day School were entertained to games and tea at the Rectory in the afternoon by the kindness of the Rector and Mrs Moyses, Mrs Paine and Mrs Hancock. A small picture of Princess Mary was presented by Mrs Moyses to the Head Teacher, to be hung in the Schoolroom.
March 1st	Re-admitted Charles Langmead, who has been excluded for treatment of suspected tuberculosis for nearly two years. This boy, though thirteen years old, is very backward.
March 6th	W. Butler, Esq., H.M.I., visited about 11.30 and remained till 3 p.m.
March 8th	A stormy morning. Several children absent.

WEARE GIFFARD CHURCH OF ENGLAND SCHOOL LOG BOOK 1900 - 1945

1922

March 9th	The Devon County Education Committee's notice regarding Examinations for Scholarships was read this morning to the senior scholars, who were requested to tell their parents of the examinations.
March 22nd	The School Nurse (Miss R. Lee) sent notice to the Head Teacher that she had excluded Frank Edworthy from school for impetigo.
April 3rd	Owing to the schoolroom being required for the Rural District Council Election, the children were granted a whole holiday.
April 12th	School closed at 3.40 p.m. for Easter Holiday.
April 24th	School re-opened this morning after the Easter Holiday with an attendance of 40.
May 15th	The school dentist, Mr R.J. Inder, visited and examined all children between five and ten years of age. Several parents were present.
May 17th	Dr Connolly, School Medical Inspector, visited and examined the children referred for treatment.
May 24th	Today being Empire Day, the head-teacher gave an address on the duties and responsibilities of children of the Empire. Patriotic songs were sung, and the saluting of the flag took place in the playground. The celebration closed with the National Anthem. A half holiday was given in the afternoon.
May 25th	School closed for the day on account of the Church Sunday School outing to Instow.
May 26th	The School Nurse, Miss Lee, visited, and examined the girls.
May 29th	Ivy Edworthy is absent, excluded from school with sores on her face by the School Nurse.
June 1st	Miss J. Grayson, the County Inspectress and Organizer of Physical Training, visited and examined the scholars in Physical Exercises and Games. She informed the Head Teacher that she was highly pleased with the work done, and with the alertness and responsiveness of the children.
June 2nd	School closed at 3.40 p.m. for Whitsuntide holiday (2 days, to re-assemble on June 7th).
June 7th	School re-opened this morning after Whitsuntide holiday.
June 21st	School closed for a half holiday in the afternoon for the Strawberry Tea and Fete.
July 19th	Diocesan Inspection this afternoon at 2 p.m. 41 children were present. The Rev. E.F. Hall was the examiner.
August 3rd	School closed for the day on account of the Chapel outing to Westward Ho!
August 4th	School closed at 3.40 for the summer holiday of four weeks.
September 4th	Re-opened school this morning with an attendance of 41.

WEARE GIFFARD CHURCH OF ENGLAND SCHOOL LOG BOOK
1900 - 1945

1922

September 5th Diocesan Report	Diocesan Report received this morning, of which the following is a copy:- Date of Inspection: July 19th 1922. No. of Scholars on books: 43 No. of Scholars present at inspection: 41 Revisiting this school after some years it was a pleasure to notice the steady progress that has been made during Mrs Mancy's headship of the school. The children respond very well and show a good grasp of their work. Their attitude is one of keenness and interest and the general character of the work is very satisfactory. Signed: E.F. Hall, Diocesan Inspector. R.H. Moyses, September 22nd 1922
September 5th	I have excluded Helen Henderson for impetigo of face.
September 6th	School closed this afternoon for Bideford Hospital Fete at Northam.
September 12th	Winifred Henderson and Cora Squire are excluded for impetigo.
October 9th	The school nurse, Miss Lee, visited and examined the children.
October 22nd	Arthur Edworthy is excluded for impetigo.
November 2nd	Ida Beer has impetigo apparently on her legs, so I have sent her home.
November 27th	The school nurse Miss Lee visited and found the children who have had impetigo all clear.
December 15th	Attendance this week much improved, being 42.3 or 98.3%.
December 20th	The river being in flood rose so rapidly, making the roads impassable, by 10.40, that the attendances were cancelled and the school meeting abandoned.
December 21st	Closed school for Christmas Holiday, to re-open January 8th 1923.

1923

January 8th	Re-opened school this morning after the Christmas holiday with 40 children in attendance.
January 10th	Mr Robbins, the County Education Committee's Inspector, visited during the morning session.
February 7th	A wet and stormy morning. Only 30 children in attendance out of a possible 41.
February 8th Land waters	Owing to the roads becoming rapidly impassable the afternoon meeting was abandoned, to allow the scholars to reach their homes in safety.
February 19th	Miss Lee, the School Nurse, visited, and examined the girls.

WEARE GIFFARD CHURCH OF ENGLAND SCHOOL LOG BOOK
1900 - 1945

1923

February 22nd	A wet and stormy morning, resulting in a very poor attendance. Several children have been absent during the week with severe colds.
February 27th	The Rector, the Rev. R.H. Moyses, visited and checked the Registers.
February 28th	The monitress, Miss B.E. Parkhouse, terminated her engagement to-day, leaving to take a post as assistant teacher at Bampton Council Infants' School.
March 2nd	The attendance during this week has been the worst recorded during the current school year, several children being absent with severe colds. Average attendance 29.2 out of a possible 40, or only 73%.
March 28th	Closed school at 3.40 for Easter holiday (till April 9th).
April 9th	Re-opened school after Easter holiday with 44 scholars in attendance.
April 13th	Mr R.J. Inder visited and examined and treated the teeth of 36 scholars. Several parents were present.
April 19th	Miss Banbrook absent from her school duties, owing to the sudden death of her mother, this afternoon.
April 26th	The school closed for the day, a whole holiday being granted by the desire of His Majesty King George V, to mark the occasion of the marriage of H.R.H. the Duke of York to the Lady Elizabeth Bowes-Lyon.
April 27th	Miss Banbrook still absent. Owing to the absence of Miss Banbrook (all classes being taken by the Head Teacher) it has been impossible to adhere strictly to the time-table.
April 30th	Miss Banbrook resumed duty.
May 4th	J.J. Draper, Esq., H.M.I., visited, and remained during morning session.
May 10th	A whole holiday granted for Ascension Day.
May 18th	School closed after afternoon session for Whitsuntide holiday of one week to re-open on May 28th.
June 14th	School closed for the day to enable teachers to attend a meeting of the Devon County Teachers at Exeter.
June 25th	Dr W.H. Scott, the School Medical Inspector, visited, and examined about 20 scholars. Several parents were present.
July 12th	Diocesan Inspection at 10 a.m.
July 18th	School closed for the afternoon on account of the Church Sunday School Outing to Saunton Sands.
July 26th	School closed for the day, for the Chapel Annual Outing to Westwood Ho!
July 27th	Closed school after afternoon session for summer holiday of four weeks.

WEARE GIFFARD CHURCH OF ENGLAND SCHOOL LOG BOOK
1900 - 1945

1923

August 27th	School re-opened this morning after summer holiday with 44 scholars in attendance.
August 30th	Miss Roote, School Nurse, visited and examined all children, boys and girls.
November 13th	H.M.I. W. Butler Esq. visited and remained during both sessions.
November 14th FLOODS	Owing to the Torridge being in flood and the roads becoming impassable before 9 a.m., the school meeting could not be held. The Correspondent was notified.
November 15th	Attendance badly affected by rough stormy weather, 10 children being absent. Diocesan Report received today. Scholars present: 43 Examiner: Rev M.H. Needham The day of the inspection was excessively hot and the atmosphere of the school intensely overpowering, so that it was impossible for the children to do themselves justice. The general standard of work as seen on this hot afternoon was below the average of what one would expect from this school, but it would be unfair to criticise too closely under the circumstances. R.H. Moyses, Correspondent.

WEARE GIFFARD CHURCH OF ENGLAND SCHOOL LOG BOOK
1900 - 1945

1923

December 4th

Received the following report from the Correspondent:
Board of Education
School: Weare Giffard C. of E. No. 510 Reg No. E.9/510/1 Inspected on November 13th 1923
Report by H.M.I. Mr J.J. Draper.
Mixed:-

Since the last report was made the attendance has been of an unusually fluctuating character, producing an effect of much unevenness in the general progress. It cannot be overlooked however that the fundamental weaknesses now evident are largely due to bad habits which should engage the Head Teacher's close attention.

1. The failure to suppress promiscuous answering has resulted not only in impeding individual effort but also in fostering slipshod thinking.
2. The prevalence of sotto voce conversation and collusion indicates a lack of self-control.

While credit is due for much of the teaching in English, Physical Training, Needlework and Handwork, there are faults which should disappear under appropriate treatment:-

1. The excellent quality of the oral Reading is marred by carelessness; the older children show but little ability to give back the substance of the matter read; and more might be done in the correction of written composition to utilize the children's mistakes to advantage.
2. Arithmetic reveals much weakness. More intensive training in the processes appears to be necessary to ensure a firm foundation in the subject, while the classification of the children should be guided by the capacity and attainments of the individuals.
3. The interest of the younger children in History and Geography needs to be further stimulated by definite association of oral composition and suitable handwork.
4. The training in Needlework would gain practical value from the encouragement of home mending in school, and also a more systematic keeping of notebooks by the older girls.
5. No material progress appears in note singing and ear training.
6. The value of keeping continuous records of progress and of making reports on the results of the Head Teacher's periodical examinations was emphasised at this visit.

The Infants continue to be sympathetically managed, and much is done to brighten their school life and training. They, however, seem reluctant to express themselves coherently, and the progress in Reading is disappointing. Some minor faults in registration were pointed out to the Head Teacher at this and the previous visit of inspection.

The Head Teacher deserves much credit for the successful progress of the School Savings Association.

It is understood that the Managers entertained plans last year for improving the surface of the playground, which continues to be unsuitable for Physical Training. No steps, however, appear to have been taken to remedy the defect.

R.H. Moyses, Correspondent.

WEARE GIFFARD CHURCH OF ENGLAND SCHOOL LOG BOOK
1900 - 1945

1923

December 14th	Miss Banbrook absent from her school duties today owing to illness.
December 17th	Miss Banbrook resumed duty.
December 20th	Closed school after afternoon session for Christmas Holiday from December 21st to January 7th.

1924

January 7th	Reopened school this morning, with 51 scholars in attendance.
January 16th	Amy Mugford fell against the wall during playtime, cutting a nasty gash across her eyebrow. Nurse Beer kindly plastered the wound.
January 25th	Bad weather and the prevalence of severe influenza colds among the children have severely affected the attendance during the past week. The percentage of attendance, 82.6%, is the lowest recorded for some time.
January 25th	I have today excluded Cyril Manning who apparently has severe impetigo of face and body.
February 6th	Albert Clarke, absent since February 4th, is reported to be ill with measles, and Dorothy Clarke and William Tyrell, who are living in the same house, are kept at home by the parents.
February 11th	Albert Clarke is reported to be suffering with scarlet fever, not measles.
February 22nd	Attendance has been badly affected by severe colds and influenza among the scholars during the past few weeks, resulting this week in a low record of 83.8%.
February 29th	The serious falling-off in the attendance has this week resulted in the low average attendance of 36.4, only 70%.
March 3rd	As, owing to increase of influenza among the scholars, only 21 (40%) were present this morning, the school was closed for one week by the Managers.
March 7th	The Rector, the Rev. R.H. Moyses, informed the Head Teacher that the authority of the School Medical Officer for the closure of the school for influenza had been granted.
March 10th	School re-opened this morning with 47 scholars in attendance.
March 17th	Miss Banbrook absent this morning owing to cold and sore throat.
March 21st	Evelyn Beer kept at home by parents for whooping cough.
March 25th	Mary Edworthy and Arthur Edworthy excluded for whooping cough.

WEARE GIFFARD CHURCH OF ENGLAND SCHOOL LOG BOOK 1900 - 1945

1924

March 26th	More cases of whooping cough, thirteen children being reported to the Medical Officer of Health and the School Medical Officer. The Correspondent has also been notified.
March 31st	School closed by order of M.O. Health, Dr E.J. Slade King from March 31st to April 21st inclusive.
April 22nd	School remains closed for Easter holiday, to re-open on April 28th 1924.
April 28th	Re-opened school this morning. Only 34 children were present out of a possible 51 on books. Most of the absentees are still suffering from whooping cough.
May 2nd	Attendance this week is the lowest recorded for several years, being only 32.9 out of a possible 49 (or 67.1%). 14 children are still excluded for whooping cough.
May 9th	The low percentage of average attendance still continues, owing to exclusions for whooping cough. The infant class attendance is especially low, being only 41%.
May 21st	The School Dentist, Mr R.J. Inder, visited and examined nearly all scholars present, several receiving treatment. Several mothers came and only one objection was made.
May 29th	School closed for the usual Ascension Day holiday, and Sunday School Outing to Clovelly.
June 6th	Attendance this week again forms a low record, being only 67.5% of average attendance. Many children who have had whooping cough and had returned to school are absent ill.
June 9th	School closed for the day, being Whitsun Bank Holiday.
June 13th	Notice was received this morning from the headmistress of Edgehill Girls' College, Miss E.O. Johnson, that Phoebe Mancy, who sat for the County Scholarship Examination on May 17th, had been successful in gaining a free place in the College.
June 20th	The attendance this week has improved, though five children are still excluded, suffering from the effects of whooping cough.
June 24th	Miss Roote, Superintendent School Nurse, visited, and examined all the children. She appeared pleased with the girls, who nearly all wear the hair bobbed.
June 27th	The Rector, the Rev. R.H. Moyses, visited and checked the registers. Today ends the first quarter of the school year, the worst quarter for attendance recorded during the past twelve years, being only 74.3% of average attendance: a bad record entirely due to epidemic sickness, whooping cough and after effects.
July 4th	Attendance much improved this week, and now appears normal. 44.7 or 97.1% of average attendance.

WEARE GIFFARD CHURCH OF ENGLAND SCHOOL LOG BOOK
1900 - 1945

1924

July 9th	A half-holiday granted this afternoon on account of Strawberry Tea and village fete in the Barton grounds.
July 17th	Alfred Tanton excluded today for ringworm of face.
July 18th	A certificate from Dr Wilson has been received, stating that Phyllis Braunton is not at present fit to attend school.
July 30th	School closed for the summer holiday after afternoon session for five weeks and to allow a day's holiday for the Chapel Outing on July 31st.
September 8th	School re-opened this morning after the summer vacation with 42 scholars in attendance. During the holiday the inside of the school building has been painted and distempered and the school yard has been resurfaced and asphalted. Dr W.H. Scott, the School Medical Inspector, visited and examined about twenty children. Many of the parents were present about 1.30 p.m.
September 10th	The Rector visited.
September 24th	A half-holiday granted this afternoon to enable children to take part in a Gipsy Fete held in the Rectory grounds in aid of school and church funds.
October 8th FLOODS	Owing to the flooded state of the river, rendering the roads impassable, the school meeting could not be held and was consequently abandoned. Notice was sent to the Correspondent, the Rev. R.H. Moyses.
October 29th	The children were given a whole holiday today, the school premises being required as a polling station for the Parliamentary Election.
November 26th	Mr Robbins, Devon County Education Committee's Inspector, visited during the afternoon session.
December 3rd	Mr T.E. Wooldridge visited and checked the registers this morning. To enable the staff to attend a conference on English arranged by the Board of Education at Geneva Girls' Council School, Bideford, at 2.15 p.m., the school is closed for the afternoon, the children being given a half-holiday.
December 19th	School closed after afternoon session for the Christmas holidays.

1925

January 5th	Re-opened school after the Christmas holiday, with 45 scholars present out of 46 on roll.
January 19th	Miss Roote, Emergency School Nurse, visited and examined all children present. She excluded Amy, Barbara and George Mugford for pediculosis.
January 26th	The children excluded by the school nurse have returned to school quite clean.

WEARE GIFFARD CHURCH OF ENGLAND SCHOOL LOG BOOK
1900 - 1945

1925

January 30th	Attendance has been affected this week by severe colds among the children, and bad weather.
February 4th	Mr Richard Gomer, Sanitary Inspector, visited, and advised the exclusion of the Edworthy family, as their sister is excluded from Torrington Girls' School, suspected of infection from mumps.
February 12th FLOODS	Owing to the flooded state of the river, making the roads impassable, school could not be carried on today, and the meeting was therefore abandoned. The Correspondent, Mr W. Bright, has been notified.
February 26th FLOODS	School could not be carried on today owing to the Torridge being in flood, rendering the roads impassable and making it impossible for the children to get to school.
February 27th	Rough and stormy weather, with 'land-waters', has badly affected the average attendance this week, resulting in the low percentage of 86.1%.
March 11th	Head Teacher absent ill with influenza. Miss Banbrook taking charge.
March 16th	Head Teacher resumed duty. Influenza is very prevalent among the scholars, 27 children being absent.
March 19th	Miss Banbrook absent, ill with influenza.
March 20th	The prevalence of influenza among the scholars has resulted in the low record of average attendance for the week, of 29.8 (only 63.4%). Two sisters, Elsie and Evelyn Beer, are excluded for mumps.
March 23rd	Miss Banbrook resumed duty.
March 24th	Miss Banbrook again absent, through personal illness.
March 25th	Miss Banbrook resumed duty.
March 25th	J.J. Draper, Esq., H.M.I., and W. Robins, Esq., Devon County Inspector, visited this afternoon and made a survey of the school buildings.
April 10th	School closed today after morning session for Easter holidays, to re-open on April 20th.
April 20th	School re-opened this morning after Easter holidays.
May 7th	School closed for the day on account of Torrington May Fair.
May 8th	The School Dentist, Mr R.J. Inder, visited and examined all children over 5 years old, giving treatment where necessary. There were objections by the parents of Winifred Henderson, James Martin and Thos Braunton to treatment being given to their children's teeth by the dentist.

WEARE GIFFARD CHURCH OF ENGLAND SCHOOL LOG BOOK
1900 - 1945

1925

May 11th	Dr W.H. Scott, School Medical Inspector, visited and saw several children referred for treatment.
May 19th	Miss Roote, the School Nurse, visited and examined all the scholars.
May 21st	School closed all day for the usual Ascension Day holiday.
June 24th	School closed for the afternoon, a half holiday being granted for the Strawberry Fete held in the village.
July 16th	School closed for the day, a holiday being granted for the Wesleyan Sunday School outing to Westward Ho!
July 30th	This month's record of attendance is, owing to sickness among the scholars, lower than usual, being only 91% of average attendance. School closed after afternoon session for the summer holiday of five weeks.
September 7th	School re-opened this morning after the summer holiday, with 35 scholars present. The Lovering Scholarship, tenable for three years at Bideford Grammar School, has been awarded to Eric James Beer by the Trustees of the Lovering Educational Foundation.
September 21st	Dr W.H. Scott, the School Medical Inspector, visited and examined about 20 children. One mother brought her infant, 3 months old, and several mothers were present. The doctor remarked on the clean and healthy condition of the scholars.
September 22nd	The Rector, the Rev. R.H. Moyses, visited and examined the registers. The attendance today has been affected by bad weather, 8 children being absent.
September 23rd	A purse of £4.10s.0d., collected by Weare Giffard School for the Children's Ward of the New Bideford Hospital, has today been presented to Lady Reardon Smith at the opening ceremony at 2.30 p.m. Phyllis Beer and Marjorie Moore made the presentation.
October 2nd	Dr G. Armstrong visited, and, in connection with the observance of Health Week, gave a lecture to the scholars on the 'Human Body' about 3 p.m.
October 6th	Received notice from the Medical Officer of Health that Ernest Becklake is to be excluded from school for 42 days, owing to infectious disease in the family (Scarlet Fever).
October 7th	Phyllis Beer is excluded for impetigo of face.
October 23rd	Owing to the rising of the Torridge this afternoon, rapidly rendering the roads impassable, school was dismissed at 3.30 p.m. to enable the children to reach home in safety.
October 25th	Doris Tanton is excluded for impetigo.
October 29th	J.R. Coulthard, Esq., H.M.I., visited, and remained during the day.

WEARE GIFFARD CHURCH OF ENGLAND SCHOOL LOG BOOK
1900 - 1945

1925

November 13th	Illness among the scholars has affected the attendance this week, the average attendance for the week being only 32 out of a possible 38, or only 84.2%.
November 26th	Visited this day. W.G. Robbins.
December 4th	Wintry weather, with severe frosts, have, together with much sickness among the scholars, caused a further falling-off in the attendance during the past fortnight, the average attendance falling off to 29.3 or only 77.1%.
December 11th	I have today received from Mr R. Gomer, Sanitary Inspector, a notice dated November 13th 1925, ordering the exclusion of Frank Wilton on account of scarlet fever in the family.
December 23rd	School closed this afternoon for the usual Christmas holiday, to re-open on January 11th. The term just ended has made the lowest percentage of average attendance recorded for some years, only 85.5%.

1926

January 11th	Re-opened school this morning with an attendance of 33.
January 18th	Dr W.H. Scott, School Medical Inspector, visited and saw several children referred for treatment.
January 25th	Harold Edworthy and Alfred Tanton are excluded, suffering from mumps.
February 25th	Miss Roote, Superintendent School Nurse, visited and examined all children present, numbering 33.
March 3rd	School closed for the afternoon on account of the Bishop of Exeter's visit to Weare Giffard.
March 31st	School closed after afternoon session for Easter holidays, to re-open on April 12th 1926.
April 12th	Re-opened school after Easter holiday. 39 children present out of a possible 40.
April 14th	10 of the elder girls began today a course in Domestic Science at the Torrington centre in the Torrington Church School.
May 6th	School closed for a day's holiday on account of Torrington May Fair.
May 13th	School closed for the usual Ascension Day holiday.
May 24th	School closed for the usual Whitsuntide Bank Holiday.
June 1st	The School Dentist, Mr R.J. Inder, visited and examined all scholars over 5 years of age. There was only one objection to treatment.
June 16th	A half-holiday was given this afternoon for the Village Strawberry Fete at the Old Mill.

WEARE GIFFARD CHURCH OF ENGLAND SCHOOL LOG BOOK
1900 - 1945

1926

June 22nd	Notice has been received today from Miss E. Cuthbertson-Hill, Headmistress of Edgehill Girls' College, Bideford, that Stella May Brownjohn has been awarded a free place in the College from September next, as a result of the Devon County Scholarship Examination in May last.
July 7th	The Head Teacher, at the request of the Education Committee, with the consent of the Managers, attended a lecture given by Mr Sayers F.R.H.S. on Rural Science, at Great Torrington Blue Coat School, this afternoon at 2.15. Miss Banbrook carried on the school during the afternoon.
July 19th	Diocesan Inspection at 2 p.m. Mr H.H. Hawkins, Diocesan Inspector of Schools, was the examiner. 35 children were present.
July 21st	J.K. Coulthard, Esq., H.M.I., visited this morning.
July 23rd	The Report on the Religious Instruction following the Diocesan Inspection by Mr H.H. Hawkins on July 19th 1926 was received this morning. The following is a copy: Diocesan Inspection July 19th 1926. Examiner: Mr H.H. Hawkins. No. on books: 39 Scholars present: Boys 13 Girls 22. The Infants have been carefully taught and the older ones had a good knowledge of the stories. A happy atmosphere prevails. In the Upper Group there was close attention and keen interest. The various problems were thoughtfully tackled and from most of the children the response was bright and ready. A very reverent attitude was displayed. Present at Inspection:- the Rector. R.H. Moyses, Correspondent.
July 29th	The Chapel Outing being fixed for tomorrow, July 29th, for which the Managers have granted a whole day's holiday, the school therefore closes this afternoon after afternoon session for the summer holiday of five weeks, to re-open on September 6th.
September 6th	Re-opened school this morning after the Summer Vacation with 33 scholars in attendance. Marjorie Moore has been awarded a Lovering Scholarship, tenable for 3 years at Edgehill Girls' College, to commence on September 17th. The free place gained by Stella May Brownjohn at the same College also begins on September 17th. Gladys and Mildred Gilbert have removed to Exmouth, consequently their names are removed from the register.
October 5th	Dr W.H. Scott, the School Medical Inspector, visited for routine inspection. There were no objections, and several mothers were present, with babies under school age for inspection.
November 9th	School could not be carried on today, owing to the Torridge being in flood. The roads at 9 o'clock were impassable, preventing children coming to school. The meeting was therefore abandoned and notice sent to the correspondent.
November 10th	A wet and stormy morning. Only 19 children present.

WEARE GIFFARD CHURCH OF ENGLAND SCHOOL LOG BOOK 1900 - 1945

1926

December 8th	Miss Roote, Superintendent School Nurse, visited, and examined all the children (31) present.
December 22nd	School closed after afternoon session for Christmas holidays, to reopen on January 10th 1927.

1927

January 10th	School re-opened after the Christmas holiday with 28 in attendance. The Head Teacher, with the consent of the Devon County Education Committee, and the School Managers, was granted leave of absence on January 10th and January 11th to attend a week-end course for rural head teachers, arranged by the Board of Education, at St Luke's Diocesan Training College, Exeter, from January 6th to January 11th. The school was carried on by Miss Banbrook during the Head Teacher's absence.
January 12th	The Head Teacher resumed duty.
January 20th	Dr W.H. Scott, the School Medical Inspector, visited, and examined children marked for reference.
February 9th	Miss Banbrook absent from duty through illness.
February 14th	Miss Banbrook resumed duty. Only 17 children are present this morning, 10 children being absent, reported ill with influenza, which is very prevalent in the district.
February 16th	Miss E. Gunnell, Organizing Inspectress of School Gardening, visited, and discussed the planning and working of the school garden with the Headmistress.
February 17th	More children are absent this morning owing to influenza, only 12 or 44% being present.
February 18th	Only 10 children present, 2 further cases of influenza being reported. Dr F. Pridham, M.O.H. for the Torrington District, requested the Managers to close the school till February 28th.
February 25th.	The Medical Officer of Health, Dr F. Pridham, has ordered the school to be closed for another week, to reopen on March 7th.
March 7th	Reopened school this morning, 27 children being present out of a possible 28.
March 10th	Miss Mann, County Instructress in Hygiene, visited this morning and gave a lesson to the Upper School on 'Personal Hygiene'. She expressed her pleasure at the satisfactory condition of the school premises and the children.
March 14th	Miss Roote, Emergency School Nurse, visited and examined all children present. She expressed great satisfaction and pleasure in the clean and well-kept condition of the scholars.
March 17th	Mr R.J. Inder, the School Dentist, visited and examined and treated the teeth of all scholars present. Several parents attended, and there were no objections.

WEARE GIFFARD CHURCH OF ENGLAND SCHOOL LOG BOOK
1900 - 1945

1927

March 31st	The Head Teacher, with the consent of the Devon County Education Authority and the School Managers was absent to attend a Refresher Course for Devon Teachers, held at the University College, Exeter, March 31st to April 2nd. Miss Banbrook was left in charge of the school.
April 4th	The Head Teacher resumed duty.
April 8th	J.J. Draper, Esq., H.M.I., visited this afternoon and checked the Registers.
April 13th	School closed for the Easter holiday, to reopen on April 25th.
April 25th	Reopened school this morning. One child admitted.
May 5th	School closed for Torrington May Fair holiday.
May 9th	Arthur Edworthy, while forking ground in the school garden, accidentally ran one of the prongs of the fork into his foot.
May 25th	School closed today for the usual Ascension Day holiday.
June 4th	Notice was received today from the Headmistress of Edgehill Girls' College, Bideford, that Ida Doreen Beer had been placed among the successful candidates for a Free Place at the College in the recent County Scholarship Examination.
June 6th	School closed for the usual Whit Monday Bank Holiday.
June 7th	Miss Banbrook absent from duty. A telegram was received from her stating that she was returning this evening.
June 8th	Miss Banbrook resumed duty. She gives personal illness as the reason for her absence yesterday.
July 19th	Ruth Manning is excluded from school as she is suffering with chicken pox. As her brother Cyril and sister Myrtle have not had the disease, they are excluded also for twenty one days.
July 27th	Florence Rookes fell in the playground and injured her right arm.
July 29th	School closed after afternoon school for the usual Summer holiday of 5 weeks, to reopen on September 5th.
September 5th	Reopened school this morning with an attendance of 30 out of a possible 33. John Thomas Braunton kept at home by parents, reported to be suffering from chicken pox.
September 13th	The school is closed from September 13th to September 16th inclusive, with the authority of the Education Committee and the Managers, to allow the Head Teacher and the Assistant Teacher to attend the Refresher Course at Barnstaple Grammar School, arranged by the Board of Education.

WEARE GIFFARD CHURCH OF ENGLAND SCHOOL LOG BOOK 1900 - 1945

1927

September 19th	Phyllis, Aubrey, Gwendoline, and Vera Braunton are excluded from school owing to infectious illness, chicken pox.
September 30th	Miss Bird visited and checked the Registers. Clara and Ernest Becklake are excluded suffering from chicken pox.
October 11th	Dr W.H. Scott, School Medical Inspector, visited and examined the 'routine' children. Several parents were present. The Diocesan Inspector, the Rev. Moore, visited during the afternoon, and expressed regret that, owing to the illness of Mr H.H. Hawkins, the school had been overlooked with regard to the annual Diocesan Inspection. No notice of an intended visit had been made, and as the Medical Inspection was taking place, Mr Moore decided to defer the Scripture examination and asked the Head Teacher to express his regrets to the Correspondent, the Rev. R.H. Moyses.
November 2nd	Miss Gunnell, the County Inspector of School Gardens, visited this afternoon.
November 8th	Diocesan Inspection this afternoon at 2 p.m. The Rev. F.W. Moore was the examiner.
December 9th	The following report has been received from the Diocesan Inspector, the Rev. F.W. Moore. Date of Inspection November 8th 1927. Scholars on Books: 28 Scholars Present at Inspection: 11 boys, 16 girls. Scholars withdrawn: None. The Infants were bright and responsive and their answering showed that they had been well taught the stories in the syllabus. In the Upper School the answering was thoughtful, and the children could follow a line of thought. In their written work, too, several of these children expressed themselves remarkably well. The tone of the school is good and the singing most pleasing. R.H. Moyses, Correspondent.
December 22nd	School closed after afternoon session for the usual Christmas holiday, till January 9th.

1928

January 9th	School reopened this morning with 24 children present.
January 13th	School could not be carried on today owing to floods. Before 9 a.m. the roads were impassable and consequently the school meeting had to be abandoned. Notice was sent to the Correspondent.
January 16th	Phyllis Squire and Betty Busby are excluded from school owing to ringworm.
January 24th	The School Medical Inspector, Dr W.H. Scott, visited and inspected several children.

WEARE GIFFARD CHURCH OF ENGLAND SCHOOL LOG BOOK 1900 - 1945

1928

February 5th	Head Teacher absent from 11.15 a.m. to attend the inquest held at the Rectory to give evidence regarding Sydney Joseph Stevens (17½ years old) found drowned in the river Torridge, through falling over the river wall, which is of a dangerously low level near the school. Miss Banbrook left in charge till noon. Head Teacher present to resume duty at 1.30 p.m.
February 17th	Mr R.J. Inder, School Dentist, visited, and examined, treating where necessary, the teeth of all the children present. Before the conclusion of his visit, he spoke to the children on the structure and care of the teeth. Several parents were present, and no objections to treatment were made.
March 23rd	An abnormally high tide flooded the Hallspill and Annery Kiln districts, preventing the children from getting to school from those parts. The attendance is consequently affected, 5 children being absent for this reason.
March 23rd	Betty Busby is reported as suffering from whooping cough and is consequently excluded.
March 26th	Joyce Stevens is excluded from school as she is suffering from ringworm on the body.
April 19th	The Head Teacher absent this afternoon, by permission of the Managers and the Devon County Education Committee, to attend the Short Refresher Course, at University College, Exeter, April 19th to 21st, arranged by the N.U.T. Miss Banbrook is left in charge of the school.
April 23rd	Head Teacher resumed duty. John Braunton is reported to be ill with measles.
April 25th	Five children of another Braunton family, Phyllis, Aubrey, Vera, Gwendoline and Kitty, are excluded from school by their doctor, owing to the illness of a little sister with measles.
May 3rd	School closed for the day on account of Torrington May Fair.
May 4th	Reopened school.
May 7th	More cases of measles are reported by parents. Ernest and Clara Becklake, James Martin, Hilda and John Henry Braunton are excluded. 12 children are now excluded.
May 11th	Owing to measles the attendance has fallen to the low average of 14.8 or only 52.8%.
May 16th	Measles still increasing, 18 children being absent, only 10 or 35% being present. School closed by order of the Medical Officer of Health for the District, Dr F. Pridham. The School Nurse visited and examined the 10 children present, before the closure of the school.
June 4th	The school is further closed by the Medical Officer of Health, Dr F. Pridham, until June 11th on account of the continued prevalence of measles.
June 11th	School reopened today, 28 children being present.
July 3rd	The School Nurse visited and examined all the children, 31 being present.

WEARE GIFFARD CHURCH OF ENGLAND SCHOOL LOG BOOK 1900 - 1945

1928

July 23rd	The Diocesan Inspection was held this afternoon at 2 p.m. The Rev. F.W. Moore was the examiner.
July 27th	School closed, after afternoon session, for the summer holiday from July 27th, to reopen on September 3rd.
September 3rd	School reopened today after summer vacation, with 33 scholars on books.
September 18th	Dr W.H. Scott, School Medical Inspector, visited and examined several children. Some parents were present.
October 18th	Miss Pester, the School Nurse, visited, and examined all children present, as to cleanliness.
October 22nd	The following report has been received from the Diocesan Inspector, the Rev. F.W. Moore:- Date of Inspection: July 23rd 1928. Scholars on Books 33. No. present: 31. The children of this small school gave a good account of themselves notwithstanding the fact that, through the inpsection taking place earlier than in 1927, they have had less than twelve months at the work of the syllabus. The answering from both the Infants and the Upper Group was very satisfactory and it is clear that good steady work is being done. The reverent tone and bright singing are worthy of mention. R.H. Moyses, Correspondent. October 30th 1928
November 1st	School closed after afternoon session for the mid-term holiday till November 6th.
November 6th	School reopened after the mid-term holiday.
November 9th	A rough, stormy day, which badly affected the attendance, 6 children being absent.
November 27th	Visit of H.M.I. J.R. Coulthard, Esq.

WEARE GIFFARD CHURCH OF ENGLAND SCHOOL LOG BOOK
1900 - 1945

1928

December 19th	The Rector visited, with the report of His Majesty's Inspector. The following is a copy of the report:- Board of Education. Local Education Authority:- Devon. School:- Weare Giffard C. of E. No. 510 Inspected on 27th November 1928. Report by H.M.I. Mr J.J. Draper. The Head Mistress has given careful attention to the recommendations made in the last report and with adequate effect in respect of most of them. Since 1923 several scholarships have been gained by children attending the school. Both teachers show interest in their work and welcome opportunities of widening their school practice. The scholars are keen and pleasant to deal with, and quite satisfactory progress is being made with the work of the school as a whole, whilst there is a definite broadening of outlook in recent years. The extension of the practical work to include Gardening, and well-finished basketry and raffia-weaving, and the encouragement of individual work in History are all good developments. In the study of Nature, also, much interest has been aroused in the top class. From Standard I (taught with the Infants) onwards bookwork is neat and Reading reaches a good level, but the oral and reasoning sides of Arithmetic seem to need more practice. The Infants are kindly and sympathetically managed. The varied Handwork and bright surroundings of their classroom are pleasing, and might well provide material for stimulating language work and greater freedom in oral narration. Further educational apparatus for the younger Infants could perhaps be supplied by the co-operation of the senior scholars. On the observational side of the training provided at this stage the simple study of natural environment might be given further emphasis. Besides the suggestions made for future possible developments of the Senior Handwork and the extension of directed individual studies, it is understood that a few routine matters discussed at the visit will receive due consideration. It is gratifying to note that the School Savings Association continues to flourish and that good use is being made of opportunities offered by the local branch of the County Rural Library. R.H. Moyses, December 20th 1928
December 20th	School closed for Christmas holiday after afternoon session, till January 7th.

1929

January 7th	School could not be reopened today as the Headteacher had been called away by a family bereavement. The Managers decided to extend the Christmas vacation for a few days longer.
January 14th	Reopened school this morning with 34 scholars on books.
January 15th	The School Nurse, Miss Pester, visited and examined all scholars as to cleanliness. No trace of pediculosis was found, the second time that the scholars have proved to be free.

WEARE GIFFARD CHURCH OF ENGLAND SCHOOL LOG BOOK
1900 - 1945

1929

January 17th	Dulcie Edworthy, during the dinner hour, injured the little finger of her right hand by getting it squeezed in the door as a little boy, John H. Braunton, was closing the door.
January 22nd	The School Medical Inspector, Dr W.H. Scott, visited, and examined several children.
January 25th	The School Dentist, Mr R.J. Inder, visited and examined the teeth of all children present over 5 years of age, giving treatment where required. There were no objections.
February 8th	The Head Teacher is absent this afternoon by permission of the Managers.
February 13th	Head Teacher resumed duty.
February 15th	Owing to severe wintry weather, with heavy snowstorms, only 15 children were present at 9.40. As most of these were wet-footed, it was decided to abandon the meeting, as allowed by regulations of Board of Education.
March 27th	School closed after afternoon session for the Easter Holiday, to reopen on Monday April 8th.
April 8th	Reopened school this morning after the Easter holiday. Six new scholars were admitted. There are now 41 children on books.
April 8th	Owing to contact with a sister who attends Edgehill Girls' College, where cases of smallpox have occurred, Joan Mancy and William Moore have been vaccinated and are excluded from attendance at school by the Medical Officer of Health, Dr F. Pridham.
April 12th	Miss A.M. Bird, one of the School Managers, visited and checked the registers.
May 2nd	School closed for the day on account of Torrington May Fair.
May 8th	Mr Robbins, the County Inspector, visited during afternoon session.
May 9th	School closed for the day to allow of Ascension Day Observance. Amongst other festivities, an hour's concert was given by the school children, in the Old Mill.
May 20th	School closed today, being Whit Monday Bank Holiday.
May 30th	The school was closed today, the premises being required for use as a polling station for the General Election.
May 31st	Four cases of suspected measles have been notified this morning. Betty Busby, Gwendoline Shute, Phyllis Squire and Marjorie Squire are consequently excluded from school.
June 6th	Mr J.R. Coulthard, H.M.I., visited during the morning session.
June 27th	The School Nurse, Miss Pester, visited and examined all the scholars. Miss A.M. Bird visited during afternoon session and checked the registers.

WEARE GIFFARD CHURCH OF ENGLAND SCHOOL LOG BOOK
1900 - 1945

1929

July 13th	An entrance examination for the Lovering Scholarship was held this afternoon in the school, Mr J.S. Fergusson, M.A., Headmaster of Bideford Grammar School being the examiner. William Moore, Wallace McKenzie and Joan Mancy were the candidates examined.
July 25th	The school was closed for the day on account of the Chapel Outing to Teignmouth.
August 1st	The school was closed for the day on account of the Church Sunday School Outing to Westward Ho!
August 2nd	School closed after afternoon session for the usual summer vacation, to reopen on September 9th (5 weeks).
September 9th	Reopened school after the summer holiday, 35 children being present. Joyce Tanton of Hallspill is excluded, suffering with whooping cough. The Lovering Trustees have awarded scholarships to Joan Mancy and Wallace McKenzie, tenable at Edgehill Girls' College and Bideford Grammar School respectively for three years.
September 24th	The School Medical Inspector, Dr W.H. Scott, visited, and examined several scholars.
November 1st	School closed after afternoon session for mid-term holiday.
November 5th	School reopened after mid-term holiday (November 2nd to November 4th inclusive).
November 6th	The School Nurse, Miss Pester, visited and examined all children present. She expressed pleasure at the clean and satisfactory condition of the children.
November 12th FLOODS	Owing to the flooded condition of the valley, due to the overflow of the river Torridge, children were unable to go to school, and the meeting was consequently abandoned. Notice has been sent to the Correspondent, the Rev. R.H. Moyses.
November 19th FLOODS	The river, in flood today, rose rapidly making the roads impassable. At 2.40 the school was dismissed, to enable the children to reach home in safety, and the afternoon's attendances were cancelled in the registers. Notice has been sent to the Correspondent, the Rev. R.H. Moyses.
November 20th FLOODS	School could not be carried on today owing to continuance of floods, making it impossible for the children to get to school; the meeting had consequently to be abandoned. This flood (November 19th to 20th) is a record for duration.
November 21st	Miss Bond, H.M.I., visited during the morning session.
November 25th FLOODS	The river again in heavy flood. By 9 a.m. the roads were impassable, and the school meeting had to be abandoned, no children being present. The roads were flooded all day.
November 29th FLOODS	The river in flood again today. By 2.30 p.m. the roads were rapidly becoming impassable, and to enable children to reach home in safety, the afternoon session had to be abandoned, and the children dismissed. The attendance marks in the registers were cancelled.

WEARE GIFFARD CHURCH OF ENGLAND SCHOOL LOG BOOK 1900 - 1945

1929

December 5th FLOODS	By 11.50 a.m. the river had risen rapidly, making roads dangerous. The children were dismissed at 11.55 and the afternoon meeting had to be abandoned.
December 20th	School closed after afternoon session for the usual Christmas Holiday, until January 6th 1930.

1930

January 9th	School reopened this morning after the Christmas holiday, with 34 children in attendance. Phyllis and Marjorie Squires are excluded from school, as they are reported by the parents to be suffering with whooping cough.
January 8th	The School Medical Inspector, Dr W.H. Scott, visited and examined several children who had been referred for treatment.
January 17th	The School Dentist, Mr R.J. Inder, visited and inspected, treating where necessary, the teeth of all children over 5 years of age. 10 children were absent owing to illness, but there were no objections, and several parents were present.
January 24th	More cases of whooping cough are reported, and the following children are now excluded from this cause: Kitty and Joan Braunton, Rosalie Beer, Gwendoline Shute and Harold Beer.
February 4th	Norman Mitchell and Winifred Lawrence are reported to be suffering from whooping cough and are consequently excluded.
February 13th	Miss A.M. Bird, one of the Managers, visited this afternoon and checked the Registers.
February 21st	During the playtime this afternoon, about 2.35 p.m., while running in the road after a ball, James Martin was knocked on the head by a stone which fell from the top of the playground wall. As the wound was bleeding profusely, first aid was rendered by the Head Teacher and the bleeding stopped. The Correspondent was notified of the mishap.
Feburary 24th	The playground wall has been repaired. James Martin is in attendance this morning.
March 3rd	Eileen and Mary Grigg are reported by their mother to be suffering with chicken pox, and are consequently excluded from school.
March 4th	Eric Busby is excluded from school as he is reported by his father to be ill with chicken pox.
March 10th	Violet Curtis and Frank and Iris Day are reported by parents to be ill with chicken pox and are consequently excluded from school.
March 23rd	Attendance much improved, 33 children being in attendance, the highest number present since January 10th.
April 16th	School closed after afternoon session for the Easter holiday.
April 28th	School reopened this morning after the Easter vacation.
May 1st	A whole day's holiday was granted for Torrington May Fair and school was consequently closed for the day.

WEARE GIFFARD CHURCH OF ENGLAND SCHOOL LOG BOOK 1900 - 1945

1930

May 16th	Mary Grigg is reported by her parents to be ill with measles and she and her brother and sister, Desmond and Eileen Grigg, are consequently excluded.
May 19th	Marjorie Squire is excluded, owing to an attack of chicken pox. Her sister Phyllis is also excluded.
May 26th	Rosalie Beer is excluded, reported to be ill with measles.
May 27th	John Wooldridge, Evelyn and Olive Cole, Harold Beer, and Frank Day are reported by their parents to be ill with measles, and are consequently excluded. 11 children are now excluded through infectious illness.
May 29th	School closed for Ascension Day Observance, a whole holiday being given. The day scholars gave a concert in the schoolroom in the afternoon, after attending Divine Service in the morning.
June 3rd	Joyce Tanton, who is ill with measles, is excluded from school. Twelve children are now excluded with infectious illness.
June 9th	School closed for Whit Monday Bank Holiday.
June 16th	School closed for the afternoon session on account of Sunday School Outing to Clovelly.
July 8th	Diocesan Inspection. Mr H.H. Hawkins was the examiner. 37 children were present.
July 14th	Dulcie Edworthy, absent from school, is reported by her mother to be suffering with chickenpox.
July 14th	Miss Banbrook is absent today owing to the serious illness of her sister.
July 17th	The Rector visited, with the Diocesan Inspection Report, which is as follows:- Exeter Diocesan Inspection of Schools. Date of Inspection July 8th 1930. No. on Books 40. Children present 37. The work has been interfered with by much sickness of the children, and many of those present had been absent for some considerable time. The Infants were quite bright and responsive and it was evident that under normal conditions the results would have been highly satisfactory. The children worked well. In the upper division the children needed some encouragement before they felt confidence in answering the questions. The attention was good and the children followed the various points with interest. Mr H.H. Hawkins was the examiner.
July 21st	Dulcie Edworthy is medically certified to be suffering with rheumatic fever and is not now excluded through infectious illness. Frank Day is also certified by his medical attendant to be unfit to attend school for at least 28 days.
July 21st	All the infants are now present, for the first time since the week ending May 9th.
July 24th	School closed for the day on account of the Chapel Outing to Paignton.
August 1st	School closed after morning session for the summer vacation - August 1st to September 5th.

WEARE GIFFARD CHURCH OF ENGLAND SCHOOL LOG BOOK
1900 - 1945

1930

September 8th	School reopened this morning after summer holiday. 36 scholars were present.
September 23rd	Dr W.H. Scott, School Medical Inspector, visited, for routine inspection, and examined several scholars. Some of the parents were present.
October 1st	The School Nurse visited, and examined all children present. She remarked on their cleanliness and freedom from pediculosis.
October 2nd	The Head Teacher paid a visit, with 22 scholars (aged 7 to 13) to the Missionary Exhibition at Bideford, during the morning school session from 10.30 to 12. As an educational journey, the consent of the Managers and the Education Committee was given.
October 17th	Norman Mitchell is absent, medically certified as suffering from fracture of the collarbone, the result of a fall while playing at home.
October 30th	School closed after afternoon session, for the mid-term holiday, October 31st to November 3rd inclusive.
November 4th	School reopened after mid-term holiday.
November 11th	Armistice Day observed by placing a wreath on the War Memorial. The two minutes' silence was observed at 11 o'clock.
December 18th	The School Dentist, Mr R.J. Inder, visited during the morning, and examined and treated where necessary the teeth of all children present over 5 years of age. Three children were absent through illness, and several parents were present.
Decmber 19th	School closed after afternoon session for the Christmas holiday, to reopen on January 5th.

1931

January 5th	School reopened this morning after the Christmas holiday. Eight new scholars were admitted.
January 6th	Dr W.H. Scott, School Medical Inspector, visited during the afternoon session and examined several children referred for treatment.
February 17th	Miss A.M. Bird, one of the School Managers, visited, and checked the registers.
March 2nd	Owing to the schoolroom being required as a polling station for the County Council Election, the school was closed for the day.
March 3rd	Edith Gordon is excluded, as she is suffering with impetigo of face.
March 27th	The School Nurse visited, and examined the children for cleanliness.
April 2nd	Mr J.R. Coulthard, H.M.I., visited during the morning session. Closed school at mid-day for the Easter vacation, to reopen on April 13th.
April 13th	Reopened school, with 44 children on roll.
May 7th	A whole day's holiday for Torrington May Fair.

WEARE GIFFARD CHURCH OF ENGLAND SCHOOL LOG BOOK
1900 - 1945

1931

May 22nd	Mr Westcott, of the County Staff, visited and saw the boys at work in the school garden. Closed school this afternoon for the Whitsun holiday (Whitmonday only).
May 26th	Reopened school after Whitmonday holiday.
June 3rd	Miss A.M. Bird, one of the School Managers, visited and checked the registers.
July 3rd	Diocesan Inspection. Mr H.H. Hawkins was the examiner. 43 children were present.
July 14th	The Rector, the Rev. A.B. Thompson, visited, with the Diocesan Inspector's report, which is as follows:- Date of Inspection: 3rd July 1931 Scholars on books: 44 Scholars present: 43 The opening assembly was a pleasing and reverent function, and the children displayed a reverent attitude. The Infants were attentive and many of them answered the questions. There was a bright response and a keenness of manner in the Senior Group. The children have been thoroughly taught and have also been encouraged to think for themselves. They were easily handled and a sympathetic contact was soon obtained. The syllabus has been well covered and most of the children were intimately acquainted with the details of the various Bible stories. (Signed) H.H. Hawkins, Diocesan Inspector. Present at Inspection: The Rector. A.B.Thompson, Correspondent.
July 31st	Closed school after afternoon session for summer holiday (5 weeks).
September 7th	Reopened school after summer holiday with 41 children present.
September 30th	Miss A.M. Bird visited and checked the Registers.
October 16th	Attendance reached the low level of 76%, owing to the prevalence of severe influenza colds.
October 20th	The School Nurse visited, and examined all children present.
October 27th	School closed today, the rooms being required as a polling station for the General Election.
October 29th	School closed after afternoon session for the mid-term holiday, to reopen on November 3rd.
November 3rd	Reopened school this morning after the mid-term holiday. Today a milk club was started with the approval of the managers. Twelve children have joined, and the milk was supplied by Mr R.C. Powell, Weare Giffard Barton, as per contract with the Devon County Education Committee.
November 4th FLOODS	School could not be carried on today owing to the Torridge being in flood. By 9 a.m. the roads were impassable and the school meeting had to be abandoned. Notice was given to the Rev. A.B. Thompson, Correspondent.
December 10th	The School Nurse visited in the afternoon and examined all children present. She reported all to be free from any sign of uncleanliness, but excluded Pert Ball, who had an abscess forming on his knee.

WEARE GIFFARD CHURCH OF ENGLAND SCHOOL LOG BOOK
1900 - 1945

1931

December 15th	Mr R.J. Inder today made his annual dental inspection of the children over 5 years old. Several parents were present and there were no objections to treatment.
December 22nd	School closed after afternoon session for Christmas holiday.

1932

January 6th FLOODS	Owing to floods rendering the roads impassable the school meeting has, with the consent of the Correspondent, been abandoned for the day. The school will therefore open tomorrow, January 7th, after the Christmas holidays.
January 7th	Owing to continued floods the school meeting had to be abandoned.
January 8th	Only 25 children present. Several of those absent reported to be ill with influenza and severe colds.
January 12th	23 children only in attendance, several more being reported ill with influenza by parents. The School Nurse visited this morning.
January 13th FLOODS	Owing to the rising floods, rendering the roads impassable, with the consent of the Correspondent, the Rev. A.B. Thompson, the school meeting for the afternoon was abandoned.
January 19th	The School Doctor, Dr Rhodes, visited with the School Nurse, Miss Hill, and examined cases referred for treatment.
January 25th	Miss Banbrook absent from duty owing to illness.
February 1st	Miss Banbrook resumed duty.
March 3rd	John T. Braunton is excluded as he is apparently suffering with mumps.
March 7th	Three more children, Aubrey Braunton, Vera Braunton and Violet Curtis are excluded, owing to suffering with mumps.
March 9th	Leslie Ball is excluded with mumps.
March 15th	Mr J.J. Draper, H.M.I., visited during the afternoon session.
March 23rd	School closed, after afternoon session, for Easter holiday, to reopen on April 4th.
April 4th	School reopened this morning with 37 in attendance out of a possible 38 on roll. Two children were admitted. Ernest Becklake is excluded, as he is reported by parents to be suffering with mumps.
April 15th	Gwendoline Braunton is excluded, apparently suffering with mumps.
April 20th	Joan Braunton has mumps and is consequently excluded from school.

WEARE GIFFARD CHURCH OF ENGLAND SCHOOL LOG BOOK
1900 - 1945

1932

May 5th	School closed for the day on account of the usual Torrington May Fair holiday, which this year coincides with Ascension Day.
May 9th	Two more cases of mumps are reported by parents. Phyllis Squire and Desmond Grigg, the sufferers, are in consequence excluded.
May 10th	Eileen Grigg and Ronald Gorvett are reported by parents to be suffering with mumps and are excluded from school.
May 11th	Leslie Ball and Richard and William Lawrence are excluded, suffering with mumps. Mrs Ball reports that the Medical Officer of Health, Dr F. Pridham, has ordered her to keep all her children from school.
May 13th	More cases of mumps reported. Average attendance for week reaches low level of 71.5%.
May 16th	School closed for the day, on account of Whitmonday Bank Holiday.
May 27th	Three more children are excluded on account of infection with mumps: Harold Beer, Marjorie Squire and Mary Grigg.
May 30th	Three more cases of mumps are reported by parents: Edith Gordon, Olive Cole and Alec Parkhouse are in consequence excluded from school. The School Nurse, Miss Hill, visited and examined all children present. She remarked on the cleanliness of all the scholars.
June 1st	William Lawrence is reported by his parents to be ill with chicken pox. He and his brother and siter, Richard and Winifred Lawrence are consequently excluded. another case of mumps, Eveline Cole, is alo excluded.
June 14th	Reginald and Marjorie Ball are excluded with mumps.
June 16th	Two fresh cases of mumps reported this morning, Joyce Tanton and Ethel Ball being excluded in consequence. Since the first case on March 3rd, the average attendance has been affected by the exclusion of 26 children for this epidemic during the past three months.
June 27th	Ronald Gorvett is reported by parents to be ill with measles, and is consequently, with his brother, Ernest, excluded from school for three weeks.
July 5th	Mr H.M. Lewis and Miss A.M. Bird, two of the managers, visited, and showed much interest in the work of the school.
July 7th	Evelyn and Lilian Stevens are excluded on account of infection with mumps.
July 13th	Eveline Beer is reported to be ill with mumps and is consequently excluded.
July 27th	Mr T. Hayes, Superintendent Attendance Officer, visited.
July 28th	School closed for the day on account of Chapel Outing to Westward Ho! and Ilfracombe. School closed for summer holiday of five weeks, to reopen on September 5th.
September 5th	Reopened school after summer holiday with 37 children present.

WEARE GIFFARD CHURCH OF ENGLAND SCHOOL LOG BOOK
1900 - 1945

1932

September 9th	Miss Hill, the School Nurse, visited and examined all children present. She remarked on the clean condition of all the children, which showed an entire absence of pediculosis.
September 14th	Joyce Tanton complained of headache and has a rash on her head and chest, so I have sent her home, and cancelled her attendance.
September 16th	Dr F.M. Rhodes, the School Medical Inspector, visited, and carried out the usual routine inspection. Several parents were present.
September 21st	Half-day holiday - school closed for the Sunday School Outing to Westward Ho!
September 22nd	Diocesan Inspection at 9 a.m. Mr H.H. Hawkins was the examiner. Three of the Managers, The Rev. A.B. Thompson, Mr Lewis and Miss A.M. Bird, were present.
September 30th	The Diocesan Inspector's report has been received from the Correspondent. The following is a copy. Date of Inspection: September 22nd 1932. No. of Scholars on Books: 34 No. present at Inspection: 12 boys, 20 girls. The past year has been an unfortunate one for the school in that there has been an exceptional amount of sickness. The continuity of the work has been much broken and the Infants Class seemed to have been the more affected. It will take much care, thought and effort to pull this class up to normal standard. More variety and life in the teaching are needed. There were many evidences that thorough and serious work has been done in the Upper Group and, although the age range is a wide one, the work has been very effectively accomplished. The children are attentive and under effective control. They answer questions well and are very interested in their work. (Signed) H.H. Hawkins, Diocesan Inspector.
October 14th FLOODS	Owing to the rapid rise of the river, with flooding of the roads, with the consent of the Correspondent, the school meeting for the afternoon session was abandoned, and the children sent home, at 1.30 p.m.
October 21st FLOODS	By 9 a.m., owing to the Torridge being in flood, the roads were impassable, and the school meeting had to be abandoned for the day.
October 28th	School closed for mid-term holiday, to reopen on November 1st.
November 1st	School reopened this morning after mid-term holiday. Vera, Gwendoline and Joan Braunton are absent, ill with influenza.
November 11th	Several children are absent, reported ill with influenza and sore throat. Percentage of attendance again down to 80%.
November 17th	Mr H.M. Lewis and Miss A.M. Bird, managers, visited and checked the registers. Desmond Grigg fell in the playground about 10.50 a.m. while at play, and sustained a nasty cut in his forehead about 1 inch long. Mr Wooldridge took him by car to Bideford Hospital but the Dr in attendance did not consider it necessary to stitch the edges of the wound.
November 24th	H.M.I. Mr Stringer visited.
December 1st	The School Nurse, Miss Hill, visited and inspected all children present. She spoke to the children and complimented them on their high standard of cleanliness.

WEARE GIFFARD CHURCH OF ENGLAND SCHOOL LOG BOOK 1900 - 1945

1932

December 22nd	The Correspondent, the Rev. A.B. Thompson, visited. The following is a copy of the report received from the Board of Education:- Inspected on 24th November 1932. Report by H.M.I. Mr J.J. Draper. This two-class school has had the advantage of a settled staff for many years, but the attainments of the children, after allowing for a period of poor attendance due to epidemic sickness, are somewhat disappointing. The syllabus of instruction is generally sound, and the higher class is under good control. The teaching methods, however, particularly in Arithmetic, have not been carefully thought out, and the incomplete record of work is an indication of ineffective revision in such subjects as History and Geography. Composition is the best subject, and Handwork and Gardening are also taught with some success. In Literature, the reading is on individual lines, but it is evident that the children's grasp of the subject matter should be more frequently tested. Singing is only moderate. The Infants are kindly managed, and the walls of their small class room are attractive. Singing, Recitation and Stories are well taught, but the children are definitely backward in fundamental subjects. The record of work in this class is also incomplete.
December 22nd	School closed this afternoon for the usual Christmas holiday, to reopen on Monday January 9th, 1933, at 9 a.m.

1933

January 9th	School reopened this morning after the Christmas holiday, 28 children out of a possible 33 being present.
January 24th	Mr R.J. Inder, the School Dentist, visited and carried out the routine inspection of the teeth of all children over 5 years old present, 25 in number. Several parents attended, but several children were absent through illness. There were no objections.
January 27th	Several children being absent through illness has reduced the attendance for the past fortnight to the low average of 77%.
February 1st	Miss Banbrook, unfit for duty owing to influenza, is absent from school this morning.
February 2nd	Miss Banbrook still absent.
February 3rd	More cases of influenza among the scholars have reduce the average attendance for the week to the low percentage of 62.1. Only 42% were present on Friday morning February 3rd, 14 out of a possible 33.
February 6th	School closed by order of Dr F. Pridham, Medical Officer of Health (from 6th February to 14th inclusive, to reopen on February 15th), on account of so many children being ill with influenza.
February 15th	School reopened this morning with 24 children in attendance out of a possible 33. Miss Banbrook resumed duty.
February 17th	The School Nurse, Miss Hill, visited and examined all children present, 24 in number. She remarked on their clean and well cared-for

WEARE GIFFARD CHURCH OF ENGLAND SCHOOL LOG BOOK 1900 - 1945

1933

March 28th	Miss A.M. Bird (Correspondent pro tem.) visited. Harold Beer was injured during the walk to school, at mid-day, by Desmond Grigg throwing a stone. After rendering first aid, the head teacher sent the boy home. He was taken to Dr Pugh at Torrington, where the wound, about 1½ in. long, was stitched.
March 21st	Dr W. Horton-Date, Deputy Medical Officer, visited, and examined children referred for treatment.
April 12th	School closed for Easter Holiday after afternoon school, to reopen on April 24th.
April 24th	School reopened this morning.
April 25th	Dr F. Pridham, M.O.H., visited.
May 4th	School closed for the usual Torrington May Fair Holiday, for the whole day.
May 24th	Empire Day was observed by singing of patriotic songs and lessons on the Empire.
May 26th	Miss A.M. Bird, Correspondent, visited and checked the registers.
June 1st	School closed after afternoon session for Whitmonday Bank Holiday.
June 5th	Reopened school after Whitsuntide Bank Holiday.
July 3rd	Diocesan Inspection at 1.30 p.m. The Rev. F.W. Moore was the examiner. 36 children were present. Miss Bird, Correspondent to the Managers, attended the inspection. The day was oppressively hot.
July 12th	A half holiday was granted by the Managers this afternoon for a fete being held at Weare Hall.
July 17th	Miss Hill, the School Nurse, visited, and examined all children present as to their cleanliness. She again complimented the children and their parents on the high standard of cleanliness of Weare Giffard scholars. No child with even a suspicion of pediculosis has been found in the school for several years.
August 3rd	School closed after afternoon session for the summer holiday of five weeks, to reopen on Monday September 11th.

WEARE GIFFARD CHURCH OF ENGLAND SCHOOL LOG BOOK 1900 - 1945

1933

September 11th	School reopened after summer holiday with 36 children present out of a possible 37 on books.
September 13th	The following is a copy of the report of the Diocesan Inspection, received today from the Correspondent, Miss Bird. Date of Inspection: July 3rd. No. on Books: 38 No. present: 36. Examiner: Rev. F.W. Moore. There was a reverent tone about the school and the syllabus is taught with care. The infants were somewhat a mixed class with some responding nicely. In the Upper group, while there was some good answering to the questions, there was rather a lack of enthusiasm and imagination, and as a class one felt these children were scarcely doing themselves justice through being afraid to let themselves go. (signed) L.H. Dukesell
September 28th	Half holiday for Sunday School Outing to Westward Ho!, the school being closed for the afternoon.
October 26th	School closed after afternoon session for the mid-term holiday, to reopen on October 31st.
November 6th	The Rector, the Rev. L.H. Dukesell, visited.
December 7th	Miss Bird, School Manager, visited and checked the registers.
December 8th	The School Medical Inspector, Dr F.M. Rhodes, visited and examined 20 scholars. Several mothers were present at the examination of their children.
December 21st	School closed after afternoon session for Christmas holiday, to reopen on January 8th.

1934

January 8th	School reopened after Christmas holiday, with 35 scholars out of a possible 35 on roll.
January 16th	Mr R.J. Inder, the school dental surgeon, visited, and examined, treating where necessary, the teeth of all children over 5 years old. Several parents were present, and no objections were made.
January 26th	The School Nurse visited and examined all children present, as to cleanliness.
February 2nd	Kathleen Braunton is reported to be suffering from impetigo and is in consequence excluded.
February 7th	L.H. Dukesell.
March 2nd	Owing to the schoolroom being required as a polling station for the County Council Election, the school is closed for the day.
March 13th	Miss A.M. Bird visited and checked the registers.
March 23rd	Dr F.M. Rhodes, School Medical Inspector, visited and examined children referred for treatment.
March 29th	School closed after afternoon session for Easter holidays, to reopen April 9th. L.H. Dukesell.

WEARE GIFFARD CHURCH OF ENGLAND SCHOOL LOG BOOK
1900 - 1945

1934

April 9th	School reopened after the Easter Holiday.
April 19th	School closed at mid-day - by permission of the Managers and the Education Committee to allow the Head Teacher and Miss Banbrook, Assistant Teacher, to attend the N.U.T. Refresher Course at Exeter, April 19th to 21st.
May 3rd	School closed for the day on account of the usual Torrington May Fair holiday.
May 9th	The Rector, the Rev. L.H. Dukesell, and Miss A.M. Bird, who checked the registers, visited.
May 10th	School closed for the Ascension Day holiday.
May 18th	School closed after afternoon session for the usual Whitmonday Bank Holiday, May 21st, to reopen on Tuesday, May 22nd.
June 15th	For the fortnight ending today, the record attendance of 100% has been made.
June 21st	The Rector, the Rev. L.H. Dukesell, visited.
June 27th	L.H. Dukesell.
July 11th	The Diocesan Inspection was held this afternoon at 1.30 p.m. The Rev F.W. Moore was the examiner. 38 children out of a possible 40 were present. Mr H. Lewis, one of the School Managers, was present.
July 24th	Miss Bird visited.
August 1st	School closed for the afternoon, on account of a Garden Fete at Weare Hall.
August 2nd	School closed after afternoon session for Summer Holiday of 5 weeks, to reopen on September 10th.
September 10th	School reopened after the summer holiday with all children on roll present.
September 12th	School closed for the day on account of Church Sunday School outing to Woolacombe.
September 13th	The following is a copy of the Diocesan report received by the Correspondent, the Rev. L.H. Dukesell. Date of Inspection: July 11th. Scholars on books: 40. Scholars present at Inspection: 13 boys, 25 girls. The examiner was the Rev. F.W. Moore. The Infants as a class were rather heavy and lacking in imagination. A few individual children, however, answered quite brightly. The Upper group was good, the answering being bright and thoughtful and the class well together. There was, too, some creditable written work from several of these children. L.H. Dukesell.
September 20th	Miss A.M. Bird, one of the Managers, visited and checked the registers.
September 24th	The School Nurse, Miss M. Goddard, visited to test the children's eyesight.

WEARE GIFFARD CHURCH OF ENGLAND SCHOOL LOG BOOK 1900 - 1945

1934

September 25th	The School Medical Inspector, Dr F.M. Rhodes, visited for routine inspection. Several children were accompanied by parents. Nancy Tucker, who has whooping cough, and her twin sister, Margaret Tucker, both in the Infant Class, are excluded from school.
October 1st	Margaret Tucker has returned, having previously suffered from whooping cough. Gwendoline Matthews is excluded owing to whooping cough. Several children absent with colds.
October 3rd	The Rector, the Rev. L.H. Dukesell, visited. *(signed)* L.H. Dukesell.
October 4th	The School Nurse, Miss Goddard, visited, and excluded Audrey Joan Smith and Jean, under suspicion of suffering from whooping cough.
October 11th	More cases of whooping cough reported by parents, Eveline, Olive, Ernest and Queenie Cole, Merlyn Matthews, Mary Prouse and Betty Beer being excluded in consequence. 12 children in all are now excluded from infectious illness.
November 1st	Ernest and Ronald Gorvett are excluded for whooping cough.
November 23rd	Owing to epidemic disease, the attendance for the sixth week in succession has reached a low level of 63.1.
November 27th	Head Teacher absent through illness. Miss Banbrook in charge.
November 29th	A whole holiday given today at the request of His Majesty King George V on the occasion of the marriage of his son Prince George, Duke of Kent, to Her Royal Highness Princess Marina of Greece.
November 30th	Head Teacher resumed duty.
December 6th FLOODS	By 1.30 p.m. the rapid rise of the Torridge had caused the roads to be impassable and the afternoon session had to be abandoned.
December 20th	School closed after afternoon session for the Christmas holiday until January 7th 1935. The percentage of average attendance for three months ending December 20th has reached the low record of 75% owing to epidemic disease, chiefly whooping cough.

1935

January 7th	School reopened after the Christmas holiday with 27 children present out of a possible 40 on books. Chicken pox is prevalent and the following children suffering with the disease are excluded from school: Ronald and Ernest Gorvett, Eveline, Olive, Ernest and Queenie Cole, Betty and Rosalie Beer, and Jean Oatway.
January 16th	Miss Goddard, School Nurse, visited, and examined all children present as to cleanliness.
January 17th	Mr R.J. Inder, School Dentist, visited for Routine Inspection and treatment. Several parents were present. 31 children were examined and there were no objections. received medical certificate from the parents of Alan Pidler (who is over 5 years of age and has not yet attended school stating that he is ill with chicken pox. L.H. Dukesell.

WEARE GIFFARD CHURCH OF ENGLAND SCHOOL LOG BOOK 1900 - 1945

1935

February 14th	H.M.I. W. Stringer, Esq., visited. Only 23 children.were present out of 40 on books.
February 14th	The average attendance has this week reached the low percentage of 64% owing to illness, influenza and colds among the scholars.
February 26th	The Head Teacher absent from duty this morning by permission of the Managers, being summoned as a witness to attend Bideford Police Court. The school is in charge of Miss Banbrook. The Head Teacher resumed duty in the afternoon.
March 12th	The Police Sergeant from Torrington gave a lecture to all the schoolchildren this afternoon on "Safety First and the Dangers of the Roads".
March 25th	Norman Mitchell fell on the school premises during the dinner-hour about 1.15 p.m., severely bruising his forehead. H.T. thought it advisable to send him home after first aid treatment had been given.
March 28th	Fire Drill - room cleared in 30 seconds.
April 11th	Head Teacher absent from 3.15 p.m. to 4 p.m. by permission of the Chairman of the Managers. Miss Banbrook in charge.
April 12th	Mr G. Kelland, Attendance Officer, visited. L.H. Dukesell.
May 2nd	School closed for the day for the usual Torrington May Fair Holiday.
May 6th	School closed for Celebration of the Silver Jubilee of their Majesties King George V and Queen Mary. To mark the occasion, a large new Union Jack, to be hoisted for the first time today, has been presented to the school by Captain Larsen, and a framed picture of their Majesties, by the Jubilee Celebration Committee, to be hung in the school room, is promised.
May 9th	Notice has been received from the parents of John Martin that he is suffering from chicken pox. He is consequently excluded from school.
May 20th	Edith Braunton and Peter Coad are excluded, owing to suffering with chicken pox. Dr Rhodes, School Medical Inspector, visited for referred cases.
May 27th	Received medical certificate regarding Alan Pidler, certifying his illness to be due to scarlatina. Mary Prouse is also excluded, suffering with chicken pox. Captain Larsen has given a gramophone and 10 records for use in school.
May 31st	Miss Goddard, School Nurse, visited. Fire Drill.
June 10th	School closed for the usual Whitmonday Bank Holiday.
June 19th	Miss West, of the National Milk Publicity Council, at 3.15 p.m. gave a talk on Food and Milk by permission of the Head Teacher.

WEARE GIFFARD CHURCH OF ENGLAND SCHOOL LOG BOOK
1900 - 1945

1935

June 21st	About 10.50 a.m. during the play interval, Norman Mitchell fell and hurt his arm while jumping in the road. After rendering first aid, the Head Teacher sent him home.
June 22nd	Dr C. Wilson certifies that N. Mitchell is suffering from a fractured radius and ulna as a result of his fall on June 21st.
July 9th	Diocesan Inspection. Miss Savage, Assistant Diocesan Examiner, inspected the scholars at 1.30 p.m. The Rector, the Rev. L.H. Dukesell, was present, and 40 children were in attendance. It has been reported to me that Desmond Grigg fell in the school playground while at play on Friday afternoon.
July 19th	The Rector visited. He had received the report of the Diocesan Inspection, of which the following is a copy:- Date of Inspection: July 9th 1935. No. on Books 43. Scholars present: 13 Boys, 27 Girls = 40. The Infants responded very easily and happily and shewed a good knowledge of the stories. Opportunities for the expression of the children's own ideas are given in drawing and modelling done in connection with the lessons. I recommend that some wall-pictures, preferably Shaw's, be provided for this group. The Seniors worked fairly well. Their New Testament knowledge was better than their Old Testament. This rather difficult part of the syllabus becomes easier if the events are centred round the lives of the great personalities of the period. The written work was satisfactory; there were several very good papers which revealed the careful teaching that had been given. It is important that these Senior boys and girls should have Prayer Books for their work on the Catechism and the Services of the Church. (Signed) Gwendoline M. Savage, Diocesan Inspector. Present at Inspection: The Rev. L. H. Dukesell.
August 1st	School closed this afternoon, after afternoon session, for summer holiday of five weeks, to reopen on September 9th. L.H. Dukesell, August 1st 1935.
September 9th	School reassembled this morning with 38 scholars present. Norman Mitchell has been awarded a scholarship by the Lovering Educational Foundation, tenable at Bideford Grammar School, for three years.
September 12th	School closed for the day on account of the Sunday School Outing to Woolacombe.
September 24th	Mr Westcott, County Horticultural Organiser, visited this morning.
September 30th	Owing to the termination of the Devon contract for milk in schools (with Mrs Powell, the Barton, Weare Giffard) no supplies have been sent, and the children are without their usual morning milk.
October 2nd	L.H. Dukesell.
October 7th	The children are now able to resume their morning milk, as Mr Hedden of the Barton has today started to supply, under the Milk Scheme, as official contractor to the Devon County Council.

WEARE GIFFARD CHURCH OF ENGLAND SCHOOL LOG BOOK 1900 - 1945

1935

October 10th FLOODS	Owing to the rapid rise of the river, the roads were becoming flooded, so it was deemed advisable at 11.45 a.m. to close the school, and send the children home, abandoning the afternoon session.
October 31st	Mr W. Robbins, Devon County Inspector, visited. School closed after afternoon session for the mid-term holiday, November 1st to 4th.
November 6th	A whole day's holiday was granted today at the command of His Majesty King George V to celebrate the marriage of his third son, Henry, Duke of Gloucester, to the Lady Alice Montagu Douglas Scott, daughter of the late Duke of Buccleuch.
November 6th	I have been notified by the Secretary to the Lovering Trustees that a Lovering Scholarship has been awarded to Eric Busby, tenable at Bideford Grammar School for three years.
November 7th	Dr F.M. Rhodes, School Medical Inspector, visited, and carried out the routine examination of 17 scholars. Miss Goddard, School Nurse, and several parents were present, about 2 p.m.
November 14th	School closed for the day, as the premises are required as a polling station for the General Election.
November 15th FLOODS	Before 9 a.m. the roads were rapidly becoming impassable, owing to the Torridge being in flood, and school had to be abandoned for the day. Notice has been sent to the Correspondent, the Rev. L.H. Duksell.
November 25th	A framed picture of the King and Queen, King George V and Queen Mary, has been today hung in the schoolroom to mark the Silver Jubilee of their Majesties.
November 26th	Mr R.J. Inder, School Dentist, visited, and examined the teeth of all children present (38 out of a possible 40). Several parents wee present.
December 19th	School closed for the Christmas Holidays, to reopen on January 6th 1936.

1936

January 6th	School reopened after the Christmas Holiday with 37 scholars in attendance.
January 20th	Death of His Most Gracious Majesty King George V.
January 21st	Proclamation of His Majesty King Edward VIII.
January 28th	School closed for the day to mark the occasion of the funeral of His Majesty King George the Fifth.
February 17th	Ernest Gorvett is reported to be suffering with measles and he and his brother Ronald are consequently excluded.
February 18th	The parents of Ernest Gorvett report that he is not suffering from measles. His brother Ronald is now in attendance.

WEARE GIFFARD CHURCH OF ENGLAND SCHOOL LOG BOOK
1900 - 1945

1936

March 2nd	By permission of the Managers, the Head Teacher is absent owing to family bereavement. The school is temporarily under the charge of Miss G. L. Banbrook, Assistant.
March 4th	Head Teacher resumed duty.
March 6th	Miss A.M. Bird visited.
March 24th	Owing to exceptionally high spring tides the children of Annery Kiln and Hallspill were unable to attend school, as those districts were flooded. 14 children were absent for this cause.
March 26th	Geoff K. Walton
April 1st	Dr F.M. Rhodes, School Medical Inspector, visited during the afternoon, and examined cases referred for treatment.
April 8th	School closed after afternoon session for the Easter holiday, to reopen on April 20th.
April 20th	School reopened after the Easter holiday.
May 4th	Miss Goddard, School Nurse, visited and examined all scholars (45 present) as to cleanliness.
May 6th	Miss Bird visited and checked the registers.
May 7th	School closed for the day. Torrington May Fair holiday.
May 18th	Iris Gibbons is reported to be suffering with measles, and she and her brother Derek are consequently excluded.
June 1st	School closed for the usual Whitmonday Bank Holiday.
June 2nd	School reopened after Bank Holiday.
June 18th	Diocesan Inspection this afternoon at 1.30 p.m. The Rev. F.W. Moore, Diocesan Inspector, was the examiner and 47 scholars were present.
July 13th	The Rector, the Rev. G.K. Walton, Correspondent, visited and checked the registers.
July 16th	Miss A.M. Bird visited and checked the registers.
July 17th	Geoff K. Walton.
July 29th	School closed after afternoon session to allow for a holiday on July 30th for the Chapel Outing to Ilfracombe, and for the summer holidays of five weeks, July 31st to September 4th inclusive.

WEARE GIFFARD CHURCH OF ENGLAND SCHOOL LOG BOOK 1900 - 1945

1936

September 7th	School reopened this morning with 41 scholars present. Four children suffering with whooping cough, Kathleen Carter, Allan Coad, Gladys Lawrence, and Sheila Short (all infants) are excluded. The School Oculist visited and examined Kathleen Braunton and Merlyn Matthews for defective vision.
September 8th	Dr F.M. Rhodes, School Medical Inspector, visited this morning for routine inspection. Several parents were present. Miss Goddard, School Nurse and Health Visitor visited and remained during the afternoon to test the vision of each child present, 41 in all.
September 17th	The School Dentist, Mr R.J. Inder, visited and examined the teeth of all children present over 5 years of age, giving treatment where required. Several parents were present, and there were no objections.
September 18th	Miss A.M. Bird visited and checked the registers.
September 23rd	School closed for the day for the Sunday School Outing to Woolacombe.
September 28th	The Rector, the Rev. G.K. Walton (Correspondent) visited. He had received the report of the Diocesan Inspection, of which the following is a copy: Date of Inspection: June 18th 1936. There was some very fair answering from the Infants, but it is difficult to get any enthusiasm from them as a class. The upper group was quite alert and I was much pleased with the bright answering from this class. The children showed a keen interest in the lessons taken, and gave a satisfactory account of themselves and evidence of good work. (Signed) F.W. Moore, Diocesan Inspector.
October 29th	School closed after afternoon session for the mid-term holiday, to reopen on Tuesday morning, November 3rd.
November 9th FLOODS	Owing to the rising of the Torridge, flooding the roads and rendering them impassable by 11.50 a.m., the school meeting for the afternoon was abandoned. Notice has been given to the Correspondent, the Rev. G.K. Walton.
November 10th	Dr Cox visited and examined Eveline Cole.
November 18th	Miss A.M. Bird visited and checked the registers. The Rector, the Rev. G.K. Walton, visited.
November 26th	J.J. Draper, Esq., H.M.I., visited, and remained during both morning and afternoon sessions.
December 14th FLOODS	By 10.30 a.m. the roads were rapidly becoming impassable, owing to the rising of the river Torridge, and the children in attendance were dismissed, and the school meeting for the morning session were cancelled. The attendances for the morning session were abandoned.
December 22nd	Dr F.M. Rhodes, School Medical Inspector, visited during afternoon session and examined children referred for treatment. School closed for the Christmas holidays after afternoon session, to reopen on January 11th 1937.

WEARE GIFFARD CHURCH OF ENGLAND SCHOOL LOG BOOK 1900 - 1945

1936

December 23rd	The scholars and teachers were today entertained to a Christmas party in the schoolroom by Mr and Mrs B.G. Lampard-Vachell of Weare Giffard Hall.

1937

January 11th	School reopened this morning, with 33 children present. Several children are absent suffering from influenza.
January 15th	Head Teacher absent through illness (influenza). A record low attendance this week owing to further cases of influenza, 72.5%.
January 18th	Head Teacher resumed duty. Only 16 children (40%) present this morning, further cases of colds and influenza being reported.
January 21st FLOODS	As the roads were impassable owing to the rise of the river, by 9 a.m. the school meeting had to be abandoned.
January 22nd	More cases of influenza reported, 30 children, out of 40 on books, being absent ill. The average for the week has fallen to the low level of 14 or 35%.
February 15th	The School Nurse, Miss Goddard, visited and examined all the children, as to cleanliness. She found no cause for complaint, and complimented the children in consequence.
February 19th	A record attendance of 100% for the week, 40 on books, present every day.
February 22nd FLOODS	By 2.30 p.m. the rapidly rising floods were rendering the roads impassable and the school meeting for the afternoon had to be abandoned and the children dismissed.
February 26th	The Correspondent, the Rev. G.K. Walton, visited.
March 1st	School closed for the day, the room being required as a polling station for Devon County Council Election.
March 24th	The School Nurse, Miss Goddard, visited. School closed today after the afternoon session for the Easter holiday, to reopen on April 5th. In calculating the average attendance for the year ending March 31st 1937, the figures for the week ended January 22nd 1937 are not taken into account, as the low percentage of attendance for that week was due to the prevalence of epidemic sickness, namely influenza. The meetings and attendances disregarded have been ruled through in the Summary register in red ink, and specially indicated in the Class Registers by means of a note "Rule 23, Exception 2".
April 5th	School reopened this morning after the Easter holidays.
April 22nd	Geoff K. Walton, Correspondent.
May 5th	Miss V.B. Mann, Devon County Organizer and Inspector, visited and examined the Needlework and Handwork.

WEARE GIFFARD CHURCH OF ENGLAND SCHOOL LOG BOOK 1900 - 1945

1937

May 6th	School closed for the day for the usual Torrington May Fair Holiday.
May 12th	School closed for three days to mark the occasion of the Coronation of their Majesties King George VI and Queen Elizabeth.
May 17th	School closed for the usual Whitmonday Bank Holiday.
May 18th	School reopened with a good attendance after the Whitsuntide and Coronation holidays.
June 2nd	Peter Coad, aged 7, fell over the railings into the roadway about 1.25 p.m. today, sustaining a scalp wound about 1 inch long which was treated with iodine and adhesive plaster by the Head Teacher.
June 7th	The School Dentist, Mr R.J. Inder, visited and examined and treated where necessary the teeth of all children present, 35 out of a possible 36 on roll. Several parents were present, and there were no objections.
June 24th	Diocesan Inspection. 36 scholars were present. The Rev. F.W. Moore was the examiner. The Rector, the Rev. G.K. Walton, was present during the inspection, which commenced at 1.30 p.m.
July 9th	School closed for the day on account of the Church Sunday School Outing to Ilfracombe.
July 22nd	School closed for the day for the Chapel Outing to Paignton.
July 23rd	Howard Curtis is reported by his mother to be suffering from chicken pox and is consequently excluded.
July 26th	Mrs Carter reports that her child Kathleen has chicken pox. She is therefore excluded. Mr Prouse called to inform me that he intended keeping Mary from school, owing to the prevalence in the village of chicken pox. The School Attendance Officer has been informed.
July 27th	Miss A.M. Bird visited.
July 29th	School closed after afternoon session for the Summer holiday, to reopen on September 6th. Notice has been received today that the Lovering Scholarship, tenable for three years at Edgehill Girls' College, Bideford, has been awarded to Rebecca Mary Grigg.
September 6th	School reopened today after the summer holiday with 34 children in attendance. Two new scholars, both infants, were admitted. One of these, Mavis Joyce Allin, has not previous attended school, excepting for a few weeks at a private school in Torrington. Though 7 years old she has no idea of reading, though, apparently, she is intelligent.
September 15th	The School Nurse and Health Visitor, Miss Goddard, visited and tested the vision of all scholars present. One child only was absent.
September 22nd	W. Robbins, Esq., Devon County Inspector, visited.
October 28th	School closed after afternoon session for the mid-term holiday, to reopen on Tuesday November 2nd.
November 22nd	The School Nurse, Miss Goddard, visited.

WEARE GIFFARD CHURCH OF ENGLAND SCHOOL LOG BOOK
1900 - 1945

1937

November 23rd	Dr F.M. Rhodes, accompanied by the School Nurse, visited, for routine inspection. Several parents were present.
November 24th	Miss A.M. Bird Visited.
November 25th	Geoff K. Walton.
November 30th	Mr Whitworth, H.M.I., visited.
December 9th	The County Architect visited, and took particulars and measurements of the stove and floor of the main classroom.
December 23rd	School closed after afternoon session for the Christmas holidays, to reopen on January 10th.

1938

January 10th	School reopened this morning with 31 on books. 29 scholars present.
January 12th	Geoff K. Walton.
January 13th	The Rev. G.K. Walton, Rector and Correspondent, visited and checked the registers. A medical certificate has been received regarding Kathleen Braunton, who has eye trouble, and is consequently absent from school for 7 days.
January 20th	Mr Kelland, Attendance Officer, visited.
January 24th	Miss Foxwell, School Oculist, visited, and examined Alan Pidler, whose mother was present. Kathleen Braunton had been under treatment and was wearing glasses provided by her own doctor.
February 7th	The Rector, the Rev. G.K. Walton, visited. Mr R.J. Inder, School Dentist, visited and examined, treating where necessary, the teeth of all children present (under 5 excepted). Several parents were present. Mr G. Kelland, Attendance Officer, visited.
February 22nd	Miss A.M. Bird (a School Manager) visited and checked the registers.
February 24th	The Rector, the Rev. G.K. Walton, Correspondent, accompanied by the County Architect, visited, with regard to repairs and refixing of the school stove. Mr G. Kelland, Attendance Officer, visited.
February 25th	B.G. Lampard-Vachell, Esq., Mayor of Torrington and one of the School Managers, visited and checked the registers. The absence of several children since the beginning of the term, owing to an epidemic of sore throats, has resulted in the low level of 80.5% for the month ending February 25th, and 70.3% of average attendance for the week ending February 25th.

…

WEARE GIFFARD CHURCH OF ENGLAND SCHOOL LOG BOOK
1900 - 1945

1938

March 4th.	School closed for the day to enable repairs and refixing of stove in the main room to be carried out.
March 7th	As the work on the stove was unfinished by Monday, a further day's closure was agreed upon by the Managers.
March 8th	School reopened this morning. Four more cases of tonsilitis are reported by parents and the attendance remains still below normal.
March 9th	The Rector, the Rev. G.K. Walton, visited.
March 16th	Mr H.M. Lewis visited and checked the registers.
March 21st	The County Architect, Mr de Courcey Hague, F.R.I.B.A., visited and inspected the work done re the stove.
March 23rd	The Assistant Superintendent of School Enquiry Officers, accompanied by Mr G. Kelland, A.O., visited and examined the registers.
March 29th	The Rector, the Rev. G.K. Walton, visited. The School Health Visitor, Miss Goddard, visited about 11.30 a.m.
April 6th	Dr F.M. Rhodes, School Medical Inspector, visited and examined several children referred for treatment.
April 13th	School closed after afternoon session for the Easter holiday, to reopen on April 25th.
April 25th	School reopened after Easter holiday. Two new scholars were admitted.
May 5th	School closed for the day for Torrington May Fair.
May 3rd	Miss A.M. Bird visited and checked the registers.
June 6th	School closed for the day, being Whitmonday Bank Holiday.
June 17th	Diocesan Inspection at 1.30 p.m. There were 31 children present. Miss G.M. Savage was the examiner.
June 27th	Mr T.E. Wooldridge visited and checked the registers.
July 4th	Miss M. Goddard, School Health Visitor, visited and tested the sight of all children present, 29 in number.
July 6th	The School Medical Inspector, Dr F. M. Rhodes, visited at 2 p.m. and carried out the annual routine inspection. The School Nurse and Health Visitor, Miss M. Goddard, was present. Several children were accompanied by their parents.
July 8th	Notification has been received from Mrs Graham, the Secretary of the Lovering Educational Foundation, that the Lovering Scholarship, tenable for 3 years at Bideford Grammar School, has been awarded to Desmond James Grigg.
July 13th	Miss G.L. Banbrook, the assistant teacher, is absent today with the written permission of the Managers, owing to family bereavement.
July 14th	School closed for the day, on account of the Church Sunday School Outing to Ilfracombe.
July 22nd	The Correspondent, the Rev. G.K. Walton, visited and checked the registers.

WEARE GIFFARD CHURCH OF ENGLAND SCHOOL LOG BOOK
1900 - 1945

1938

July 28th	School closed for the day on account of the Chapel Outing to Exmouth. School closed for the Summer holiday from July 29th to September 2nd inclusive, to reopen on September 5th.
August 1st	Geoff K. Walton.
September 5th	School reopened this morning after the summer holiday, with 29 on roll. 28 children were present. The Attendance and School Enquiry Officer, Mr G.T. Kelland, visited during the afternoon.
September 13th	The School Dentist, Mr R.J. Inder, visited and examined, treating where necessary, the teeth of all children present over 5 years old. Several parents were present. Glenys Grigg is excluded from school with impetigo of face.
September 26th	Edith Braunton has impetigo of face and is consequently excluded.
September 30th	Mr G.T. Kelland, School Enquiry Officer, visited during afternoon session.
October 10th	George Prouse is excluded for impetigo of face.
October 12th	Miss V.B. Mann, County Assistant Organizer for Domestic Subjects, visited during the afternoon.
October 13th	Miss A.M. Bird visited and checked the registers during morning session.
October 23rd	Kathleen Carter has impetigo of face and is consequently excluded.
October 26th	Miss Goddard, School Nurse and Health Visitor, visited during morning session. Mrs Rcy, A.R.P. Instructor, fitted all the children present during the afternoon, from 2.30 to 3.30 p.m., with respirators. The Rev. G.K. Walton, Correspondent, and two Air Wardens, Mrs Bazeley and Mr H. Lewis, were present.
October 27th	School closed, after afternoon session, for the mid-term holiday, to reopen on Tuesday morning, November 1st.
November 1st	School reopened after the mid-term holiday. 23 children were present, the remaining 6 on roll being absent through illness.
November 3rd	G.K. Walton.
November 18th	The School Nurse and Health Visitor visited this morning and examined all children present as to cleanliness. They were found clean, still keeping the good record of Weare Giffard School in this respect. One child only is absent, excluded with infectious disease (impetigo) for the past eight weeks.
November 25th	Mr G. Kelland, School Enquiry Officer, visited.

WEARE GIFFARD CHURCH OF ENGLAND SCHOOL LOG BOOK 1900 - 1945

1938

December 16th	Miss Bird visited and checked the registers.
December 21st	The School Medical Inspector, Dr F.M. Rhodes, visited and examined all children present as to nutrition. Four were found below par, and Queenie Cole and Edith Braunton had so much improved in health that free milk for them is to be discontinued.
December 22nd	School closed after afternoon session for the Christmas holidays, to reopen on January 9th 1939.

1939

January 9th	School reopened this morning after the Christmas holiday, with 22 out of a possible 30 on roll. Several scholars are reported to be ill. John and Mary Martin are excluded suffering from impetigo.
January 10th	The Rector, the Rev. G.K. Walton, visited.
January 12th	Mr G. Kelland, School Enquiry Officer, visited.
January 13th	The Rector, the Rev. G.K. Walton, visited. The attendance for the week has been affected by illness among the scholars and reaches the low level of 71.3%.
January 18th	Dr F.M. Rhodes, School Medical Inspector, visited this afternoon and examined children referred for treatment. Several were absent through illness, chiefly influenza and chill.
January 23rd FLOODS	Before 9 a.m. the Torridge in flood rendered the roads impassable, and the school meeting for the day had to be abandoned.
January 30th	Miss G.L. Banbrook is absent from duty owing to the illness of her sister at Exeter.
February 6th	Miss Banbrook resumed duty.
February 8th	Miss Goddard, School Nurse and Health Visitor, visited. She excluded Mary Prouse (with a septic gathering on her eyelid, to enable it to be attended to at home) until February 10th.
February 10th	Mr G. Kelland, School Enquiry Officer, visited.
February 17th	Mr Kelland visited.
March 1st	Mr Kelland, School Enquiry Officer, visited.
March 2nd	Miss Goddard, School Nurse and Health Visitor, visited.
March 8th	Miss M. Foxwell, School Oculist, visited about 10.15 a.m., and examined Ernest Gorvett and Ena Trathen for defective eyesight.
March 17th	Mr G.T. Kelland, School Enquiry Officer, visited.

WEARE GIFFARD CHURCH OF ENGLAND SCHOOL LOG BOOK
1900 - 1945

1939

March 21st	The Rector, the Rev. G.K. Walton, School Correspondent, visited, and checked the registers.
March 31st	Miss M. Foxwell, School Oculist, visited about 3 p.m. and examined the children with defective eyesight, Queenie Cole and Kathleen Braunton, who were absent through illness when she visited on March 8th. The average for the year reached the lowest on record, being 26.2 average attendance. The number on books on the last day of the school year was also the lowest recorded, being only 25 (on roll).
April 5th	Mr G.I. Kelland, School Enquiry Officer, visited. School closed this afternoon for the usual Easter holiday, to reopen on Monday April 17th.
April 5th	Today, on retirement, I resign my appointment as Headmistress of Weare Giffard C.E. School, after over 26 years' service. (Mrs) T.W. Mancy.
April 17th	School reopened with Miss P.M. Tuckett as temporary Headteacher. The Rector signed the registers.
April 25th	Mr Inder, School Dentist, examined and treated the children.
April 27th	Notice received that elder girls are to resume cookery classes at Torrington.
May 4th	Holiday for Torrington Fair.
May 5th	Cookery classes commenced for 6 girls.
May 15th	The County Architect inspected the water supply. As there are no nibs in stock, Standard II are all using pencils, and some of the other children have to do so also. The order for requisitions was sent in on May 5th.
May 24th	The last hour was spent in celebrating Empire Day, with a reading of a suitable play, songs, and Viscount Bledisloe's message to children.
May 26th	School closed for Whitsun holidays. P.M. Tuckett, Supply Head Teacher.
June 5th	I take temporary charge of this school from today. H.C. White (County Unattached Staff) Miss Goddard, Health Visitor, visited. Afternoon session times altered from 1.30 to 4 to 1 to 3.30 (by permission of the Rector).
June 9th	The Rector visited.
June 14th	G.C. Whitworth, Esq., H.M.I., visited a.m.

WEARE GIFFARD CHURCH OF ENGLAND SCHOOL LOG BOOK 1900 - 1945

1939

June 23rd	Report received.
June 23rd	Following is a report on the school after an inspection on November 30th 1937 by J.J. Draper Esq., H.M.I. - omitted at the time, it was entered from a copy as dated. The school shows little change since the last report was issued. It still has merit in a few rather limited directions, whilst in others there is a good deal of unsatisfactory work. The two underlying but not disconnected causes of this weakness are:- 1. The spirit of routine which infects much of the teaching. 2. The failure to prepare the lessons. The absence of Notes of Lessons and of forecasts of work to be attempted has been pointed out to the Head Mistress at several visits of Inspection. Until these two important matters receive proper attention no substantial progress can be made in the work of the school. Geoffrey K. Walton, Correspondent, 26.6.39
June 26th	Rector visited.
June 28th	Received notice of Scripture Exam. to be held on July 13th.
July 7th	Eleven plus return forwarded.
July 13th	Diocesan Inspection by Rev. F. W. Moore.
July 19th	Dr Rhodes, S.M.I, visited for routine inspection p.m.
July 20th	School closed for today owing to Chapel Sunday School outing.
July 27th	The Correspondent checked registers and found them correct. G.K. Walton.
July 26th	School closed today owing to Church Sunday School outing.
July 31st	The Rector visited.
August 2nd	School closed today (on instructions from the office, to allow of transfer of desks, etc., to Senior School at Torrington) for the Summer Holiday. Monthly return forwarded.
August 3rd	Staff present today. Miss G.L. Banbrook gives up service in this school as she has been placed on the Supply Staff, owing to reorganisation. Stock book, Record book, and Registers are completed to date. I resign charge of this school from today. H.C. White.
September 11th	I take charge of this school today. A.M. Vousden (County Unattached Staff).
September 12th	The Rector visited.

WEARE GIFFARD CHURCH OF ENGLAND SCHOOL LOG BOOK 1900 - 1945

1939

September 16th	S.E.O. visited.
September 25th	S.E.O. visited.
October 5th	S.E.O. visited.
October 6th	School Nurse visited.
October 9th	Reported break in railings on frontage.
October 15th	S.E. Officer visited.
October 23rd	S.E. Officer visited.
October 25th	Registers and Record Book completed to date. I resign charge of this school from today. A. M. Vousden.
November 1st	I take temporary charge of this school from today. Ida P. Bow. Dr F.M. Rhodes visited the school this afternoon to make the Nutrition Survey.
November 3rd	I resign charge of this school from today. Ida P. Bow.
November 6th	I resume temporary charge of this school today. A.M. Vousden. School Enquiry Officer visited.
November 13th	M.O.H. visited.
November 14th	School Nurse visited.
November 16th	School Enquiry Officer visited.
November 24th FLOODS	School marooned by floods. No attendance.
November 27th FLOODS	School meeting again abandoned.
November 28th	School resumed.
November 29th FLOODS	At 9 a.m the river was rising rapidly and the children were dismissed on the advice of the Correspondent.
November 30th	School Enquiry Officer visited. Children dismissed at 3.15 having had no break.

WEARE GIFFARD CHURCH OF ENGLAND SCHOOL LOG BOOK
1900 - 1945

1939

December 8th	School Enquiry Officer visited.
December 15th	Dental Inspection.
December 18th	Mr Kelland visited.
December 21st	School closed this morning to allow children to attend the Christmas market. Break up for Xmas vacation.

1940

January 8th	I take up duty today as temporary supply. Gertrude I. Arnold. Twelve children present. The morning session started at 9.40 a.m. on account of my not being able to be here (by bus) before that time. The time was made up by 15 minutes each session. The Rector visited the school this afternoon to inform the children of a school treat at Torrington given by the Mayor on Wednesday at 2.15 p.m. Notice was sent both to H.M.I. and Education Secretary.
January 12th	Mrs Bazley visited the school this afternoon but remained only for ten minutes. The children were out in the playground.
January 15th	The School Nurse visited this morning to examine children for cleanliness. All satisfactory. The Rector visited school also.
January 16th	Full attendance for two days - 17. Received Scholarship Forms. Three children entering (County). All forms sent to parents.
January 18th	Received Scholarship Forms from parents filled in. As the big room is too cold for small number of children the class room is used. The big room is used for Lunch Drill and games and singing. The ventilators being unable to close the snow and wind is penetrating indoors. The severe weather has caused the attendance to drop to 12 today. Percentage for week 89%. Phyllis Prouse not able to attend in the cold weather (satisfactory reason).
January 22nd	Severe cold and frost today but attendance fairly good.
January 26th	This week the attendance has been fairly good in spite of very dangerous roads. Percentage 82.3%. This afternoon school started at 12.45 p.m. in order that the closing of session might take place at 2.15. No play in either session (time made up). Received permission for this earlier closing from the Rector.
February 1st	The playground wall has broken down during the week-end owing to the frost. Word has been sent to the Correspondent.

WEARE GIFFARD CHURCH OF ENGLAND SCHOOL LOG BOOK
1900 - 1945

1940

February 12th	Mr Wooldridge visited the school this morning and checked the Registers. He listened to the children singing; also was interested in the general work. One scholar (Edith Braunton) reported as absent through measles. Necessary forms sent to M.O.H., D.M.C. and Nurse. Two scholars entered. 19 on Registers.
February 19th	The Rector visited the school this afternoon and remained to the end of session. After looking at some of the scholars' work he took the closing prayers. Attendance is improved this week.
February 27th	The attendance this week has dropped. Today only nine present, German measles cases with contacts the cause.
February 28th	Only eight present today. Coal 1 ton received.
March 1st	The attendance this week has fallen to 50% on account of German measles and influenza.
March 4th	Attendance still low - only eight present. The Scholarship Forms for candidates received.
March 5th	Miss Bird visited the school this afternoon and remained for a short time. Registers were checked. Eight present.
March 7th	Miss Foxwell, School Oculist, visited the school and examined Allan Pidler and Allan Coad. Attendance for week 43%.
?Date?	The Rector visited this morning. 8 present.
?Date?	H.M.I. Mr Whitworth visited this morning. The attendance still very low - 50% for the week.
March 11th	Received 1 Register.
March 15th	Miss Lawrence, P.T. Organiser, visited the school this afternoon but the children had left. She arranged to send some apparatus for the Drill.
March 18th	The Rector visited the school this morning and remained for the first session (Religious Instruction).
March 20th	The school closed this afternoon for the Easter holidays. The latter part of the afternoon was given to games. Attendance this week 65%. Average attendance for year 19.8. Received notice from Educational Secretary that the three weeks ending March 1st, 8th, 15th be cancelled for adding the attendance in the annual Returns as the percentage was below 60%. "Rule 23 Exception 2". The weeks have been crossed through on Summary Register according to instructions.

WEARE GIFFARD CHURCH OF ENGLAND SCHOOL LOG BOOK
1900 - 1945

1940

April 1st	School started after the Easter vacation with full attendance - 20. One new scholar.
April 4th	Miss Bird visited the school this morning. Register checked. 20 present.
April 10th	Exclude George and Phyllis Prouse for impetigo.
April 11th	Nurse Goddard visited school this morning for cleanliness. The school closed for the afternoon on account of Head Teacher attending Torrington Senior School opening by President of Board of Education.
April 19th	Miss Bird visited the school this morning at 9.30 a.m. and remained for the Scripture Dramatisation. Registers checked and signed. Bettine Grigg absent, as she was sitting for Scholarship examination at Bideford. An attendance mark given.
May 1st	This afternoon the children during the 2nd session had games and singing to celebrate May Day.
May 2nd	Nurse Goddard visited the school this morning.
May 10th	Today I relinquish my duties here as Temporary Supply Head Teacher after 5 months. G.I. Arnold.
May 14th	Mrs E.M. Turner takes charge of this school. As the children had been told that school would not reopen there were none present. The Rector decided to extend the holiday by one day.
May 15th	Owing to difficulties of transport, I am unable to arrive until 9.15. This time will be made up. Only 7 children present. This is due to the fact that the school had been closed for the Whitsun holiday but was reopened owing to the gravity of the European situation. Many of the children have apparently gone away on holiday.
May 16th	Today Mr Robbins called about lack of equipment. He has promised to make enquiries about this.
June 3rd	Mr Kelland called. All children who were present were weighed and measured.
June 5th	Scripture Examination taken by Mr Hawkins.
June 7th	Miss Brown. H.M.I., called re accommodation for evacuated children.
June 10th	The Rector called today. He spoke to the children and saw some of their work; also made final arrangements for the Sunday School Outing.
June 11th	The Rector called to say that the Outing has been postponed. There is some difficulty about buses, owing to the fact that evacuation of London children to Devon is about to start.
June 17th	School will now commence at 9 a.m. as I am able to arrive by that time. Lunch 12-1 p.m. Afternoon session 1-3.30 p.m.

WEARE GIFFARD CHURCH OF ENGLAND SCHOOL LOG BOOK
1900 - 1945

1940

June 18th	Report of Scripture Examination taken by Mr H.H. Hawkins on June 5th. The children in this school are very natural and friendly, and they seem to be happy in their work. The present teacher who is doing Supply Duty is taking a keen interest in their welfare and doing a great deal for them. Sound and effective religious teaching is being given and the lessons are presented in an attractive manner. Questions are freely and accurately answered and in some cases individuality of thought is shown. Attention is good and the children have the ability to follow closely a fresh line of thought. The atmosphere is quiet and reverent.
June 24th	Today children evacuated from several London schools joined us, 39 in all. Classes have been arranged by which Miss Hobill and Miss Cooper, the teachers in charge of the children, are taking Infants and Lower Juniors in the schoolroom. I am now taking the upper section of the Juniors, in the classroom.
June 25th	School nurse visited. Measles very prevalent. Nine children are absent owing to this.
July 4th	Mr Wooldridge (Manager) called today and signed registers.
July 9th	Nurse Goddard visited and inspected all children.
July 15th	Received notice that the attendances for week ending June 28th are to be cancelled (Rule 23, Exception 2): measles.
July 26th	Received permission from Rev. Walton the correspondent to close at 3.15 p.m.
July 29th	Miss Bird called in and listened to Mental Arithmetic. In the afternoon we took all the children to see the corn cut in Mr Hedden's field.
August 1st	End of school term. Owing to the war schools are to be kept open. Children are invited to attend school, to take part in various organised activities.
August 16th	Today I relinquish charge of this school.
August 16th	Today I take up duties at the school. F. Christopher.
September 5th	In the absence of the Vicar, I obtained permission from Miss Bird to close the school tomorrow, Friday, September 6th, to give the caretaker an opportunity to clean the building. Today I relinquish charge of this school.
September 9th	Resumed charge of this school. E.M. Turner.
September 18th	Dr Rhodes, S.M.I., visited and examined some of the children. The remainder will be examined on October 11th.
September 27th	The Rector visited today and watched the Physical Training Lesson. Miss Martin (Physical Training Organiser) came and discussed the P.T. lessons.
October 2nd	Mr Kelland, S.E. Officer, visited today.

WEARE GIFFARD CHURCH OF ENGLAND SCHOOL LOG BOOK 1900 - 1945

1940

October 4th	Miss Martin, P.T. Organiser, paid us a visit and demonstrated with the Juniors.
October 7th	Miss Bird called to check registers.
October 11th	Dr Rhodes, S.M.I., paid a visit and examined evacuees and two local children. John Martin's mother refused to allow John to be re-examined.
October 24th	School closed today until Tuesday October 29th (Mid-term holiday).
October 29th	Reopened this morning.
November 4th	River Torridge in flood. No path to the school. Meeting abandoned.
November 12th	Unable to reach school owing to floods. School abandoned.
November 14th	Floods at Chope's Bridge end of the village. Children unable to reach school. Meeting abandoned at 10 a.m.
November 15th	The Rector visited at 9.30 a.m. and stayed to hear children sing hymns.
November 15th	Owing to an epidemic of mumps the attendance is falling. 58.6%. Cancelled, Rule 3, Ex. 2.
November 22nd	Attendance only 52.8% and is cancelled (Rule 3, Ex. 2).
November 29th	Attendance 52.8%. Cancelled (Rule 3, Ex. 2).
December 6th	Attendance has fallen to 50.4% - many more cases of mumps. Cancelled (Rule 3, Ex. 2).
December 12th	Dr Pridham, M.O.H., called about the epidemic of mumps.
December 13th	Attendance 51.2%. Reported.
December 20th	Attendance 59.3%. Reported. Closed for Xmas holidays.

1941

January 6th	Reopened school at 9.30 a.m.. Received letter stating that attendances for weeks ending December 13th and 20th must be cancelled (Rule 3, Ex. 2).
January 30th	Mr Robbins (C.I.) visited with Mr Bell (L.C.C.).
February 3rd	Attendance very low owing to snow. Local children 59%. L.C.C. 82.3%.
February 18th	Left school soon after 3 p.m. owing to illness at home. Miss Hobill supervised my class until closing time.

WEARE GIFFARD CHURCH OF ENGLAND SCHOOL LOG BOOK
1900 - 1945

1941

March 13th	School was closed yesterday by permission of the Managers to enable Miss Hobill to escort children to L.C.C. Scholarship Examination. This was reported to Exeter and H.M.I. (Whitehall) by telegram.
March 28th	School closed for Easter holidays.
April 22nd	School reopened. Times 9.30 a.m. - 12.30 p.m., 1.30 - 4 p.m.
April 25th	Mr Inder (School Dentist) visited and attended to teeth of local children and "unofficial" evacuees.
May 9th	School closed this afternoon, by permission of the Rector, to enable children to go to Bideford to see the dancing display for War Weapons Week.
May 28th	Mr Hawkins visited to examine children in Scripture. 50 children present.
May 30th	Closed until Tuesday June 3rd (Whitsun Holiday). End of War Weapons Week.
June 3rd	Reopened after weekend holiday. A holiday was granted on Friday afternoon - War Weapons Week.
June 11th	Dr Leavey attended to immunise children against diphtheria. Forty-seven children were immunised.
June 18th	L.C.C. Supplementary Scholarship Examination. Three children, Ronald Waite, Hazel Hanson and Jean Jeffery, sat for this Examination.
June 20th	Copy of the Report on the Scripture Examination held on May 28th 1941. The Infants are in charge of an experienced London Head Teacher and the Head Mistress (Mrs Turner) is teaching the Junior children. There is a very quiet and reverent atmosphere in this school, and the children are very happy in their work. They are keenly interested and very appreciative. Fresh lines of thought appeal to them and they are evidently accustomed to having the Bible stories presented to them in a realistic and attractive manner. Questions were readily answered and the children were acquainted with a good selection of Bible stories and simple church teaching.　　　H.H. Hawkins, Diocesan Inspector.　　　Read and received: G.K. Walton, 20.6.41
June 25th	Mr Gross, School Enquiry Officer, called.
June 27th	Received permission to leave school at 3 p.m.
July 1st	Mr Gross, S.E.O., called.
July 7th	Allan Coad reported suffering from diphtheria and has been removed to hospital. Joan Griffin absent as a contact.
July 8th	Mr Gross, S.E.O., called.
July 9th	2nd Immunisation for diphtheria by Dr Killard-Leavey.
July 14th	Mr Gross, S.E.O., called. Average attendance for week ending July 11th is poor owing to many children being affected by immunisation.

WEARE GIFFARD CHURCH OF ENGLAND SCHOOL LOG BOOK 1900 - 1945

1941

July 16th	Sheila Short absent - appendicitis.
	School closed tomorrow (July 17th) - Sunday School Outing.
August 1st	Closed this afternoon until Tuesday August 5th, there being a general holiday on August 4th.
August 15th	School closed at the end of the afternoon session for the first part of the summer holiday (August 15th - September 1st). Much whooping cough prevalent. Attendance 58.2%.
September 1st	School reopened today.
September 4th	Received notice to cancel the attendance for week ending August 15th (Rule 3, Ex. 2).
September 19th	School closed at the close of the afternoon session until Monday October 13th. This is the second part of the summer holiday.
October 13th	Reopened this morning. Miss Bird called.
October 17th	Dr Rhodes, S.M.I., examined some local children and a few special cases amongst evacuees.
October 22nd	The Dentist visited to attend to the teeth of all "official evacuees".
November 3rd	Dr Rhodes visited the school and examined all those children who were not examined on October 17th.
November 18th	Took charge of this school. E.M. Gow.
December 1st	Resumed duty today after being absent since November 11th (through illness).
December 9th	Took charge of this school. B.L. Watkins. G.K. Walton 9.12.41.
December 18th	School closed at end of afternoon session for Christmas holidays.

1942

January 5th	Resumed duty today. E. Turner.
January 22nd	S.M.I. called re Margaret Duncan.
March 31st	School closed for Easter holidays.
April 20th	School reopened.
April 24th	Children weighed and record of height taken.

WEARE GIFFARD CHURCH OF ENGLAND SCHOOL LOG BOOK 1900 - 1945

1942

April 29th	S.M.I. called and saw several children - special cases.
May 12th	School nurse examined heads of all children.
May 14th	Mr H.H. Hawkins, Diocesan Inspector, examined the children in Scripture Knowledge (at 1.30 p.m.). Twenty five children out of thirty one were present. The absentees were mainly very young children.
May 22nd	School closed for Whitsun. As the school bus did not run on Tuesday, permission given by the Rector to close on that day.
May 26th	Reopened school.
June 1st	Registers checked by Miss Bird.
June 9th	Nurse Tuck (L.C.C.) called. One child excluded with suspected impetigo.
June 18th	Nurse Tuck visited.
June 22nd	Notice was received today from Miss Cuthbertson-Hill, Headmistress of Edgehill College, that Margaret June Gilder has been awarded a Special Place at the College, as a result of a County Examination held on March 15th.
June 26th	Nurse Tuck inspected heads of all the children. Two children, recent admissions, found with dirty heads.
June 29th	Two children excluded on account of dirty heads by Nurse Tuck.
July 2nd	Scripture Report received.
July 14th	Letter received from the Secretary suggesting that the school be organised as a one-class school.
July 16th	I replied to the letter pointing out that as there are six five year old children and two retarded six year olds it would be difficult to teach them in one class. I suggested that a Supplementary Teacher be sent to take the younger ones.
July 20th	Exeter inform me that Miss Hobill, the L.C.C. Head Mistress, is to remain.
July 23rd	Mr Gross, S.E.O., called. The attendance is very poor (70%) owing to a number of children suffering from severe head colds. Brian Isaacs has impetigo.
July 27th	Examined by managers. Geoff K. Walton.
July 31st	School closed for summer holidays.
August 31st	Reopened today. There are now 17 local children and only 9 evacuees.
September 1st	Mr Lewis attended to the teeth of evacuated children.
September 3rd	National Day of Prayer. School closed. Service for children held in church at 11.30 a.m.

WEARE GIFFARD CHURCH OF ENGLAND SCHOOL LOG BOOK 1900 - 1945

1942

September 18th	School closed at mid-day. Sunday School outing.
September 14th	Five children immunised against diphtheria.
September 28th	Mrs Bazeley checked registers.
October 1st	School closed to enable stove to be repaired. Mr Robbins called on September 30th re numbers of children.
October 12th	Today I posted to the Head Teacher of Welcombe School a parcel of readers, etc., which were too advanced for a junior school. The books concerned have been duly set off in Stock Book 24.
October 22nd	2nd Immunisation (Diphtheria). E. Tucker absent. I sent his mother a message to take him to have his second immunisation on Saturday October 24th.
October 26th	Miss Bird checked reigsters. The Rector called. Mr O. Halstead, the School Oculist, called. There were no cases. E. Tucker was immunised on October 24th.
October 27th	The School Nurse inspected the children's heads. All were clean. Geoff K. Walton.
October 29th	Return of L.C.C. Scholarship Candidates forwarded. School closed at the end of the afternoon session for mid-term holiday.
November 2nd	School reopened.
December 3rd	Mrs E.M. Turner absent owing to a bilious attack.
December 7th	Permission given to Mrs E.M. Turner to leave school early, having received news of the death of father.
December 17th	Mrs E.M. Turner absent - indisposed. Dennis and Christine Hardy returned to London. There are now only seven evacuated children in the school.
December 23rd	School closed for Xmas Holidays at end of morning session. School party held in the afternoon. Miss Hobill L.C.C. leaves today to return to London.

1943

January 11th	Reopened school today. Number of children now as follows: Local 13 . Evacuated children 4. A Parker, D. Bate, B. Bate did not return from London, The children are now taught in one class. Mr Gross, S.E.O., called.
January 20th	Medical Inspection by Dr Rhodes, S.M.I.
January 25th	Arnold Parker re-admitted. Evacuees 5.

WEARE GIFFARD CHURCH OF ENGLAND SCHOOL LOG BOOK
1900 - 1945

1943

February 1st	There was no school today. The village was flooded and only five children had arrived.
February 2nd	Floods subsided. School opened.
February 9th	School assembled, but as the river was rising rapidly the children were sent home.
March 1st	The School Nurse examined all heads. Two children, Donald and Jean Huxham, were admitted. The boy - who is nearly 9 - is very backward in Arithmetic, having no knowledge of money sums.
March 2nd	Examination papers for Glenys Grigg received.
March 6th	Special Place Examination supervised by the Rector and the Head Teacher.
March 11th	The Rector checked the Registers.
March 17th	G.C. Whitworth Esq., H.M.I., visited p.m. G. K. Walton.
April 2nd	On completing the Summary for year ending March 1943 I find that as I omitted to allow for 2 weeks holiday in April 1942 the Summary needed adjusting. This I have done by means of loose sheets, attached to the pages in question. Numbers are correct.
April 16th	Closed for Easter Holiday.
May 3rd	Reopened.
May 11th	Visited. B.G. Lampard-Vachell. W.E. Philip.
May 14th	The Rector called and checked registers.
May 26th	Diocesan Inspection by H.H. Hawkins Esq. School closed for remainder of day.
May 31st	Nurse Tuck visited and inspected all children.
June 3rd	Ascension Day service in church at 9.30 a.m. School closed for remainder of day.
June 11th	School closed until Tuesday June 15th for the Whitsun Holiday.
June 15th	School reopened.
July 12th	Holiday granted. Anniversary at Monkleigh.
July 30th	School closed for Summer Holidays.

WEARE GIFFARD CHURCH OF ENGLAND SCHOOL LOG BOOK 1900 - 1945

1943

August 16th	Reopened school.
September 8th	School closed for Sunday School Treat.
September 13th	Torrential rain. The few children who came to school were soaked. The school too was very wet, the water having come in from the rear. The Rector thought it advisable to send the children home.
September 16th	Visited the school and found 16 children present. B.G. Lampard-Vachell. Closed at 4 p.m. for 3 weeks holiday.
October 11th	Reopened school. Devon children 14. Evacuees 4. Total 18.
October 19th	Visited to make arrangements for meals from Torrington. N. Penfold.
October 20th	Equipment for canteen dinners checked and entered in stock book no. 2.
October 27th	Log book read. G.K. Walton.
November 5th	Closed at end of the afternoon session for half-term holiday granted by the Managers.
November 9th	Today hot dinners were served to the children. Sixteen children had dinners which were excellent.
November 18th	The School Nurse inspected heads and reported all were clean. All the children partake of school dinners.
December 6th	Attendance very low, 43%. Three cases of whooping cough. The other children suffering from influenza colds. Miss Bird called at 10 o'clock and told me to close the school and go home as I was feeling ill.
December 13th	Returned to school after a week's absence due to influenza. Attendance still very low (only 57%).
December 22nd	Closed for Xmas holidays.

1944

January 10th	School reopened.
January 20th	I visited. S. Gross, S.E.O.
January 21st	F.M. Rhodes, A.C.M.O.
February 1st	Received information that the attendance for week ending December 10th is to be cancelled (Rule 23 Ex. 2) (Influenza).
February 8th	Result of Book Drive sent to Torrington. About 600 books were collected.

WEARE GIFFARD CHURCH OF ENGLAND SCHOOL LOG BOOK 1900 - 1945

1944

February 9th	School will be closed tomorrow so that I may attend a Refresher Course for Teachers at Bideford Art School. Reopen Friday February 11th.
February 11th	I visited. S. Gross, S.E.O.
February 15th	I visited. S. Gross, S.E.O.
February 18th	F.W.C. Peete, S.R.N., visited.
February 23rd	M.H.Goddard vision testing (School Nurse).
February 24th	I visited. S. Gross, S.E.O.
March 3rd	I visited. S. Gross, S.E.O.
March 4th	Special Place Examination held. One entrant, William Grigg. The Rector was present.
March 6th	Admitted 4 children, three girls and one boy evacuated from London. The number of evacuees is now 8.
March 9th	I visited. S. Gross, S.E.O.
March 16th	I visited. S. Gross, S.E.O.
March 23rd	I visited. S. Gross, S.E.O.
March 30th	I visited. S. Gross, S.E.O.
April 5th	Closed for Easter Holidays.
April 24th	Reopened school. Two more London children entered, Joan and Connie Stubbings. This makes the total Devon 15, Evacuees 8. Miss Bird called in the morning. Mr Gross called in the afternoon.
May 1st	School was closed today. Permission given by the Managers to enable the teacher to go to London on personal business.
May 11th	School will be closed tomorrow, May 12th, for teacher to attend a course on "The Backward Child" at Torrington.
May 18th	School will be closed on May 19th for teacher to attend further course at Torrington. The school has been badly neglected this week. I have written to Mrs Short pointing this out. Lavatories are in a very unsatisfactory condition.
May 26th	School closed for Whitsun holiday until Wednesday May 31st. School still very dirty.
May 31st	School reopened

WEARE GIFFARD CHURCH OF ENGLAND SCHOOL LOG BOOK
1900 - 1945

1944

July 5th	The Diocesan Inspector (Mr Franklin) examined the Scripture. Twenty one children were present. Received notice that William L. Grigg has been awarded a Special Place at Bideford Grammar School. He has been a very satisfactory pupil and should benefit greatly from a higher education.
July 21st	Mr Hutton, School Oculist, visited and examined the eyes of Linda Tanton and Phyllis Prouse.
July 25th	School will be closed tomorrow for the Church Fete.
July 29th	Sent in my resignation today. School closed for Summer Holidays.
September 4th	Reopened school. There are now 15 Devon and 13 evacuated children, ages 4½ - 10+.
October 20th	School abandoned on Wednesday 18th owing to rising floods and very small attendance. Four children sent home at 3.30 as water is again rising. Attendance poor.
October 26th	Half-term holiday, 26th - 31st October. Today I relinquish my post as Head Teacher in this school, after 4½ years, during which time I have been very happy. The school has become very difficult owing to an influx of young children and the London children who are rather backward. E.M. Turner.
October 30th	Examined. G.C.F. Edwards.
November 1st	School reopened after half term holiday. Mr K.G. Gerry, Unattached Supply Staff, in charge of school. School closed on October 31st - no teacher.
November 13th	Received Needlework Requisition.
November 17th	School abandoned at 12.20 p.m. owing to rapidly rising floods. Would have preferred to have kept children until the mid-day meal was over but water rising very quickly. Dinners were accordingly cancelled. Figures in red ink in Canteen Register to be taken as correct.
November 21st	Miss Goddard, School Nurse, called.
November 24th	No school on Thursday November 23rd owing to heavy floods. Mr Gross, School Enquiry Officer, called.
December 4th	Miss K.T. Prideaux took over charge of the school from Mr Gerry.
December 5th	Received new stock and entered it in stock book.
December 7th	Mr Gross, School Enquiry Officer, called.
December 19th	After notifying children that the School Dentist would be visiting today, he failed to put in an appearance. Mr Gross, School Enquiry Officer, called.

WEARE GIFFARD CHURCH OF ENGLAND SCHOOL LOG BOOK
1900 - 1945

1945

January 8th	School reopened. Mrs Zappelkri (temporary supply staff) in charge.		
January 9th	Visit at 10 a.m. by school dentist.		
January 10th	Mr Gross called 11.45 a.m.		

WEAR GIFFORD

CHURCH OF ENGLAND SCHOOL

MISCELLANEOUS DOCUMENTS

Form No. 61.

CHANGE OF SCHOOL IS ALLOWED.
(a) At the beginning of the School Year on 1st April, and on the re-opening of the Schools after the Christmas and Summer Holidays.
(b) When after change of residence a child is to be admitted for the first time to a School in a new district.

DEVON COUNTY EDUCATION COMMITTEE.

To the Head Teacher of the _Weare Giffard C.E._ School.

Please admit the undermentioned Child as a Pupil in the above-named School. I certify that the particulars here given are correct.

Date _September 5th_ 19 38. Signed _F. W. Martin_
(Parent or Guardian of the said Child).

(1) Address of Parent _Marsh Brooke Cott._
   Weare Giffard.

(2) Full Name of Child _Betty Florence Mary Martin_

(3) Date of Birth _17-7-34._
   (If the Child has not attended any Public Elementary School before, a Certificate of Birth should be produced. Such Certificate can be obtained on payment of 6d., provided that application is made to the Registrar on a Form which can be obtained from the Attendance Officer.)

(4) Name of last School (if any) attended by Child ____

(5) Cause of leaving ____

(6) Has the Child ever attended a School in Devon? If so, state name of School _No._

Please mark X against the name of each disease from which the child has suffered.

Measles ____
Scarlatina ____
Diphtheria ____
Whooping Cough ____
Chicken Pox ____
Mumps ____
Rheumatism _X_
Brain Fever ____
St. Vitus Dance ____
Fits ____
Rupture ____

10,000—16/5/27.
368

FORM No. S.E.17

CHANGE OF SCHOOL IS ALLOWED.
(a) On the re-opening of the Schools after the Christmas, Easter, and Summer Holidays.
(b) When after change of residence a child is to be admitted for the first time to a School in a new district.

DEVON COUNTY EDUCATION COMMITTEE.

To the Head Teacher of the _Weare Giffard C of E._ School.

Please admit the undermentioned Child as a Pupil in the above-named School. I certify that the particulars here given are correct.

Date _Sept: 9th_ 19 40. Signed _M. K. Isaac_
(Parent or Guardian of the said Child).

(1) Address of Parent _I Annery Kiln_
   Weare Giffard

(2) Full Name of Child _Brian Ernest John Isaac_

(3) Date of Birth _28-11-1935_
   (If the Child has not attended any Public Elementary School before, a Certificate of Birth should be produced. Such Certificate can be obtained on payment of 6d., provided that application is made to the Registrar on a Form which can be obtained from the School Enquiry Officer.)

(4) Name of last School (if any) attended by Child ____

(5) Cause of leaving ____

(6) Has the Child ever attended a School in Devon? If so, state name of School {

Please mark X against the name of each disease from which the child has suffered.

Measles ____
Scarlatina ____
Diphtheria ____
Whooping Cough _X_
Chicken Pox _X_
Mumps ____
Rheumatism ____
Brain Fever ____
St. Vitus Dance ____
Fits ____
Rupture ____

10,000—B.388.

Form No. S.E.17

CHANGE OF SCHOOL IS ALLOWED.
(a) On the re-opening of the Schools after the Christmas, Easter, and Summer Holidays.
(b) When after change of residence a child is to be admitted for the first time to a School in a new district.

DEVON COUNTY EDUCATION COMMITTEE.

To the Head Teacher of the _Weare-Gifford_ School.

Please admit the undermentioned Child as a Pupil in the above-named School. I certify that the particulars here given are correct.

Date 26. 4. 1942. Signed _A. Prouse_
(Parent or Guardian of the said Child).

(1) Address of Parent _Annery Kiln, nr. Bideford, N. Devon._

(2) Full Name of Child _Albert John Prouse._

(3) Date of Birth _June 6th 1937._
(If the Child has not attended any Public Elementary School before, a Certificate of Birth should be produced. Such Certificate can be obtained on payment of 6d., provided that application is made to the Registrar on a Form which can be obtained from the School Enquiry Officer).

(4) Name of last School (if any) attended by Child _none._

(5) Cause of leaving _none._

(6) Has the Child ever attended a School in Devon? If so, state name of School { _none._

10,000—B.388.

Please mark X against the name of each disease from which the child has suffered.	
Measles	X
Scarlatina	
Diphtheria	
Whooping Cough	X
Chicken Pox	
Mumps	X
Rheumatism	
Brain Fever	
St. Vitus Dance	
Fits	
Rupture	

Form No. S.E.17

CHANGE OF SCHOOL IS ALLOWED.
(a) On the re-opening of the Schools after the Christmas, Easter, and Summer Holidays.
(b) When after change of residence a child is to be admitted for the first time to a School in a new district.

DEVON COUNTY EDUCATION COMMITTEE.

To the Head Teacher of the _Weare Giffard_ School.

Please admit the undermentioned Child as a Pupil in the above-named School. I certify that the particulars here given are correct.

Date _June 28th_ 1943. Signed _E. London_
(Parent or Guardian of the said Child).

(1) Address of Parent _C/o Rockmount, Weare Giffard_

(2) Full Name of Child _James Anthony Abraham London._

(3) Date of Birth _23rd Oct. 1936_ (RODING SCHOOL DAGENHAM ESSEX)
(If the Child has not attended any Public Elementary School before, a Certificate of Birth should be produced. Such Certificate can be obtained on payment of 6d., provided that application is made to the Registrar on a Form which can be obtained from the School Enquiry Officer).

(4) Name of last School (if any) attended by Child _RODING SCHOOL DAGENHAM ESSEX_

(5) Cause of leaving _ON HOLIDAY_

(6) Has the Child ever attended a School in Devon? If so, state name of School { _NO._

10,000—B.388.

Please mark X against the name of each disease from which the child has suffered.	
Measles	X
Scarlatina	—
Diphtheria	X
Whooping Cough	X
Chicken Pox	—
Mumps	—
Rheumatism	—
Brain Fever	—
St. Vitus Dance	—
Fits	—
Rupture	—

FORM No. S.E.17

CHANGE OF SCHOOL IS ALLOWED.
(a) On the re-opening of the Schools after the Christmas, Easter, and Summer Holidays.
(b) When after change of residence a child is to be admitted for the first time to a School in a new district.

DEVON COUNTY EDUCATION COMMITTEE.

To the Head Teacher of the ~Weare Gifford Church~ School.

Please admit the undermentioned Child as a Pupil in the above-named School. I certify that the particulars here given are correct.

Date 20th April 1942   Signed S. F. Sucker, (mother)
(Parent or Guardian of the said Child).

(1) Address of Parent Annery Kiln, WEARE GIFFARD, nr Bideford.

(2) Full Name of Child Ernest Henry George Sucker

(3) Date of Birth 24-1-1934
(If the Child has not attended any Public Elementary School before, a Certificate of Birth should be produced. Such Certificate can be obtained on payment of 6d., provided that application is made to the Registrar on a Form which can be obtained from the School Enquiry Officer.)

(4) Name of last School (if any) attended by Child —

(5) Cause of leaving —

(6) Has the Child ever attended a School in Devon? If so, state name of School { — }

10,000—B.388.

Please mark **X** against the name of each disease from which the child has suffered.

Measles ___
Scarlatina ___
Diphtheria ___
Whooping Cough **X**
Chicken Pox ___
Mumps ___
Rheumatism ___
Brain Fever ___
St. Vitus Dance ___
Fits ___
Rupture ___

FORM No. S.E.17

CHANGE OF SCHOOL IS ALLOWED.
(a) On the re-opening of the Schools after the Christmas, Easter, and Summer Holidays.
(b) When after change of residence a child is to be admitted for the first time to a School in a new district.

DEVON COUNTY EDUCATION COMMITTEE.

To the Head Teacher of the ~Weare Gifford Church~ School.

Please admit the undermentioned Child as a Pupil in the above-named School. I certify that the particulars here given are correct.

Date April 21st 1942   Signed L. E. Grigg
(Parent or Guardian of the said Child).

(1) Address of Parent Heatherdowns, Weare Gifford

(2) Full Name of Child Hilerie Juanita Grigg

(3) Date of Birth May 15th 1938.
(If the Child has not attended any Public Elementary School before, a Certificate of Birth should be produced. Such Certificate can be obtained on payment of 6d., provided that application is made to the Registrar on a Form which can be obtained from the School Enquiry Officer.)

(4) Name of last School (if any) attended by Child —

(5) Cause of leaving —

(6) Has the Child ever attended a School in Devon? If so, state name of School { — }

10,000—B.388.

Please mark **X** against the name of each disease from which the child has suffered.

Measles **X**
Scarlatina ___
Diphtheria ___
Whooping Cough ___
Chicken Pox ___
Mumps ___
Rheumatism ___
Brain Fever ___
St. Vitus Dance ___
Fits ___
Rupture ___

Form D.

School **Weare Gifford** Deanery of **Hartland** Archdeaconry of **Totnes**

Exeter Diocesan Inspection of Schools.

22 May 1943

Dear Sir,
 I have the pleasure of forwarding to you, for the information of the Managers, the accompanying Report on the Religious Instruction of this School, inspected by me
 This Report should be passed on to the Head Teacher and entered in the School Log-book.

Yours faithfully, H. H. Hawkens

Date of Inspection 20 May 1943
To the Correspondent.
Diocesan Inspector.

STATISTICS: Scholars on Books **18** | Scholars present at Inspection— B. **9** G. **6** | Withdrawn from all Religious Instruction — | Withdrawn from only part of Religious Instruction —

	Infants.	I.	II.	III.
Teacher responsible for Instruction		Mrs Turner		
Additional Instruction				

Since my last visit the evacuated teacher has been recalled and the Head teacher is now alone. To teach a number of children, even a small one, with a wide range of age is no easy task and demands effort, energy and careful planning. Mrs Turner is tackling the problem in a praiseworthy manner and the children are receiving a useful Christian training.

The teaching is thorough and sincere and the children are keenly interested in it. Reality has been given to the Bible stories and they have been translated into terms of daily life. The children are very friendly and it is a pleasure to talk to them. They answer questions readily, accurately and thoughtfully.

Present at Inspection

Devon County Education Committee.

(Postal Address) Weare Giffard School

Oct 27th 1940

.... School.   No. ....

I hereby certify that I have left matters in such a state that the working of the school will not be unduly disrupted.

The Stock Book is in order — A few books are missing —
    1 Blackies' Study Reader
    1 Atlas
    1 Roads of Dreamland (reader)

The Needlework Balance Sheet has been Completed and Canteen money paid to H! Lancekwell Savings Stamps value £1. are left in the drawer.

L. M. Turner.

Reader's Notes

Reader's Notes

Reader's Notes

Reader's Notes

Reader's Notes